The Art of Exegesis

The Art of Exegesis

An Analysis of the Life and Work
of Martin Hans Franzmann

MATTHEW E. BORRASSO

WIPF & STOCK · Eugene, Oregon

THE ART OF EXEGESIS
An Analysis of the Life and Work of Martin Hans Franzmann

Copyright © 2019 Matthew E. Borrasso. All rights reserved. Except for brief quotations in critical publications or reviews, no part of this book may be reproduced in any manner without prior written permission from the publisher. Write: Permissions, Wipf and Stock Publishers, 199 W. 8th Ave., Suite 3, Eugene, OR 97401.

Wipf & Stock
An Imprint of Wipf and Stock Publishers
199 W. 8th Ave., Suite 3
Eugene, OR 97401

www.wipfandstock.com

PAPERBACK ISBN: 978-1-5326-7200-2
HARDCOVER ISBN: 978-1-5326-7201-9
EBOOK ISBN: 978-1-5326-7202-6

Manufactured in the U.S.A.   JANUARY 10, 2019

For Holly, Enzo, Anastasia, and Theo

"The Christian interpreter must remain a beggar if he would be a true interpreter of God's Word, remembering that it is *given* to men to know the mysteries of the kingdom of Heaven."

—Martin Hans Franzmann

Contents

Permissions | ix
Preface | xi
Acknowledgements | xv

1 Theology Must Sing | 1
2 Beggars Before God | 25
3 The Posture of the Interpreter | 50
4 Words of Life | 84
5 Grace Under Pressure | 109
6 Weary of All Trumpeting | 132

Appendix | 161
Bibliography | 193

Permissions

Image of Martin H. Franzmann courtesy of Concordia Historical Institute, Department of Archives and History, The Lutheran Church—Missouri Synod, St. Louis, Missouri.

Material: Text of Thy Strong Word (LSB #578)

Copyright notice: Text © 1969 Concordia Publishing House. Used with permission. www.cph.org

Material: Text of In Adam We Have All Been One (LSB #569)

Copyright notice: Text © 1969 Concordia Publishing House. Used with permission. www.cph.org

Material: Text (65 words) from the Preface and text of *To Respect Language* (page 44–46) from *Pray for Joy*

Copyright notice: From *Pray for Joy* © 1970 Concordia Publishing House. Used with permission. www.cph.org

Material: Text (1293 word excerpts) from *Ha! Ha! Among the Trumpets*

Copyright notice: From *Ha! Ha! Among the Trumpets* © 1966, 1994 Concordia Publishing House. Used with permission. www.cph.org

Material: Text (1101 word excerpts) from *Toward a More Excellent Ministry*

Copyright notice: From *Toward a More Excellent Ministry* © 1964 Concordia Publishing House. Used with permission. www.cph.org

Material: Text (507 word excerpts) from *New Courage for Daily Living*

Copyright notice: From *New Courage for Daily Living* © 1963 Concordia Publishing House. Used with permission. www.cph.org

Material: Text (60 word excerpts) from *Alive with the Spirit*

Copyright notice: From *Alive with the Spirit* © 1974 Concordia Publishing House. Used with permission. www.cph.org

Material: Text (166 word excerpts) from *Grace Under Pressure*

Copyright notice: From *Grace Under Pressure* © 1969 Concordia Publishing House. Used with permission. www.cph.org

Text of *The British Lutheran*. Used with permission.

Text of Weary of All Trumpeting © 1972 Augsburg Fortress/1517 Media. Used with permission.

Preface
The Art of Exegesis

MARTIN HANS FRANZMANN WAS more than a servant of the church, he was the church's poet. In serving the Wisconsin Evangelical Lutheran Synod at Northwestern College, The Lutheran Church—Missouri Synod at Concordia Seminary, and the Evangelical Lutheran Church of England at Westfield House in Cambridge, Franzmann dedicated himself toward a singular goal, teaching people to hear the voice of Christ. His work as a New Testament scholar was rooted in the idea that one never sits over the text as lord, but always under it as servant. His devotion to the church led to service of it in various capacities, ones that ultimately put him in the middle of difficult disputes. While people tend to remember him for his hymnody, it is his hermeneutical, exegetical, and ecumenical work that form the foundation from which that hymnody sprang. To know Franzmann only through his hymnody is to know him partially. This work seeks to introduce to a new generation that which may have been forgotten in time.

Scholarly work engaging Franzmann is limited primarily, if not exclusively, to his hymnody.[1] As stated above, the present work seeks to widen the exposure of Franzmann beyond that. Thus, there is relatively little attention given to his hymnody. The bulk of the work will attend to his exploits as a scholar and ecumenical figure. These aspects of his life were not compartmentalized. His theological perspective was not limited to classrooms, scholarly articles, or board rooms, it found its way into the

---

1. A recent S.T.M. thesis from Rev. Daniel Burfiend of Concordia Theological Seminary in Ft. Wayne, Indiana, is also bucking the trend of dealing primarily with Franzmann's hymnody. To be sure Richard Brinkley's work has touched on specific passages of Franzmann's literary output, but it has remained largely focused on the biography and origin of Franzmann's hymnody.

homes and lives of people. It is necessary, then, to engage with a variety of his writings meant for a variety of audiences. The investigation will center on his scholarly articles and books as well as his published devotional material. While the two types of writing are distinctively different in their scope and purpose, it will be shown that for Franzmann there is an interconnectivity. His scholarly work focuses primarily on hermeneutics, isagogics, and exegesis of the New Testament. It is not, however, limited to those areas as it also speaks to ecumenical and confessional interests. His devotional and sermonic material are often comprised of concise and poetic expositions of scripture that demonstrate a beloved Franzmann axiom, "theology is doxology, theology must sing."[2]

While it is clear that the present inquiry will orbit primarily around Martin Franzmann's own writings, there will also be interaction with other published and unpublished materials that concern him. A limitation of this inquiry is that it cannot deal with everything. As the bibliography amply demonstrates, it is not possible to spend significant time on every piece he wrote and this is not simply because of the limited interaction with his hymnody. The intention of this exploration is to give an in depth overview of his work as a scholar and ecumenical figure, not a point by point analysis of each piece of his literary output.

The opening chapter focuses on Martin Franzmann's biographical information. It touches on his hymnody, as that is how most know him, as well as his early poetry. Finally, it sets the stage for his work as a New Testament scholar and ecumenical figure.[3] The chapter that follows unpacks Franzmann's hermeneutical perspective in relation to his origins in the Wisconsin Synod and his work as a professor. It addresses his understanding of how to approach the biblical text and offers a possible explanation as to why Franzmann held such a perspective. Chapter three further dissects Franzmann's hermeneutical perspective as it relates to his own exegetical work. There is also a discussion concerning the reception of his commentaries on Matthew, Romans, and Revelation as well as his New Testament introduction. The fourth chapter demonstrates how Fran-

---

2. Franzmann, *Ha! Ha! Among the Trumpets*, 92–97.

3. Franzmann's definition of this term will be explored in chapter five. For now, it is important to note that he understood the ecumenical task, as well as ecumenicity in general, in broad terms. Such work included interaction not only with church bodies of different confessions but also with those church bodies that claim the same confession. In other words, ecumenical work is Lutherans dialoging with American Evangelicals as well as Lutherans dialoging with other Lutherans.

zmann's hermeneutical and exegetical work were given practical application. The focus therein is limited to his sermons and devotional material. The next chapter explores Franzmann's work as an ecumenical figure. It wrestles with his writings about and participation in the conferences in Bad Boll, the Lutheran World Federation, and the National Lutheran Council. The concluding chapter ponders the end of Franzmann's life as a scholar and church figure. It concludes with an analysis of his role in repairing the breach at Concordia Seminary in the wake of the walkout.

At the memorial service held on the campus of Concordia Seminary in St. Louis on April 2, 1976, Professor William Schmelder offered the following reflection:

> For us who knew him as a teacher, he was one who opened for us the fullness and depths of the Biblical texts; who taught us as his students to emulate Moses when reading the word of God; whose posture as an interpreter was: take off your shoes, the ground on which you are standing is holy ground. He was a man of culture, whose eloquence is noted in the hymns which appear in the *Worship Supplement*. If anyone had a way with words Martin Franzmann did, but always in the service of the Word. But I suppose most of all we shall remember him as a Christian gentleman, one whose teaching and preaching, whose life, whose being, whose poetry, whose elegance and eloquence had been given shape because of the death and resurrection of Jesus Christ.[4]

It is the contention of this work not only that his voice was once exceedingly valuable, but that it is one sorely needed in the church today. In part, that is because of his trademark poetic flair. Franzmann believed that, "the language of poetry is the most powerful, the most moving, and in the last analysis, the truest and most accurate form of speech."[5] The church today could use a dose of powerful, moving, and true eloquence. His poetic flair, however, is not the only reason. Franzmann speaks with power not because of his eloquence, but because he speaks from a place

---

4. Robin Leaver also quotes this in his introduction using Fred L. Precht's transcription from Lutheran Worship Hymnal Companion (St. Louis: Concordia Publishing House, 1992), 609. The audio recording of Prof. Schmelder's message still exists in the archives of Concordia Seminary in St. Louis. The quote above has been rendered to match the audio recording as opposed to the transcription used in Precht and Leaver. While the difference is minimal, it should be noted.

5. Franzmann, "The Hermeneutical Dilemma: Dualism in the Interpretation of Holy Scripture," 531.

of deep conviction, because his speech was formed and shaped by a book that grabbed him and would not let him go. That devotion to the scriptural word is refreshing, not just in terms of scholarship, but also in speaking to the hearts of people in need of hope.

Personally, I should note that I am not a disinterested observer. Franzmann is, academically and theologically speaking, my grandfather. That is to say, his students were my professors. But more than this, I have come to revere him as a father in the faith, as one who taught me to take off my shoes when approaching the biblical text and to hear in those pages the very voice of God that grabs me and will not let me go.

Acknowledgements

A WORK OF THIS sort is rarely, if ever, the product of a single person's effort. It is fitting, then, to recognize the efforts of those who made this particular one possible. My appreciation belongs first to Wipf & Stock for taking a chance on my work. Thanks is due also to those groups who allowed previously published materials to appear in this publication. Without my Master of Sacred Theology thesis advisor at United Lutheran Seminary, Maria Erling, I never would have thought to choose Martin Hans Franzmann as a subject and the completion of that effort would have taken much longer. Her encouragement and counsel were invaluable. Thanks are also due to Michael Krentz, the additional reader, whose willingness to participate meant that it would be read, evaluated, and approved by someone with ties to the Franzmann family.

Of course, there are several people who offered anecdotes and advice throughout the research and writing phases to whom, even if they are not named specifically, I am indebted. Prominent among them is Carol Feuerhahn. Her willingness to speak and her generosity of time and material will never be forgotten. Richard Brinkley proved to be a source of support and insight in the early stages of my research. James Voelz, and Robert Mordhorst gave of their time and memories to help me understand Franzmann's perspective and the impact he had in the life of his students. Martin's living children, Peter and Alice, also generously gave by sharing a part of their lives, a trust which I do not take lightly.

To their credit, the staff of Concordia Historical Institute, especially Jonathan Lange and Mark Bliese, through their concerted effort and continued willingness to lend assistance, made the research possible. The same should be said of the staff at the libraries on the campuses of Concordia Seminary in St. Louis, Missouri, Martin Luther College in

New Ulm, Minnesota, and United Lutheran Seminary in Gettysburg and Philadelphia, Pennsylvania.

Several more people made the writing possible. Among them are the congregation I am privileged to serve, Redeemer Evangelical Lutheran Church in Parkton, Maryland, who afforded me the time and continually nurtured the effort. Without Brooks Schramm, Thurman Frey, and James Sharp some translation efforts would have been futile. Linda Shaffer and Stacey Parker graciously proofread the manuscript, any mistakes that remain are because I failed them. Three individuals who read and critiqued portions should also be mentioned. My dear mentor, Jon Diefenthaler, whose expertise as an American church historian and depth of insight were beyond valuable. Harrison Parker and Matthew Gerzevske, who are by rights, even if not by birth, my brothers. Their input and encouragement undergirded this entire endeavor.

Finally, and most importantly, my family. Without my in-laws, Mark and Bonnie Hughes, the publication would not have been feasible. Chief among all others are my dear wife, Holly, and my children, Enzo, Anastasia, and Theo. They encouraged, supported, and sacrificed for me more than any other. There are no words to express the depth of gratitude I feel. It is only fitting, even if it is not enough, that this is dedicated to them.

1

Theology Must Sing

DOXOLOGICAL ENDINGS

> God the Father, Light-Creator
> To Thee laud and honor be;
> To Thee, Light of Light begotten,
> Praise sung eternally;
> Holy Spirit, Light-Revealer,
> Glory, glory be to Thee;
> Mortals, angels, now and ever
> Praise the Holy Trinity.[1]

A HYMN THAT ENDS doxologically is an unsurprising and indeed common occurrence in Lutheran hymnody. It is far rarer, however, that a hymn has the greatest doxological ending in all of western hymnody. Bruce Backer, in his introduction to worship for Wisconsin Synod Lutherans, makes such a claim for the hymn verse above.[2] At first glance it seems outrageous, especially considering the fact that there are relatively few published works that deal directly with the hymn writer, Martin Hans Franzmann, and his hymnody. One that does is written by Robin Leaver

---

1. Franzmann, "Thy Strong Word," *Lutheran Service Book*, 578.

2. Backer, *Lutheran Worship: A Course Guide*, 129. Quoted in Brinkley, *Thy Strong Word*, 110.

titled, *Come to the Feast: The Original and Translated Hymns of Martin H. Franzmann*. In it Leaver, who is a European trained academic specializing in music history, claims that Franzmann "was the John the Baptist, the forerunner of twentieth-century American hymnody."[3] This is high praise considering Leaver's own scholarly work that focuses primarily on the musical contributions and legacies of Bach and Luther. Who is this somewhat unknown forerunner poet? Why do his words endure with such a legacy?

The goal of this chapter is to answer those questions. In doing so, however, it will be argued that the hymnody Franzmann generated was itself a distillation of his life and work, i.e., his hymnody reflects something deeper. To demonstrate this, a thorough examination of his biographical information is necessary. This includes an exploration of what is known factually, e.g., he was a Lutheran who spent his life in three different Lutheran church bodies beginning with the Wisconsin Evangelical Lutheran Synod, moving to The Lutheran Church—Missouri Synod, and ending with the Evangelical Lutheran Church of England. It also includes, more importantly, the impact he had on those who knew him. Requisite, then, is an exploration of the matrix between personal relationships and work as a scholar, hymn writer, and ecumenist as this forms the basis for the entire work in which this chapter is situated. Martin Franzmann was indeed a hymn writer, but he was not only a hymn writer. His hymns reflect his relationships to people, to institutions, and to language. Failure to understand those relationships is failure to understand not only the hymns, but the hymn writer.

DOXOLOGICAL BEGINNINGS

Martin Franzmann was born on January 29, 1907 to William and Elsie (Griebling) Franzmann in Lake City, Minnesota. One of nine children born to the Wisconsin Synod pastor of the St. John's Lutheran Church and the daughter of an immigrant Milwaukee businessman, Martin grew up in a home that emphasized learning, music, and the Christian faith.[4] Richard Brinkley, among others, notes that "his parents [worried] over Martin's constant reading. He would read for hours on end, even late into the evening when the light was poor. Mrs. Franzmann was always

---

3. Leaver, *Come to the Feast*, 9.
4. Brinkley, "Of Four Rivers," 123.

encouraging her son to go out, get some exercise, and play with other children."[5] It was also from his mother Elsie that Martin developed a love for music.[6] By the end of his life, he would write twenty original hymns and provide translations for another nine.[7] Daily life in that Minnesota home of his youth was enveloped in music. Devotions made regular use of hymnody and summer evenings on the porch had their fair share of folk singing.[8] Like some of his siblings, Martin would learn to play instruments, in his case the cello and piano.[9] It is undeniable that what he would become, both as a hymn writer and a scholar, began there on the shores of Lake Pepin.

The voracious reading that worried his parents would prove fruitful in his development. Martin's teachers at preparatory school remarked on his "facile mind" and "an almost limitless vocabulary."[10] At Northwestern Preparatory School and then Northwestern College, his growth as a poet and maturation as a scholar would also begin in earnest. Franzmann affectionately recalls, "There I received that part of my education which formed me most decisively."[11] The preparatory school and college shared a publication known as *The Black and Red* of which Martin would eventually become the editor. It contains Franzmann's earliest published works, a combination of prose and poetry. No less than twenty-two original poems were printed, composed in English and German. "My father was a German immigrant and reared us bilingually."[12] The bilingualism in which he was reared is evidenced in that poetry and undoubtedly aided his ability in translating hymns.

One of the poems gives insight into another language that would occupy his life, Greek. While he would eventually pursue graduate studies in classics at the University of Chicago, it was at Northwestern, "under the tutelage of men with a passion for excellence,"[13] that his skills and

---

5. Brinkley, "Of Four Rivers," 124.

6. Brinkley notes that Elsie Franzmann impacted both Werner and Martin as both became hymn writers. See Brinkley, *Thy Strong Word*, 13.

7. This counting follows the work of Robin Leaver cited above. A complete list is part of the Appendix: Another Franzmann Bibliography.

8. Brinkley, "Of Four Rivers," 123–24.

9. Brinkley, "Of Four Rivers," 124.

10. Brinkley, *Thy Strong Word*, 13–14.

11. Franzmann, "Of a Man and Four Rivers," 6.

12. Franzmann, "Of a Man and Four Rivers," 6.

13. Franzmann, "Of a Man and Four Rivers," 6.

passion were developed. In his "Apology for Greek Syntax" Franzmann writes:

> Of many roads that lead to Troy,
> Where Helen is, where every one
> That e'er had dreamings, man or boy,
>
> Deems his life shall have begun,
> I know of none that brings much joy,
> That knows not storms and heat and sun,
>
> Cold nights and sirens decoy
> And mountain tops scarce to be won
> And dragons waiting to destroy.
>
> But of them all that have begun
> Their journey on that road to Troy,
> Until these headlands shall be won,
> Until they have the golden fleece
> There's not a man of them will cease.[14]

The road to learn and understand a new language may be difficult, but it is one worthwhile. For Franzmann, it is one that proved most profitable as he would spend the remainder of his life enmeshed in a multitude of languages: Greek, Hebrew, Latin, German, and of course English.[15]

Poetry was an integral part of Franzmann's life. The poems that adorn the pages of *The Black and Red* are but a fraction of the evidence that demonstrates how integral poetry was to him. The year before he joined the faculty at Concordia Seminary in St. Louis he wrote a series of articles for the *Northwestern Lutheran* on Christian poetry. In that series he argues for its value in general as poetry and specifically its value in the life of a believer. His purpose in doing so was clear, "It is the intention of this and succeeding articles to seek and win a wider audience for Christian poetry."[16] To understand why Franzmann advocated so vigorously for poetry, why he wanted "to seek and win" that wider audience, a longer

---

14. Franzmann, "Apology for Greek Syntax," 169.
15. Franzmann, "Of a Man and Four Rivers," 6.
16. Franzmann, "Christian Poetry I," 134.

quotation, this one from a sermon twenty-seven years after the publishing of that series of articles, is illuminating.

> God makes music. It is inevitable, therefore, that the men of God whose words we hear in Scripture are singers and poets. They are not poets accidentally, not "also" poets, but poets *because* they are men of God, the prophets and apostles whose word the church receives and embraces. It is misleading to speak of "poetic" books of the Bible; the books are all poetic, for poetry is not the icing on the cake but the cake itself.[17]

This notion of the poetic nature of the scriptures and of theologians will be explored further in succeeding chapters.[18] For now, however, it suffices to note that what will be true of Franzmann throughout his life was nurtured and displayed during his formative years in the preparatory school and college in Watertown, Wisconsin.

It was at that same Northwestern College that Martin Franzmann would begin his professorial career. Graduating with an A.B. in 1928, Franzmann immediately began to teach Greek as well as English literature at his alma mater.[19] In 1930 Franzmann enrolled at Wisconsin Lutheran Seminary, though he would not graduate until 1936. This is not because Franzmann was a poor student, rather, it had to do with the affects of the Great Depression.[20] He said of his interesting predicament, "I am, I believe, the only man living who finished the Wisconsin Synod's prescribed three years of study at its Seminary in two years, five years apart, single in the first year and married in the second."[21]

His marriage was to Alice Beatrice Bentzin. She was, in his words, "the lady who (saving all their lovely reverences) made all other ladies seem a bit pale by comparison."[22] The two, who were wed on July 6, 1933, had met during Martin's time in Watertown. Their plan was to wed upon

---

17. Emphasis original. Robin Leaver published a copy of this sermon, the quotation of which is cited above. Leaver found the manuscript in the archives of Concordia Historical Institute. An identical manuscript was given to this author by Carol Feuerhahn from her late husband's library. Martin H. Franzmann, "The Devil Has All The Good Tunes?" in Leaver, *Come to the Feast*, 127.

18. See especially chapters 2–4.

19. Brinkley, *Thy Strong Word*, 14.

20. Brinkley notes that this is part of the reason why Franzmann's education was interrupted on several occasions, op. cit., 14.

21. Franzmann, "Of a Man and Four Rivers," 6–7.

22. Franzmann, "Of a Man and Four Rivers," 6.

Martin's completion of seminary.[23] Rev. Arthur Katt, the husband of Martin's sister Helen, had a different plan in mind. He wanted Martin and Alice, who was teaching in Cleveland at the time, to teach in Shaker Heights, Ohio. Katt was pastor at St. Peter's Lutheran Church and needed both to teach at the attached school. Not being able to turn down their combined salary of $1,200 a year, Martin and Alice consented.[24]

WRITING DOXOLOGY

The American Lutheran landscape was also changing rapidly during the early twentieth century. Not only was the switch from German to English taking place in The Lutheran Church—Missouri Synod, there were also overtures from disparate Lutheran bodies to begin the process of exploring further cooperation and merger. Martin's legacy as a hymn writer and translator was born during this time at St. Peter's. His brother-in-law, Arthur Katt, made use of Franzmann's linguistic and poetic skills. It was he who first suggested that Martin should try his hand at translating hymns.[25] "I encouraged him, who is by nature modest and retiring, to employ his gifts in service of the church, so sorely in need of good translations for its new hymnal."[26] Six translations and one original hymn would comprise a publication by St. Peter's in 1934 called *Christian Hymns*.[27] Katt's praise for Franzmann's ability in handling language is unabashed. "Inspite [sic] of his youth he is destined to rise to high rank and recognition on account of his exceptionally fine gifts and strenuous labors. His special field is LANGUAGE . . . He has an unusually fine and rare understanding of language, literature, poetry, and art."[28] It is because Katt saw this in Franzmann that his suggestion to translate hymns was made.

Katt, however, did not want to keep Franzmann's skills all to himself or to St. Peter's. It was Katt's contention that Franzmann be given a platform in the development of the new Lutheran hymnal. In 1929 The Lutheran Church—Missouri Synod, in convention, "authorized the revision

---

23. Brinkley, "Of Four Rivers," 126.
24. Brinkley, "Of Four Rivers," 126.
25. Brinkley, *Thy Strong Word*, 14. The knowledge of this is confirmed via an interview with Helen (Franzmann) Katt in 1992.
26. Katt, *Critical Comments on the Proposed New Hymnal*, 88.
27. Katt, *Critical Comments on the Proposed New Hymnal*, 14.
28. Katt, *Critical Comments on the Proposed New Hymnal*, 88. Emphasis original.

of the Evangelical Lutheran Hymn-book of 1912 [and] stipulated that the sister synods of the Synodical Conference of North America be requested to cooperate in order that the final result might be a common English hymnal."[29] This hymnal, which would be published by the Intersynodical Committee on Hymnology and Liturgics for the Evangelical Lutheran Synodical Conference of North America in 1941, is *The Lutheran Hymnal*. Katt was not alone in his assertion. Well known for his work *Church Symbolism*, Frederick Roth Webber was another Missouri Synod pastor and also member of the Architectural Committee of the English District. In June of 1937 Webber lavished high praise upon both Katt and the young Franzmann.

> Pastor Katt, as many of our readers know, is one of our most able authorities on hymns and hymn tunes . . . Our readers ought to know more about Pastor Katt's long and scholarly labors, as well as that astonishing genius, Professor Martin Franzmann, a highly gifted young clergyman of the Wisconsin synod, whose beautiful poetry and hymn translations will compare with the great masters of classical English. Franzmann may well be called the Tennyson of the Lutheran Church.[30]

As evidence to validate such a lofty claim, Webber tells a personal story. The entirety of the story and the translation have here been reproduced.[31]

> Two or three years ago, when depressed at the prospect of singing our wretched translation "Awake, My Heart, with Gladness," the writer of these lines went to Prof. Franzmann with our troubles. Within a few days he gave us a translation that is not only beautiful as poetry, faithful to the original text, but which sings gloriously. We have used it during three Easter seasons. Here it is, and we hope that our readers will file it away for use hereafter, and make a note in their hymnals so that it may not be forgotten:
>
> HYMN-AUF, AUF, MEIN HERZ, 7,6,7,6,6,6,6,6
>
> 1
>
> To songs of joy awake thee,
>
> My heart, O rise, behold

---

29. Polack, *The Handbook to the Lutheran Hymnal*, IV.

30. Webber, "Fine Arts in the Service of the Church," 9.

31. Instead of merely quoting Webber, it is important to see why Webber argued so forcefully in favor of Franzmann. Thus the entirety of the translation needs to be seen and read in the context of his comments.

What light hath dawned to take thee
    From pain and darkness cold.
My Saviour had Him laid
    Upon that final bed,
Whereunto we must come,
    The cold and silent tomb.

2

The deeps of hell rejoiced,
    The Foe's dark jubilee,
Deep-throated, myriad-voiced,
    Proclaimed the victory,
But ris'n in hell's despite
    Forth flashed in garments bright
Our Champion, on the grave
    To plant His banner brave.

3

Triumphant He ascendeth
    To realms beyond the sky;
And whither my Lord wendeth
    Triumphant follow I;
For this I know full well,
    By no proud prince of hell,
By none of woman born
    Shall I be from Him torn.

4

Nor fear nor doubting shakes me,
    I follow calm and bold
To Heaven's high gate He takes me
    Whereon is writ in gold:
"Since thou on earth hast borne
    For me rebuke and scorn,
Since thou has died with Me,
    Here shalt thou crowned be."

Trans. Martin Franzmann, 1935.

> Even though this issue may reach our readers after the Easter season is quite over, yet it will do no harm to mimeograph this marvelous translation, and let the congregation try it, so as to be convinced of its wonderfully singable quality.[32]

Both Katt and Webber were convinced that Franzmann's translations were far and away superior to already existing ones. They were not merely poetic, but "singable," and if Webber is to be trusted, favored by pastor and congregation alike.

Arthur Katt fought to have his voice heard in the construction of *The Lutheran Hymnal*. Compiling an analysis of the materials that would eventuate in the hymnal, Katt self-published and distributed a multi-chapter work, *Critical Comments on the Proposed New Hymnal*. He is so convinced of Martin's prowess that an entire chapter of this work is devoted to bringing Franzmann's translations to light. Not only does he include the translations themselves but an explanation as to why they are superior. Katt is unequivocal about the need for using not just any translation, but a Franzmann translation in the introduction to that chapter:

> There is one man in the Synodical Conference, whose merits as poet and translator far surpass the attempts of all others in this direction. I refer to Prof. Martin H. Franzmann, professor at Northwestern College, Watertown, Wis. While others may have tried their hand at this work, their products at best are but smooth, fluent prose rhymings,—metrically, rhythmically, mechanically correct. They do not soar. They reach no heights. I have yet to be shown one such hymn or translation, which really approaches the exalted level of poetry, stirring the emotions, thrilling the worshipper with exalted beauty of thought and poetic expression. As one of our synodical officials had said: "it is mostly of very light weight." It is "Edgar Guestian" at best, homely verse. Quite different is the work of Martin H. Franzmann. I say this, not because Prof. Franzmann is my friend, but because his hymns really have that certain something, which the others lack. And I stand not alone in this opinion.[33]

---

32. Webber, "Fine Arts in the Service of the Church," 9.

33. Katt, *Critical Comments on the Proposed New Hymnal*, 84. Katt goes on to cite the same paragraph from Webber that is cited above. No doubt that Katt and Webber knew of one another, and perhaps even knew one another personally.

The verdict rendered by Katt and Webber is the same. Franzmann's translations are of a better sort, not only for the linguistically minded, but for the worshipping congregation.

Sadly, Katt and Webber's defense of Franzmann fell mostly on deaf ears. Although one translation of Franzmann's would find its way into *The Lutheran Hymnal*, "Rise Again, Ye Lionhearted," much of the work he put into translating would be forgotten or ignored for some years. This is surprising, and worth noting, because of the definition of a hymn used by the committee. Quoting Harvey B. Marks the committee says, "A hymn is a sacred poem expressive of devotion, spiritual experience, or religious truth, fitted to be sung by an assembly of people."[34] Polack goes on to say, "A church-hymn, then, must, be a song, a popular poetic expression of that which the believers have in common."[35] On the basis of that definition it is unknown why Franzmann's original and translation work would not have been included. There were three hundred forty-seven translated hymns included, mostly from German origin but also from Latin, Scandinavian, Greek, Slovak, French, Italian, Dutch, Welsh, and Finnish origins.[36] There were three hundred thirteen original hymns from British, American, and Canadian sources.[37] Polack clearly states that those numbers "indicate that the editorial committee covered a wide field in search of hymns suitable for inclusion."[38] The precise reason why Franzmann's work was not suitable enough for inclusion seems to be lost to history. It should be noted, however, that people have been singing Franzmann unaware in the form of "O Lord, We Praise Thee, Bless Thee and Adore Thee." This hymn was originally cut from the final composition of *The Lutheran Hymnal* but was added back before production began.[39] Elements of Franzmann's translation, especially the first line of the hymn, were included, but not in entirety.[40]

After leaving Shaker Heights, Ohio, Martin finished his seminary training, graduating in 1936. As has been alluded to in the quotes from Katt and Webber above, Franzmann would indeed inhabit the position of

---

34. Polack, *The Handbook to the Lutheran Hymnal*, IX.
35. Polack, *The Handbook to the Lutheran Hymnal*, IX.
36. Polack, *The Handbook to the Lutheran Hymnal*, XI.
37. Polack, *The Handbook to the Lutheran Hymnal*, XI.
38. Polack, *The Handbook to the Lutheran Hymnal*, XI.
39. Brinkley, *Thy Strong Word*, 59.
40. Brinkley, *Thy Strong Word*, 59.

professor at Northwestern College in Watertown where he would teach for eleven years. Combined with the two previous years as a professor, thirteen years of his life were spent "teaching English literature to those pliable and amiable boys."[41] While teaching at Northwestern he also continued his studies at the University of Chicago. In 1933 he received the Shorey Travelling Fellowship in Greece from the university as part of his studies in classics there.[42] The focus of his doctoral work was "Legal Language and Imagery in Greek Tragedy."[43] Franzmann would never finish his doctoral work. In personal correspondence to Robin Leaver from Ronald Feuerhahn[44] revealed that "On his second and final attempt to finish that degree, he was summoned once again by Dr. Behnken, president of the church, to help with some major project or crisis. Martin, always the servant, obeyed the bishop's call."[45]

A DOXOLOGICAL CAREER

Lack of a doctoral degree did not inhibit his career as a scholar, professor, and churchman. On November 3, 1946 Martin was installed alongside Lewis Spitz, to the faculty of Concordia Seminary in St. Louis.[46] This was a change in synods for Franzmann who had spent nearly[47] his entire life in the Wisconsin Evangelical Lutheran Synod. The now defunct Synodical Conference of North America provided the avenue for the switch to The Lutheran Church—Missouri Synod.[48] More than a change in synod, it was also geographically that the Franzmann family would have to shift. Martin, Alice, and their two boys, John and Peter, moved from Wisconsin

---

41. Franzmann, "Of a Man and Four Rivers," 6.

42. Franzmann, "Of a Man and Four Rivers," 7.

43. Gurgel, "The Life and Legacy of Martin Hans Franzmann: Lutheran Poet, Scholar, and Professor," II-1.

44. Leaver was also a friend of Martin Franzmann, having developed a relationship while Martin lived in England. See the introduction of *Come to the Feast* for further information. Rev. Dr. Ronald Feuerhahn developed a relationship with Martin Franzmann while the two lived in England near the end of Martin's life. Additionally, Rev. Feuerhahn served as Martin's pastor.

45. Leaver, *Come to the Feast*, 147.

46. Kretzmann, "News From Concordia Seminary," 410.

47. St. Peter's Lutheran School also belonged to The Lutheran Church—Missouri Synod.

48. Hereafter referred to as LCMS.

to Missouri. John William Franzmann had been born on January 9, 1937 and his brother Peter Bentzin Franzmann entered the world on December 27, 1940. By all accounts Martin was a devoted father.[49] Peter remembers him as, "the one who helped me put up the basketball goal on the back of the house, who helped me put up the mattress for the high jump . . . playing catch, bicycling. He enjoyed bicycling himself and got both me and my brother into it."[50] Martin was, in the words of his son, "A loving father . . . a father who enjoyed his kids and was involved."[51]

Those close to the Franzmann family also remember Martin in this way. Constance Buszin Seddon, daughter of Concordia Seminary professor Walter Buszin, said, "he never hesitated to leave his desk if one of the children needed his attention."[52] Constance and her family became close with the Franzmanns. When Walter Buszin and Martin Franzmann were called to the seminary there were no vacancies in the faculty homes on campus. This resulted in the families living across the street from each other on nearby Alamo Ave.[53] Eventually, when homes became available, the Buszins and Franzmanns would move in next door to each other on Seminary Terrace.[54] To know the Franzmanns was "like nothing you had known before . . . Martin was always the gentleman, welcoming us into his home and making us feel that each of us was a uniquely important guest."[55] Seddon's description of Alice is even more illuminating.

> Alice Franzmann, Martin's wife, was a tall, stately woman of striking appearance. She wore dresses of colorful cotton that were cut in a deep "V" at the neck, with skirts that reached almost to the floor. She tied her long, black hair at the back of her head in a smart knot; her ears were pierced and adorned with large hoop earrings, far from common practice in the 1950s.

---

49. Brinkley, "Of Four Rivers," 127.

50. Interview with Peter Franzmann, August 30, 2017.

51. Interview with Peter Franzmann, August 30, 2017.

52. Seddon, "Memories of the Franzmann Family and the Origins of Thy Strong Word," 140.

53. Seddon, "Memories of the Franzmann Family and the Origins of Thy Strong Word," 140.

54. Seddon, "Memories of the Franzmann Family and the Origins of Thy Strong Word," 140. The Buszin family moved into the former home of Walter Meyer, 11 Seminary Ter. The Franzmann family moved into the former home of Theodore Graebner, 9 Seminary Ter.

55. Seddon, "Memories of the Franzmann Family and the Origins of Thy Strong Word," 140.

Alice was unique in every way, with a warmth and personal charm that endeared her to the Seminary community. It would be a mistake, however, to believe that Alice was only an interesting personality. In fact, she had been an accomplished teacher before marrying Martin, and was the backbone of the Franzmann family, so that Martin could be free to be the scholar. It was Alice, for example, who drove the family car, and Martin who never learned to drive.[56]

On April 11, 1950, Martin and Alice welcomed Alice Louise Franzmann, or "Little Alice," into the family.[57] Serving as godparents for Little Alice were none other than Walter and Margaret Buszin. The relationship between the two families was a strong one, even more so between Walter and Martin. "Not only did the two men have a mutual respect, but they shared a ready knowledge of each other's work."[58] Margaret Buszin's sister was married to a colleague of Martin's when he was teaching at Northwestern College. This meant that "Walter understood Martin's deep roots in the Wisconsin synod, and so there was an immediate and comfortable connection between the two families."[59] Walter was also aware of the early translation work Martin had undertaken at the request of Arthur Katt, as he had served on a subcommittee for the formation of *The Lutheran Hymnal*.

Walter Buszin's academic interest was in hymnody and liturgics. When the seminary had need for a processional hymn for the baccalaureate service, Buszin entrusted the task to Franzmann. One day, while sitting at his desk, Buszin came across a tune he felt perfect for the yet to be written hymn. He promptly got up, walked across the lawn, and gave the tune to Martin, asking him to do something with it because Buszin was too busy.[60] Whether he truly was too busy or just wanted to make use

---

56. Seddon, "Memories of the Franzmann Family and the Origins of Thy Strong Word," 140.

57. Constance Seddon mentions this nickname for the youngest Franzmann child. In interviews with Carol Feuerhan and James Voelz it was confirmed. Also, this necessitated a nickname for the elder Alice Franzmann. Feuerhahn and Voelz referred to her as "Mama Alice" and "Big Alice" respectively. Cf. Brinkley, "Of Four Rivers," 128.

58. Seddon, "Memories of the Franzmann Family and the Origins of Thy Strong Word," 141.

59. Seddon, "Memories of the Franzmann Family and the Origins of Thy Strong Word," 140.

60. Seddon, "Memories of the Franzmann Family and the Origins of Thy Strong Word," 143.

of his talented colleague and neighbor is irrelevant. Franzmann would fulfill the request, writing four verses based on the motto of the seminary, ανοθεν το φος, "Light from Above." The hymn was first sung in chapel on October 7, 1954.[61] Eventually two more verses would be added, including the verse that began this chapter.[62] "Thy Strong Word," arguably the hymn for which Martin Franzmann is best known, came about as the result of that request from Buszin.

Franzmann's career as a scholar and ecumenist[63] flourished during those years serving on the faculty, and unsurprisingly, his hymn writing would continue. Leaver tracks the chronology of Franzmann's hymn writing and demonstrates that the period of time spent at Concordia Seminary in St. Louis was his most prolific period of composition. Of the twenty-nine original and translated hymns connected with Franzmann, nine were completed before the end of 1938 and five would be finished after 1969. A total of sixteen would be written during his tenure at Concordia Seminary.[64] Franzmann's second to last hymn was called, "Preach You the Word,"[65] and was written for Concordia Theological Seminary in Springfield, Illinois,[66] the sister seminary of Concordia in St. Louis. It was this seminary, a place where he would spend one year teaching, that awarded him a Doctor of Divinity degree in 1956.[67]

Although honorary, doctor was a title Franzmann demonstrated he deserved not only because of the quality of his work but also the quantity.

61. "Light from Above," 362.

62. Brinkley in *Thy Strong Word* and Leaver in *Come to the Feast* track the development of this hymn. It is interesting to note that while both have theories as to how the hymn developed, how the verses were ordered, and who wrote them, Constance Seddon's analysis in her aforementioned essay lays any debate to rest (see page 143). Franzmann wrote every verse as the content in the archives of Concordia Historical Institute will demonstrate.

63. It should be remembered that Franzmann understood ecumenicity in broad terms. See footnote 3 in the Preface or chapter 5 for more information.

64. Franzmann served as professor at Concordia Seminary from his installation in the fall of 1946 until his retirement from the seminary at the end of the 1968–69 academic year. He would begin his time in Cambridge in October of 1969.

65. The hymn was written in conjunction with his time spent there as a professor in 1973.

66. That seminary has since moved to Fort Wayne, Indiana.

67. Franzmann spent a portion of the 1972–73 academic year at the seminary in Springfield. His degree was awarded on June 1, 1956. Seminary President Walter Baepler and president of the Board of Control Alvin W. Mueller's signatures appear on the diploma. That diploma is extant in the archives of Concordia Historical Institute.

The sheer output of his literary work is impressive in its own right.[68] He was a regular contributor to the seminary's journal *Concordia Theological Monthly* and the synod's publication *The Lutheran Witness*. What makes it even more astonishing is that this output happened at the same time he taught a full load at the seminary and served on various committees across ecclesiastical institutions. A brief list of those committees and his position on them includes: Bad Boll Commissioner (1949, 1953, 1956), Synodical Advisory Committee on English Bible Versions (1950–1956), Secretary, Synodical Conference (1952–1956), Chairman, Department of Exegetical Theology at Concordia Seminary (1956–1969), Vice-chairman of the Committee on Doctrinal Unity (1950–1962), LCMS Representative to the Lutheran World Federation (1962), and Member of the Commission on Theology and Church Relations of the LCMS (1962–1969).[69] In addition, he routinely served as essayist at conventions and convocations nationally and internationally.[70]

It was Little Alice's marriage to a Royal Naval officer that brought Martin and Mama Alice to the shores of England in 1969. Martin had earned a sabbatical year in 1967 and spent it overseas where Alice and her eventual husband were. Peter Franzmann believed that Lutherans in Cambridge availed themselves of the opportunity to convince his father to join their ranks.[71] It was not nearly as difficult as one might think. Martin Franzmann was a "committed Anglophile" and credited those early years reading and teaching English literature to have generated such a love.[72] He would be installed as Tutor at Westfield House in Cambridge on Saturday October 4, 1969 at the Abbey Church on Newmarket Road. This day bears significance for another reason; at the same service, Martin Franzmann would also be ordained by the Evangelical Lutheran Church of England. For years Martin was "deemed to be the Missouri Synod equivalent of Melanchthon. This kind of exception that proves the rule."[73] The "rule" referred to is the Missouri Synod's insistence that any-

---

68. See Appendix: Another Franzmann Bibliography.

69. "Service Bulletin: Martin Hans Franzmann."

70. This includes the 1952 Synodical Conference Convention and the 1952 Northern Illinois District Convention. Not only were the audiences different, the essays themselves were different. For an example of international exploits, see Koch, *When the Murray Meets the Mississippi*, 217.

71. Interview with Peter Franzmann, August 30, 2017.

72. Franzmann, "Of a Man and Four Rivers," 6.

73. Interview with James W. Voelz, July 25, 2017.

one called to preach or teach theology should be ordained. While some may have assumed Franzmann was, his Wisconsin synod formation and employment did not require him to be. Additionally, no one tried to hide this fact. "He would preach in chapel and wear a cassock and surplice, but with no stole."[74] What explanation might there be for this situation? "Sometimes genius is enough."[75]

His lack of ordination does not seem to have made any difference with the students he taught during those years at Concordia Seminary. After Martin's death a former student made the following assertion: "It is too rare in professorial lectures that learning and truth are combined with a language that is rich and fat, like a great harvest, or delightful and hilarious, like a burst of joy. Franzmann often achieved that union."[76] His style would be remembered, even if at times some of the content was forgotten. "It was kind of like this: Man that was a great class, what did he say?"[77] That is not to speak ill of Franzmann, rather it is an affectionate description of how students were captivated by him. "He had incredible insights. I still use [one] to this day. He would say, 'The most thorough going proof for the doctrine of original sin is in a subordinate clause in Matthew,' and we would ask, what is it? [and he said] 'If you who *are* evil, know how to give good gifts to your children . . .' and it stuck."[78] The captivation with Professor Franzmann spilled outside of the classroom too. Two students, Dean Wenthe and James Voelz, met once a week of their own accord in Franzmann's office just to read metaphysical poetry like Spencer and John Donne.[79] For some, the connection between professor and student verged on the pastoral. One student has fondly remarked, "We were his congregation."[80]

In Cambridge Franzmann would officially serve in pastoral roles. Although called to the position of Tutor at Westfield House, during vacancy periods he would regularly travel across the country to military bases and conduct services for the troops.[81] He would also participate

---

74. Interview with James W. Voelz, July 25, 2017.
75. Personal correspondence with Richard Brinkley, 2017.
76. Korby, "Notes from the Editor's Notebook," 5.
77. Interview with James W. Voelz, July 25, 2017.
78. Interview with James W. Voelz, July 25, 2017.
79. Interview with James W. Voelz, July 25, 2017.
80. Interview with Robert Mordhorst, August 25, 2017.
81. Interview with Carol Feuerhahn, September 25, 2017.

in at least one church building dedication ceremony, not just wearing the cassock and surplice, but also the stole to match the office he now inhabited.[82] The dedication of the outdoor pulpit at St. Peter's Lutheran Church in Sunbury had historical significance for the Evangelical Lutheran Church of England.[83] Stones from the first building used some three hundred years earlier by Lutherans to officially worship in England were used in the construction of an outer wall and outdoor pulpit.[84] Why Martin was asked to participate in this is unknown. The sermon was delivered by chairman of the ELCE, Rev. Dr. E. George Pearce, which means Martin was there for some other reason, perhaps only to pull back the red curtain that had veiled the commemoration foundation stone.[85] His participation in this event, and in his travelling around the English countryside, speaks to the fact that Martin was involved not merely in the life of Westfield house, but in the life of the ELCE as a whole. That life would see Martin participate in conferences, delivering papers as well as providing commentary on recent events in the life of his former church body, the LCMS.[86]

To be sure, his work at Westfield House as tutor would take up most of his time. It was not, however, only the New Testament that Martin would spend time teaching. Franzmann was quite adept at Hebrew as well, even penning a set of introductory notes published by Concordia Publishing House on the Minor Prophets.[87] Westfield House would make use of this talent when Martin taught a course on Obadiah.[88] The focus of his work in Cambridge would continue to be what it was in St. Louis, the formation of pastors as holistic theologians. One of the ways this was achieved was through weekly pericope studies. "On every Tuesday afternoon all the students of Westfield House gather for an hour and a half to study the Propers . . . Each man contributes to the study according to his ability, and all are encouraged to join in the discussion."[89] Some students

82. Pearce, "The Stones of All Hallows—Speak," 6–9.
83. Hereafter referred to as ELCE.
84. "Ancient Stone Used in Lutheran Ceremony," 11.
85. "Ancient Stone Used in Lutheran Ceremony," 11.
86. "News from Our Churches," 8.
87. See Franzmann and Roehrs, *Concordia Self-Study Commentary: An Authoritative In-Home Resource for Students of the Bible*.
88. Interview with James W. Voelz, July 25, 2017.
89. Franzmann, "Westfield's Window," 2. This was a column of sorts in the *British Lutheran* that ran regularly and had various authors. Franzmann penned four entries

would prepare for an extended discussion of the readings on the basis of Greek or Hebrew while others might be asked to find a hymn that matches the day and still others would prepare a sermon.[90]

"What goes on here is not very dramatic; nor is it, at this stage, necessarily profound. But it is felt that what this hour is trying to achieve is most important for the theology of both students and instructors."[91] Important because of what the traditional divisions of theology can create. Whether it is Exegetical, Historical, Systematic, or Practical, there is a temptation to let "divisions become separate compartments of study, not clearly and organically related to one another and to the whole."[92] In Franzmann's estimation, what happens then is that,

> Each part becomes a fascinating branch of scholarship, pursued for its own sake and unmindful of the fact that it is part of a ministry and exists only for that ministry; the whole loses its coherence and thrust—it becomes a collection of arrows displayed in separate cases, not the quiverful [sic] of arrows slung across the shoulder of the Church to serve the Church's conquest, with all the arrows destined to be pointed at and to pierce the heart of man.[93]

The Tuesday afternoon sessions were an attempt to mitigate such a danger.

> Our aim is to keep theology whole, that mind and heart, according well, may make one music. Our aim is to keep theology practical, an arrow poised for shooting. Our aim is above all to keep theology doxological, a song of praise to Him who loves us, has redeemed us and made us kings and priests in the service of His majestic love.[94]

A theologian asserting that theology should be doxological is an unsurprising, and indeed common, occurrence. It is far rarer, however, that a theologian's output reflects such a doxology in all its manifestations.

---

all noted in the bibliography by the same title. All citations in this chapter are from the November 1969 issue.

90. Interview with James W. Voelz, July 25, 2017. It should be noted that Voelz was a student of Franzmann's at both Concordia Seminary in St. Louis and at Westfield House while Voelz was pursuing doctoral work at the University of Cambridge.

91. Franzmann, "Westfield's Window," 2.

92. Franzmann, "Westfield's Window," 2.

93. Franzmann, "Westfield's Window," 2.

94. Franzmann, "Westfield's Window," 3.

"It was on the morning of Laetare Sunday 1976 that Martin Franzmann died. The congregation at Resurrection Lutheran Church in Cambridge was singing 'Jesu Meine Freude' at the time. Laetare, that is, Rejoice Sunday, was an appropriate day for Martin's home going."[95] In the winter of 1975 Martin's health began to rapidly deteriorate.[96] On the death certificate the cause was attributed to "exhaustion."[97] The deterioration of Martin's health was due in part to the role he played in repairing the breach at Concordia Seminary.[98] It was only four years prior, in 1972, that Martin retired from his position as tutor. He and Alice moved to a cottage in Wells and sought to live out their retirement in the same country as two of their children.[99] Little Alice, now Mrs. Ian Fletcher, and John Franzmann both lived in England as John succeeded his father as tutor at Westfield House. That John followed in his father's footsteps is not surprising. After all, it was John who learned Greek while sitting on his father's knee while Martin shaved.[100] During his retirement Martin still kept busy, authoring two books and taking time to teach at the seminary in Springfield, Illinois. There he would teach courses and advise students much the same as he had done for years.[101] Martin died in Cambridge on March 28, 1976, the morning where, "the Psalm verse of the Introit and of the Gradual [were], 'I was glad when they said unto me, let us go to the house of the Lord.'"[102] Mama Alice would continue to live in England, having buried their son John in 1990. She passed away in 1996.

95. Ronald Feuerhahn, "A Festival of Hymns of Martin Franzmann," audio recording.

96. Brinkley, "Of Four Rivers," 133.

97. Interview Peter Franzmann, August 30, 2017.

98. His role is explored in chapter 6 and so it will not be dealt with in detail here.

99. Cf. Brinkley, "Of Four Rivers," 132. He notes that they also maintained a flat in Cambridge.

100. Personal correspondence with Carol Feuerhahn, February 2018.

101. Cf. Daniel Burfiend, "A Third Way? Martin Franzmann's Contributions to Discussions on the Nature and Interpretation of Scripture in The Lutheran Church—Missouri Synod" (Master of Sacred Theology Thesis, Concordia Theological Seminary, Fort Wayne, Indiana). Burfiend spent time interviewing Walter Maier Jr. whose master's thesis was supervised by Franzmann at that time. Two courses that Franzmann taught were "The Art of Exegesis" and "Revelation." During this time Martin would also give a lecture on poetry. Cf. Robin Leaver, *Come to the Feast*.

102. Feuerhahn, "A Festival of Hymns of Martin Franzmann," audio recording.

Martin passed away in the assurance of his faith in God, something he possessed from his days beside Lake Pepin. His early poetry reflects this beautifully.

> Remember not our youthful sin,
>   The follies we have gloried in.
> Be with us still, as Thou hast been
>   When we go forth.
>
> And soften the regretful pain,
>   The aching wish to do again.
> Let us forget the hopes we've slain
>   When we go forth.
>
> Give Thou Thy peace into each heart
>   That we may play the manly part.
> And with Thy blessing bid us start
>   When we go forth.
>
> What's done, or well, or ill, is done,
>   But in what is to be begun
> We look to Thee, almighty One,
>   When we go forth.[103]

Some might suggest this trust in the "almighty One" reflects the naivety of youth. Perhaps it does, Martin was only seventeen at the time it was written. It is clear that Martin believed that looking to God in the days that lie ahead is a wise course of action. Doing so provides peace in the heart and a confidence despite folly and pain. This perspective does not, however, seem to have been something he abandoned in his latter days.

> If ever a man had cause to cherish a cheerful hope in God's mercy, I am that man. And so I face the challenges and opportunities of my new life beside the Cam with all the trepidations, naturally, that flesh is heir to, but also with the overriding conviction and confidence . . . that He who has led me hitherto will shepherd me also beside the still waters of the Cam, and will of His grace bring me to my last river, the "river of water of life,

---

103. Franzmann, "When We Go Forth," 61.

clear as crystal, proceeding out of the throne of God and of the Lamb."[104]

As he went forth into his last years, Martin continued to look to God. He saw the work of God that had carried him from Minnesota to Wisconsin, from St. Louis to Cambridge, and he was sure that same God would carry him to the end.

THEOLOGY MUST SING

Among other things, the above shows how practical he understood the theological task to be. It was not something to put on a shelf, it was not "a collection of arrows [to be] displayed in separate cases."[105] Theology for Franzmann was something that should touch the heart of a person. It was doxology. It must sing. His friend and colleague Walter Buszin first introduced the axiom to Franzmann that, "theology is doxology."[106] Famously Franzmann used the phrase in a sermon based on Colossians 3:16 intended for Reformation Sunday. "Theology is doxology. Theology must sing."[107] What he meant by this is articulated in the final paragraph of the sermon.

> The song of the church must be an unending song. The church must cherish the best, but its song should not be a mere repetition of the song of the past. Then shall we sing with grace, with all the emphasis on God and a most unsentimental subordination of ourselves. We shall sing to the Lord. With our song we shall guide one another continually to the center and fountain of the Christian's life and thus really teach and admonish one another. We shall sing in our hearts; the whole man will sing. We shall see then realized the ideal of all Christian song: the whole man with all his powers, with all the skills and gifts that God has bestowed upon him wholly bent on giving utterance to the peace that rules within him, wholly given to the purpose of letting the Word of Christ that dwells in him richly become articulate and

---

104. Franzmann, "Of a Man and Four Rivers," 7.
105. Franzmann, "Westfield's Window," 2.
106. Seddon, "Memories of the Franzmann Family and the Origins of the Franzmann Hymn 'Thy Strong Word,'" 144.
107. Franzmann, *Ha! Ha! Among the Trumpets*, 92.

audible through him to the upbuilding of the church and the glory of God. Then shall our theology be doxology.[108]

Franzmann believed that articulation is integral to understanding doxology.[109] Theology must sing in that it must speak eloquently of what God has done in Christ for humanity. In doing so, it uplifts the church and honors God, not simply for who God is, but for what God has done. This can be seen clearly in the hymn "In Adam We Have All Been One."

> In Adam we have all been one,
> One huge rebellious man;
> We all have fled that Evening Voice
> That sought us as we ran.
>
> We fled Thee, and in losing Thee
> We lost our brother too;
> Each singly sought and claimed his own;
> Each man his brother slew.
>
> But Thy strong love, it sought us still
> And sent Thine only Son
> That we might hear His shepherd's voice
> And, hearing Him, be one.
>
> O Thou who, when we loved Thee not,
> Didst love and save us all,
> Thou great Good Shepherd of mankind,
> O Hear us when we call.
>
> Send us Thy Spirit, teach us truth;
> Thou Son, O set us free
> From fancied wisdom, self-sought ways,
> To make us one in thee.
>
> Then shall our song united rise
> To thine eternal throne,
> Where with the Father evermore
> And Spirit Thou art one.[110]

---

108. Franzmann, *Ha! Ha! Among the Trumpets*, 97.

109. See footnote 117 of Robin Leaver, *Come to the Feast*, 151.

110. Franzmann, "In Adam We Have All Been One," *Lutheran Service Book*, 569. Both Brinkley and Leaver in their aforementioned works also record this hymn.

Even a brief analysis of this hymn reveals the theology to which Franzmann gave voice. In Adam's fall, all humanity fell. This was not merely a break between God and humanity, it was a break within humanity too. God did not, however, leave humanity to its own devices. The love of God sought, it called out with the shepherd's voice that humanity might be brought back to God and to one another. Only God can free a person from their own self-interests. One does not have to agree with Franzmann's theological position in this hymn to appreciate his eloquence and perspective of how theology can sing when it truly is doxology.

"As long as Martin Franzmann's hymns are sung, he will be remembered."[111] Of all the hymns that Franzmann wrote "Thy Strong Word" seems to have garnered the most attention as it has found a place in no fewer than nine hymnals of various denominational background.[112] One sees in that hymn, Franzmann's eloquence that calls forth those things which God has done for humanity. The problem, however, is that it is not only his hymns that reflect such things. While other writers have delved into his hymnody, scant attention has been paid to the vast literary output that bears his name.[113] As has been demonstrated, Franzmann was not one who compartmentalized theology. The hymns reflect something deeper, something that lies well beneath the surface. His work as a scholar and ecumenical figure, his place as a child before God, these things formed the basis from which the hymnody sprang. To know him only as a hymn writer, to know only his hymns, is to know him partially, fragmentally. To know only the hymns is to compartmentalize him.

Although the context is unknown, in and among the papers of Franzmann's pastor and friend was the following:

> Dr. Martin Franzmann
> A son of the Wisconsin Synod,
> A brother of the Missouri Synod, and
> A father to the Evangelical Lutheran Church of England.
> A servant to all Confessional Lutheranism.

---

111. Seddon, "Memories of the Franzmann Family and the Origins of the Franzmann Hymn 'Thy Strong Word,'" 146.

112. Brinkley, *Thy Strong Word*, 125.

113. For a further exploration of Franzmann's hymnody the following resources are suggested: Brinkley, *Thy Strong Word: The Enduring Legacy of Martin Franzmann*; Brinkley, "The Hymns of Martin Franzmann: A Perspective"; Leaver, *Come to the Feast*; Stuempfle, "Hymn Interpretation."

A faithful listener and loyal teacher.[114]

One might expect that somewhere in this should be included the words, "poet" and "hymn writer." Clearly he was both of those, in fact, in his own estimation no greater compliment could be paid than for someone to be a poet of the church.[115] It is fitting, however, that those words do not appear, because he was more than a poet, more than a hymn writer. He was a son, a brother, a husband, a father, a friend, a servant, a teacher, and above all a listener. He was a man whose theology sang in every area of his life, not just in the hymns for which he is remembered.

---

114. Personal correspondence with Carol Feuerhahn, September 2017.

115. See Franzmann, "The Devil Has All the Good Tunes?" in Leaver, *Come to the Feast*, 137.

2

Beggars Before God

THIEVES IN THE NIGHT

"On a Friday night in March 1924 at Wisconsin's Northwestern College in Watertown, a routine examination of theft led to a chain of confessions, 'squealing' and further investigations, until dormitory tutors assembled 27 boys guilty of stealing."[1] The faculty took swift action against the students involved, meting out punishments befitting the involvement, which included "expulsions, suspensions, and campus arrests."[2] These punishments, however, were "subject to the approval of the Board" because only the board of directors had the power to expel.[3] This caveat proved more than superficial when the board countermanded the faculty-imposed punishments, in some cases "commuting the suspensions to campus arrests and requiring a review of each expulsion."[4] Such a move did not bode well for the faculty. The response to the board's actions was

---

1. Braun, "The Protes'tant Controversy and Its Impact on the Wisconsin Synod," 81.
2. Braun, "The Protes'tant Controversy and Its Impact on the Wisconsin Synod," 81.
3. Braun, "The Protes'tant Controversy and Its Impact on the Wisconsin Synod," 81. Braun, a Wisconsin Evangelical Lutheran Synod historian, notes that this quote is recorded in a letter from E. E. Kowalke to John Brenner, dated April 10, 1924. Brenner was a member of the Board of Directors and Kowalke was not only Northwestern's president but the parent of an accused student. Cf. Peter Prange, "Pastor E. Arnold Sitz and the Protes'tants: Witnessing to the Wauwatosa Gospel," 23.
4. Braun, "The Protes'tant Controversy and Its Impact on the Wisconsin Synod," 81.

less than charitable, several claiming, "that the board was incompetent to judge the actions of either students or professors."[5] Gustav Bergemann, Wisconsin Synod President and ex-officio member of Northwestern College's board, inserted his voice into the discussion. Speaking concerning what the faculty considered to be a perfunctory caveat, he allegedly said, "If that is not the statute, then it is high time that it be made the rule and that the law is laid down to this faculty."[6] The law was laid down, the board overruled the faculty, and tensions began to rise in the Wisconsin Synod.

In the fall of that same year, Martin Franzmann matriculated into Northwestern College from the Preparatory school. While these formative years would be spent cultivating his intellect and developing scholarly interests, they would also be set during one of, if not the most, tumultuous time in his church body. When Martin graduated in 1928, he was offered a teaching position that had been vacated by a Protes'tant.[7] In 1930 when he began his seminary studies at the Wauwatosa campus, it is on the heels of the dismissal of the seminary's president. It is helpful, then, to explore in brief this Protes'tant Controversy and the perspective of Wauwatosa theologians. The goal of this exploration is not to render a value judgment but to offer the context that shaped Martin Franzmann's hermeneutical perspective. Through such observation one is better equipped to understand and investigate his hermeneutical framework.[8]

PROTES'TANTS CLAMOUR

The dispute between the faculty and board at Northwestern College over the guilty students was not about the students' guilt. Everyone involved agreed that those who had been investigated and found to be in possession of stolen goods, whether because they had stolen it or had received

---

5. Braun, "The Protes'tant Controversy and Its Impact on the Wisconsin Synod," 81.

6. Braun, "The Protes'tant Controversy and Its Impact on the Wisconsin Synod," 81. Prange, in his aforementioned essay, quotes the president but does not name the source of the quote. Here Braun quotes Prange without making note of the lack of substantiated evidence.

7. This is not a misspelling; it is the preferred designation of some of those involved in the events to be explored.

8. This framework will be explored in brief in this chapter. A subsequent chapter explores it in depth and provides examples of how the framework can be seen in his exegetical works.

it, were guilty of the things for which they were accused.[9] The controversy was about how the board responded to the actions of the faculty. The board's repudiation of the expulsions and suspensions resulted in the resignation of two faculty members. This was due to the fact that several faculty members felt that the board's intervention undermined the authority of the faculty. "All the professors, except Dr. Ott, stated that they were convinced that, under the conditions, it would be detrimental to the college if the faculty rescind its former action, as they were still of the opinion that the action of the faculty was justified."[10] Karl Koehler and Herbert Parisius resigned when the board further refused to affirm the decisions of the faculty. Their letter of resignation is illuminating.

> We herewith resign as teachers in your employ, our resignation to go into effect at once. Added to what we protested and pleaded in the course of the recent proceedings, there now weighs upon us the utterly ruthless and unchristian nature of the Board's procedure, persisted in, against our fervent hopes, to the very end. We so charge you before God and shall bring this and all other charges respecting your incompetence before the body which you profess to represent.[11]

The resignation caused further controversy. Koehler and Parisius did not want their resignation to impact the rest of the faculty's workload and so offered to remain teaching until the end of the term. While the faculty was amenable to this, the board refused to allow it, citing that in allowing the faculty to accept the free assistance of their now resigned colleagues, they were usurping the board's ability to hire faculty.[12]

News of the struggle at Northwestern College began to spread and in June of 1924 a meeting was held "for the announced purpose of hearing

---

9. On this point there seems to be wide agreement. Mark Braun, Peter Prange, and Leigh Jordahl all affirm it in their own explorations of the topic. See Braun, "The Protes'tant Controversy and Its Impact on the Wisconsin Synod"; Prange, "Pastor E. Arnold Sitz and the Protes'tants: Witnessing to the Wauwatosa Gospel"; and Leigh Jordahl, "Introduction," in John Philipp Koehler, *The History of the Wisconsin Synod*.

10. Northwestern College faculty minutes, April 23, 1924. Quoted in Prange, "Pastor E. Arnold Sitz and the Protes'tants: Witnessing to the Wauwatosa Gospel," 24.

11. Karl Koehler and Herbert Parisius, letter to the Northwestern College Board, April 29, 1924. Quoted in Prange, "Pastor E. Arnold Sitz and the Protes'tants: Witnessing to the Wauwatosa Gospel," 24.

12. Prange, "Pastor E. Arnold Sitz and the Protes'tants: Witnessing to the Wauwatosa Gospel," 25. Cf. Leigh Jordahl, "Introduction," xxv.

the Faculty's side to the story."[13] Gerhard Ruediger, a professor at the Wisconsin Synod seminary in Watertown, called the meeting.[14] While the board of directors were informed of the meeting, only one member chose to attend. "The Board regarded the meeting as objectionable in principle."[15] In attendance were "several pastors . . . those later identified as Protes'tants."[16] This meeting did little to bring the faculty and board back together; it seems, rather, to have driven the sides further apart.[17] "Wisconsin Synod leaders have frequently maintained that this meeting marked the emergence to public view of a 'determined and united clique.'"[18] Because of his role in calling the meeting, Ruediger fell under suspicion as a troublemaker. "It was also maintained that Ruediger had discussed the case in his seminary classes, had made slanderous charges against Synod officials and had neglected his academic duties."[19] Despite Ruediger's confession of guilt and absolution, he was removed from the seminary faculty in 1927.

The Protes'tant controversy is rooted also in two subsequent events. The first involved two schoolteachers, Gerda Koch and Elizabeth Rueter, of St. Paul's Lutheran School in Fort Atkinson, Wisconsin. These women "expressed growing disappointment at the worldliness of some church members and dissatisfaction at the lack of spirituality in congregational activities."[20] At the forefront of the attacks was a condemnation of "particularly prevalent sins of the time: women's bobbed hair and inappropriate dress, declining church life, lack of interests in missions and growing materialism."[21] The two women would study the scriptures on their own, which was not in and of itself a problem. Rather, the problem was that they would take their studies back into the classroom, espousing their views to the children in their care. They became so vocal that "they were fast becoming the preachers in the congregation. Life was beginning to

13. Jordahl, "Introduction," xxv.

14. Jordahl, "Introduction," xxv.

15. Jordahl, "Introduction," xxv.

16. Jordahl, "Introduction," xxv.

17. Prange, "Pastor E. Arnold Sitz and the Protes'tants: Witnessing to the Wauwatosa Gospel," 28. Cf. Jordahl, "Introduction," xxv.

18. Jordahl, "Introduction," xxv. Jordahl quotes a 1938 *Report of the Committee of Twelve of the North Wisconsin District of the Wisconsin Synod*.

19. Jordahl, "Introduction," xxv.

20. Braun, "The Protes'tant Controversy and Its Impact on the Wisconsin Synod," 82.

21. Braun, "The Protes'tant Controversy and Its Impact on the Wisconsin Synod," 83.

grow from this leaven."²² Their vocalizations created enemies. Not only would the teachers begin "to absent themselves from choir rehearsals, Ladies' Aid, Walther League, and ultimately worship. They encouraged their pupils to do the same."²³ When the teachers would bring concerns to their pastor, A. F. Nicolaus, he would encourage them that such matters as bobbed hair were something neither commanded nor forbidden by God. By December of 1924, things had deteriorated so much that during a council meeting Koch whispered to Rueter "Beware of false prophets."²⁴ This comment was aimed directly against their pastor. When asked to repeat the comment for the entire group to hear, Koch did so. At that moment Nicolaus responded calling her a "saucy greenhorn."²⁵ Until the women apologized for the remark, the council and pastor would not permit the women to continue teaching.

Instead of asking for a release from their current positions, they contacted a mentor at Dr. Martin Luther College in New Ulm, Minnesota, who helped arrange for their hiring at a different school.²⁶ This aggravated the congregation in St. Paul. The women, at the urging of their new pastor, appealed their suspension at St. Paul's to the district president. Consistently the women refused to retract their comment and ended up being suspended from the roster of teachers in the Wisconsin Synod. The public announcement of this final decision was made in an effort to appease St. Paul's pastor who was still not happy with the fact that not only had the women been allowed to teach at Immanuel in Marshfield, but also in two other schools, Koch at St. John in Wauwatosa and Rueter at Christus in Milwaukee,²⁷ during the 1925–1926 academic year.

> This "officious" action on the part of district officials "to keep the peace" enraged a number of people; some perhaps did not even

---

22. William Beitz, letter to Immanuel Frey, May 19, 1926. Quoted in Prange, "Pastor E. Arnold Sitz and the Protes'tants: Witnessing to the Wauwatosa Gospel," 34.

23. Prange, "Pastor E. Arnold Sitz and the Protes'tants: Witnessing to the Wauwatosa Gospel," 34.

24. William Beitz, letter to Immanuel Frey, May 19, 1926. Quoted in Prange, "Pastor E. Arnold Sitz and the Protes'tants: Witnessing to the Wauwatosa Gospel," 34.

25. William Beitz, letter to Immanuel Frey, May 19, 1926. Quoted in Prange, "Pastor E. Arnold Sitz and the Protes'tants: Witnessing to the Wauwatosa Gospel," 34.

26. Prange, "Pastor E. Arnold Sitz and the Protes'tants: Witnessing to the Wauwatosa Gospel," 34–35.

27. Prange, "Pastor E. Arnold Sitz and the Protes'tants: Witnessing to the Wauwatosa Gospel," 35.

have an intimate knowledge of the situation. They flooded the two synodical magazines with letters of complaint and seemed to single out one man in particular as the "devil" behind the public announcement, Professor August Pieper.[28]

Furthermore,

> The teachers' original concerns were soon overshadowed by complaint over how the issue had been handled. When the West Wisconsin District at its 1926 convention in Beaver Dam voted to ratify the teachers' suspension, a group of fifteen pastors and two laymen protested the action in writing, voicing for the first time what became a Protes'tant slogan: less important than the particular details of the Fort Atkinson case itself were *"hoehere Fragen"* ["higher questions"]. The protesters sought to get at the *grundlegenden Prinzipien*—the underlying principles.[29]

While the events regarding the faculty of Northwestern and the teachers of Fort Atkinson seem to have no direct relation to each other, both became touchstones for members of the Wisconsin Synod who were becoming increasingly suspicious and disaffected of Synod officials who acted dogmatically instead of evangelically. That is to say, observers of these events were concerned with the method by which the events in question were handled by Synod officials. In the case of Northwestern College, the Synod president's insistence that the faculty be brought in line, and in the case of Fort Atkinson, with the public dissemination of the suspension and subsequent efforts in one district to ratify the suspension. In handling the cases, the synod demonstrated to "protestors" the dogmatic spirit, which is understood as an intractable legalistic spirit, of the synod. Such a spirit is in opposition to the evangelical spirit, which concerns itself with the love and care of individuals. The strong preference for an evangelical spirit coalesces in "The Just Shall Live By Faith, a paper presented by William Beitz at a joint conference of Missouri Synod and Wisconsin Synod pastors in 1926."[30]

The first time Beitz presented his paper was actually in September of 1926 at a conference for only Wisconsin Synod pastors. Although Beitz

---

28. Prange, "Pastor E. Arnold Sitz and the Protes'tants: Witnessing to the Wauwatosa Gospel," 35. Pieper was a professor at the seminary in Wauwatosa.

29. Braun, "The Protes'tant Controversy and Its Impact on the Wisconsin Synod," 85.

30. Braun, "The Protes'tant Controversy and Its Impact on the Wisconsin Synod," 86–87.

had been assigned a different topic for that gathering,[31] he presented "The Just Shall Live By Faith." It would be presented several more times during the course of 1926–1927 in private gatherings.[32] The joint Missouri and Wisconsin conference in October of 1926, however, was the intended audience.

> Assigned an exegetical study of Galatians 3, Beitz instead used the Reformation pericope to launch an assault on the spiritual shortcomings of the synod. Beitz's writing was regarded by some as inflammatory, his judgments sweeping and severe. In its seminary training, its preaching and teaching and its congregational life, the Wisconsin Synod failed, Beitz charged, to "live by faith."
>
> Protesters rallied around his paper, finding in it the substance to address their "higher questions." One even called it "our Bible."[33]

Not everyone was as enthralled with the Beitz paper as the protesters. While some saw benefit in Beitz's accusations and arguments, the harsh tone alienated others.[34] G. M. Thurow, West Wisconsin District President, solicited the faculty of the seminary at Wauwatosa for an opinion on the validity of the paper.[35] "The faculty found three major faults with the Beitz paper: 1) it confused the distinction between justification and sanctification; 2) it obscured the roles of Law and Gospel in repentance; and 3) it judged heart and slandered."[36] The *Gutachten der Theologischen*

---

31. Prange notes, "Beitz had also been assigned a paper on Christian Citizenship for the Wisconsin River-Chippewa Valley Conference, held in Schofield on September 14–15, 1926. When he didn't complete it, Beitz explained 'that he had his Mixed Conference paper . . . with him, which he was willing to submit here, since, after all, it was fundamental, too, to the problem of Christian citizenship.'" Prange, "Pastor E. Arnold Sitz and the Protes'tants: Witnessing to the Wauwatosa Gospel," 46.

32. Braun, "The Protes'tant Controversy and Its Impact on the Wisconsin Synod," 87.

33. Braun, "The Protes'tant Controversy and Its Impact on the Wisconsin Synod," 87.

34. Braun, "The Protes'tant Controversy and Its Impact on the Wisconsin Synod," 87.

35. Leigh Jordahl notes that, "a solicitation of opinions from a theological faculty had been common practice among Missourians. The practice had never been favored by the Wauwatosa Theology. Nevertheless, in this instance the request was entertained." Jordahl, "Introduction," xxvi. Likely the aversion alluded to by Jordahl is due to the fact that one of the hallmarks of "Wauwatosa Theology," which should not be confused with an official position of the seminary but rather understood as the perspective of certain professors from 1900 to 1930, is that people should do the historical and exegetical investigation themselves and not rely on the dogmatic pronouncements of others.

36. Braun, "The Protes'tant Controversy and Its Impact on the Wisconsin Synod," 88.

Fakultaet von Wauwatosa was written by two of the seminary's professors, August Pieper and J. P. Meyer but was signed by all of them, including the seminary president J. P. Koehler.[37]

WAUWATOSA PERSPECTIVE

At this point it is helpful to give a brief sketch of John Philipp Koehler and August Pieper because of their association with what is known as the Wauwatosa Theology. Koehler and Pieper were classmates during their years at Concordia Seminary in St. Louis. Although Concordia was the seminary for The Lutheran Church—Missouri Synod, the existence of the Synodical Conference allowed students of the Wisconsin Synod to train there. During their years in St. Louis both Koehler and Piper, as well as a third Wauwatosa colleague, John Shaller, studied under C. F. W. Walther.[38] Walther is a prominent figure in Missouri Synod history, not only because of his role in its founding, but because he served as President of both the synod and the seminary at various times. Moreover, his voice on the American Lutheran landscape was a loud one. His didactic approach, however, left something to be desired.

> During his first year in St. Louis, Koehler studied under C. F.W. Walther and experienced first-hand the dominance of dogmatics in the curriculum. August Pieper later remembered that "New Testament exegesis consisted mainly of dictated quotations from the Lutheran exegetes of the 16th and 17th centuries" and that the hermeneutics course was taught by Walther using a Latin textbook that had been published in 1754.The hermeneutics class also included "cursory reading of a gospel in German." In other words, the Bible itself was seldom used. The textbook for the dogmatics class was Baier's Compendium, which led to student complaints about *"Baier ochsen"* (slaving away at Baier).[39]

This experience was foundational for Koehler, Pieper, and Schaller in that it cemented in them a desire to keep dogmatics secondary to exegesis. This is because they had experienced the reverse so intensely.

37. Jordahl, "Introduction," xxvi.

38. Space does not permit here to give a full explanation of C. F. W. Walther and his place within American Lutheranism. For further information about Walther, see Barnbrock et al., *C. F. W. Walther: Churchman and Theologian*.

39. Albrecht, "John Philipp Koehler (1859–1951) and the Wauwatosa Theology," 427.

Koehler wanted to read the Holy Scriptures historically, yet without relativizing them, and he insisted that the exegete must learn to hear the music and poetry of the Bible in order to appreciate the aesthetic qualities that are essential to the Word of God. This scriptural conviction was central to what became known as the Wauwatosa Theology. To some extent, this movement within the Wisconsin Synod was a reaction against the repristination theology that C. F. W. Walther and Francis Pieper[40] fostered in the Lutheran Church—Missouri Synod, but Prof. Koehler did not aspire to make a name for himself by means of theological innovations. The Wauwatosa Theology was not so much anti-Missouri as it was a positive and winsome invitation to fresh historical and exegetical study of the Holy Scriptures. Koehler was convinced that fresh, firsthand study of the Scriptures is better than learning the doctrine second-hand from our fathers in the faith. This applies especially to preachers, because sermons that are based on second-hand theology inevitably become third-hand theology in the ears of the congregation.[41]

Wauwatosa Theology, then, should best be understood as an attitude, a perspective, or way of doing theology as opposed to a specific method, theological judgment, or dogmatic assertion.[42] Central to the concerns of the Wauwatosa theologians is the notion that dogmatic pronouncements not be read back into the scriptural text. Those pronouncements, as important as they were for the conservative confessional Wauwatosa faculty, are in reality historical developments and should be treated as such. This means that the exegesis of the biblical text is not, and should not be, bound by past judgments. Even if the exegesis of a particular text is in accord with previous dogmatic pronouncements, dogmatics is always secondary to exegesis. The result of the primacy of exegesis is fresh expression of theological truth that benefits the faith and life of the church, as opposed to a stale restatement of ideas that is only intellectually grasped, if it is grasped at all.

Leigh Jordahl has argued that the Wauwatosa perspective did not shape the Wisconsin or Missouri Synods in any foundational way.

---

40. Francis Pieper is the brother of August Pieper.

41. Albrecht, "John Philipp Koehler (1859–1951) and the Wauwatosa Theology," 424.

42. Jordahl puts it this way, "The Wauwatosa Theology was not then a doctrinal system or even a hermeneutical methodology and certainly not an attempt to replace old forms with new forms. At its best it was rather an attitude and a style." Jordahl, "Introduction," xxiv.

It would appear, however, the most that can be said without forcing the evidence is that during a certain period of time there existed within the Wisconsin Synod and its Wauwatosa Seminary a situation which allowed John Philipp Koehler the freedom to develop and set forth an approach to the theology and church life which differed notably from prevailing trends in the Midwestern Lutheran environment. During a good part of that time Koehler happily found himself in association with colleagues who shared something of his vision and aims. And there was at least some students who were willing to listen and learn. Beyond this the evidence will not support many claims. There is much to indicate that the Wauwatosa Theology never struck root within its denomination. Certainly it never exerted an influence comparable to that of the "St. Louis Theology" as fathered by C.F.W. Walther. This is only to state the historically obvious.[43]

What is important to note is that Koehler is the primary figure associated with Wauwatosa Theology. It was his life's work.[44] Koehler, who would eventually become the Wauwatosa seminary president, pioneered the attitude his colleagues August Pieper and John Schaller shared. "This is not to say that Koehler's two colleagues were devoid of talent or that they made few significant contributions. By no means! There is no question that August Pieper was often an effective popularizer of the Wauwatosa Theology . . . John Schaller [was] a faithful teacher . . . he also served as a stable balance wheel within the Faculty."[45] Although Schaller died in 1920 from complications related to influenza, a conflict between his colleagues Koehler and Pieper significantly affected the Protes'tant Controversy.

One final element of Wauwatosa Theology must be noted before returning to conflict surrounding the *Gutachten* signed by Wauwastosa faculty, namely, a disdain for legalism. This disdain is part of what sits behind the demand that exegesis maintain primacy over dogmatics.[46] In his work as a historian, Koehler attempted to demonstrate that "Christ and the Apostles . . . knew nothing about any dogmatic control of exegesis."[47] The motive was not simply to reverse the dogmatic dominance that

43. Jordahl, "Introduction," xxiv.
44. Jordahl, "Introduction," xxiv.
45. Jordahl, "Introduction," xxiv.
46. Jordahl, "Introduction," xxi.
47. Jordahl, "Introduction," xxi.

sought to treat the scriptures ahistorically, but also to demonstrate that faith, not dogma, is a sufficient check on the exegete. There is no need to understand the ancient *regula fidei*[48] as a rule or interpretive principle to be applied, i.e., a body of doctrine into which the scriptures must pressed. Koehler recognizes that faith is multileveled, namely that it is both that which is subjectively experienced and objectively understandable, i.e., that it is both the trust a person has and the things that a person believes to be true. "Koehler's point is that the New Testament is not constructing a doctrinal system but rather proclaiming God's acts in man's behalf. Paul and his contemporaries were not dogmaticians but preachers."[49] There are implications, then, for the would-be interpreter of a biblical text. "The interpreter as a believer is doing his work in the Church and in the service of the Church."[50] The aspect of faith that rules is the subjective trust, not the objective doctrine. That does not mean the interpreter is free to interpret things as he or she pleases, rather, that person is bound in faith to the text. What Koehler would argue in terms of scriptural exegesis as a whole, that the words must be understood in terms of their historical and linguistic context, he would also argue for in any instance of controversy. "Fairness demands that we seek to understand our opponent not as his words can or even must be understood, but as he wants them to be understood."[51] Faith that rules the heart does so by means of the gospel, by means of that which Paul and his contemporaries preached, namely of God's action on man's behalf. In short, it is the gospel that governs the behavior of Christians not the law. "Legalism among Christians consists in drawing the motivations and forms of their life from the Law, instead of allowing them to grow from the Gospel."[52]

48. "rule of faith"

49. Jordahl, "Introduction," xxiv.

50. Jordahl, "Introduction," xxii. Cf. the successively published articles of the same name from October 1951 to May 1952 by Koehler, "Analogy of Faith."

51. Koehler, "Analogy of Faith," (October 1951): 11.

52. Koehler, "Legalism and the Evangelical Church," 131. The editorial note at the beginning is important enough to be quoted in full. "John Philip Koehler (1859–1951), professor of church history at the theological seminary of the Wisconsin Evangelical Lutheran Synod at Wauwatosa, Wis., from 1900 to 1930, was one of the most original church historians in American Lutheranism. He delivered this essay in German on Jan. 20, 1914, at Milwaukee. It was subsequently printed in *Theologische Quartalschrift*, 11, 4–12, 3 (1914–15). William J. Hassold, associate professor of religion at Concordia College, Ann Arbor, Mich., has prepared and edited this new translation for CONCORDIA THEOLOGICAL MONTHLY. Major omissions are indicated by

WAUWATOSA OPINION

Legalism is the deadly sin against which Beitz wrote in his paper "The Just Shall Live By Faith." One sees clearly that Beitz had been influenced by Wauwatosa Theology during his years at that seminary. His commitment to fresh exegetical appraisal of a biblical text combined with a disdain for dogmatic legalism as he sought to address the *hoere fragen*, i.e., the higher questions, in front of that mixed group of pastors. In July of 1927, when the faculty that had produced Beitz was asked to render their opinion, or *Gutachten*, of his paper they did so with scathing condemnations. Although both Pieper and Koehler signed the *Gutachten*, their relationship fractured. Koehler predicated his signature on the condition that the document not be presented to Beitz until Koehler had a chance to speak privately with him. Pieper agreed to the demand, but released the document to Beitz anyway. This was not just a matter of ethics for Koehler, but also a demonstration of the commitment he had to his own perspective, namely, "we seek to understand our opponent, not as his words can or even must be understood, but as he wants them to be understood."[53] Koehler withdrew his signature and demanded that all pastors of the synod receive a copy of a brief letter explaining his actions and stating emphatically that the *Gutachten* "was published without my knowledge and consent."[54] In November of that year, the West Wisconsin District affirmed the *Gutachten*, thereby declaring Beitz's paper heretical.[55] As was the case with the protests that followed the suspension of Koch and Gerda, so too did others protest this action. Those protesters, and eventually those who associated with them, were suspended and adopted the moniker "Protes'tants."[56] The following year, while on sabbatical, Koehler produced *Beleuchtung*, his clarification of his understanding of the Beitz paper. He declared that the Beitz paper, though flawed, could be rightly understood, and he rejected the *Gutachten* he had previously

---

ellipses, and section headings have been added. The fact that the essay reflects both the situation obtaining when Koehler wrote it and some of the author's own biases and prejudices does not diminish the value of the article for the perceptive reader as a significant explication of the Law-Gospel polarity as Lutherans understand it."

53. Koehler, "Analogy of Faith," (May 1952): 11. Cf. Jordahl, "Introduction," xxvi–xxvii.

54. Jordahl, "Introduction," xxvii.

55. Jordahl, "Introduction," xxvii.

56. Jordahl, "Introduction," xxvii.

signed. This move "was regarded as a direct attack on Pieper."[57] After only eight days Pieper and Meyer responded with their answer, or *Antwort*. Before Koehler had even seen the *Antwort* he received notification of his suspension as president of the seminary.[58] The break between Koehler and his colleagues was finalized in 1930 when the yearlong suspension became permanent. In 1933, because he would not sever fellowship with Protes'tants, Koehler was removed from the Wisconsin Synod entirely.

WAUWATOSA IMPACT

It is not clear what Martin Franzmann thought about these events in the life of his church body. It is clear, however, that his life was directly impacted by them. One of the Protes'tants suspended in 1927 was professor Elmer Sauer of Northwestern College. His suspension was the result of preaching at St. Matthew's Lutheran Church in Oconomoc, Wisconsin.[59] The pastor of St. Matthew's had been suspended previously as Protes'tant. "Anyone who practiced fellowship with a suspended pastor was himself immediately put under discipline and unless he repented was also suspended."[60] Although Martin had planned to take a year off and work in Milwaukee after his graduation in June of 1928, the vacancy left by Sauer needed to be filled and so Martin availed himself of the opportunity.[61] After teaching Greek and English for two years, he left Northwestern and enrolled at the seminary, which had just moved from Wauwatosa to Thiensville. In 1930, which was after Koehler left, Martin spent a year studying. From there Martin's studies took him to the University of Chicago as well as Greece as his understanding and love of language and history continued to develop.[62]

In 1936, at the retirement of Professor Huth, Martin returned to Northwestern College to teach classics.[63] Classics has been aptly defined as "a subject that exists in the gap between us and the world of the Greek and Romans . . . the questions raised by our distance from 'their' world,

---

57. Braun, "The Protes'tant Controversy and Its Impact on the Wisconsin Synod," 88.
58. Jordahl, "Introduction," xxviii.
59. Jordahl, "Introduction," xxvii.
60. Jordahl, "Introduction," xxvii.
61. Gurgel, "The Life and Legacy of Martin Hans Franzmann," II-1.
62. See previous chapter for a fuller explanation of this era of his life.
63. Gurgel, "The Life and Legacy of Martin Hans Franzmann," II-4.

and at the same time by our closeness to it."⁶⁴ The discipline would prove foundational for Franzmann in his later exploits with The Lutheran Church—Missouri Synod. For example, when discussions were being had about what should be included in the curriculum for one of the colleges of the Missouri Synod, Franzmann had the following to say, "the classics are not only useful, they are indispensable," because, "in studying the classics the budding theologian will learn to submit himself to a mode of thought and expression foreign to him to enter sympathetically into a world whose norms and axioms are sometimes startling remote from his own; he will learn rigorously to exclude himself and to let the text speak to him on its own terms, not on his."⁶⁵ It is here, but not only here, that one sees the impact Wauwatosa Theology must have made on him, even if he only entered the seminary after Koehler left.

Martin would teach at Northwestern for a decade before accepting the call to be a professor in St. Louis at Concordia Seminary. Martin's name was considered in large part because of Arthur Katt who had recommended him to fill the vacant position.⁶⁶ The decision to accept the position is worth brief exploration. Werner Franzmann, Martin's brother, commented on his acceptance saying, "the idea of being wholly in the field of theology appealed to him."⁶⁷ Alice, Martin's wife, noted, "He took the call where he thought (was told) he could help many more young men with his ability to teach and write."⁶⁸ Even the president of The Lutheran Church—Missouri Synod, John Benken, encouraged Martin to leave his alma mater and join the faculty in St. Louis.⁶⁹ While these factors alone might be enough to understand why Martin accepted the position, there was another factor at play, relating once again to controversy at Northwestern College. In the early to mid 1940s, a professor, E. Berg, and the business manager, Mr. Bilse, became embroiled in a dispute related to matters involving the dormitory.⁷⁰ The nature of the dispute is difficult

---

64. Beard and Henderson, *Classics: A Very Short Introduction*, 6.

65. Franzmann, "Classics in the Senior College," 523.

66. Gurgel, "The Life and Legacy of Martin Hans Franzmann," II-6. It should be remembered that Katt was Martin's brother-in-law.

67. Gurgel, "The Life and Legacy of Martin Hans Franzmann," II-6–II-7. Gurgel quotes the interview he conducted.

68. Gurgel, "The Life and Legacy of Martin Hans Franzmann," II-7. Gurgel quotes the interview he conducted.

69. Gurgel, "The Life and Legacy of Martin Hans Franzmann," II-7.

70. Gurgel, "The Life and Legacy of Martin Hans Franzmann," II-8.

to ascertain, however, it divided the faculty. A majority, including the president, sided with Mr. Bilse. Martin, however, sided with the minority supporting Professor Berg. Two years after the dispute, Berg left the college. Some have speculated that this may have left Martin feeling isolated, but that is a matter of speculation only.[71] It seems likely that the impact of the dispute, however, affected Martin's decision to leave.

> This goes beyond objective history, but one more thing is significant. Almost all who knew Martin, including his brother Werner, mention his dislike of controversy. Martin was not one who gloried in the heat of a battle. Even as a student, his schoolmates noticed this tendency. It lies in the realm of speculation, but one with considerable support of acquaintances and subsequent history, that a contributing factor in the acceptance of the call to St. Louis was the chance to put behind him an unpleasant situation.[72]

This understanding of Martin's distaste for controversy persists to this day. A student of Franzmann's once remarked that, "he was the most irenic individual I have ever met."[73] Whatever Martin's reasons were for accepting the position to teach at Concordia Seminary, one sees the affect of the events of the Protes'tant Controversy as well as the roots of the theological posture of Wauwatosa theologians, a posture confirmed and enhanced by his own study of classics.

HEAR YE HIM

In 1964, during Martin's eighteenth year of teaching in St. Louis, Concordia Seminary celebrated its 125th anniversary. As one might suspect, the faculty celebrated this occasion with the compilation of essays that sought to describe what it meant to train pastors. They hoped that this published work would "share the vision of what the ministry to God's people is, that [the people of the church] may be infected with a sense of urgency of it and pass it on to their sons, and that they may realize what is going on in their name in a school which is very much their own."[74] As chairman of the exegetical department and professor of New Testament

---

71. Gurgel, "The Life and Legacy of Martin Hans Franzmann," II-8.
72. Gurgel, "The Life and Legacy of Martin Hans Franzmann," II-8.
73. Interview with James W. Voelz, July 25, 2017.
74. Caemmerer, "Foreword," *Toward A More Excellent Ministry*, v.

Exegesis, Martin penned the essay "Hear Ye Him: Training the Pastor in the Holy Scriptures." He began the essay with a personal story:

> "What do you do, Daddy? I never know what to tell people when they ask me," my son once told me. I know a nine-year-old needs something that sounds impressive, and so I told him, "Tell them your father teaches hermeneutics, isagogics, and exegesis." He memorized that, and the thing served very well to keep the snobs in third grade in their place. But when I am not helping my son to impress third-grade snobs, I much prefer to use something less mysterious and generally more understandable than "hermeneutics, isagogics, and exegesis" to describe my ministry. We have our own technical language, of course, just as carpenters, plumbers, TV-repairmen, and lawyers do, but what we who instruct future pastors in the Holy Scriptures do is at bottom very simple. We teach men[75] to listen.[76]

It was to this task that Martin dedicated his life and teaching. The value of exploring this essay in the paragraphs that follow is that it offers a view that is simultaneously retrospective and prospective. Franzmann explores what he has done over the course of his time as a professor and sets up how he understands that work going forward. In doing so, he exposes his hermeneutical lenses.

The question, however, is not how did he teach? His method of teaching is less important than the content and perspective of what he taught. The focus of the remainder of this chapter is the exploration of his hermeneutical framework on the basis of the aforementioned essay. In order to understand the profound nature of his hymnody, his scholarly work as an exegete, his preaching and devotional material, or his ecumenical work one must first understand Franzmann's hermeneutical perspective. How he conceived of the scriptures, and the presuppositions he held concerning their proper exegesis, formed the basis for his life's work in all areas.

---

75. This masculine language demonstrates that Martin was a man in keeping with his time. Although conventional in his era, effort will be made to avoid such language when possible. In exact quotations the language will be preserved. It is also worth noting that Concordia Seminary, during his time and currently, does not train women for the pastoral ministry as women's ordination is not allowed in The Lutheran Church—Missouri Synod. Concordia Seminary does accept women for deaconess studies or advanced theological degree programs, but not in an effort toward ordination within the church body.

76. Franzmann, "Hear Ye Him: Training the Pastor in the Holy Scriptures," 81.

The manner in which he approached the scriptures was as a hearer, as a listener, first and foremost. "We must learn to listen. We who teach exegesis, the interpretation of the Holy Scriptures, must teach men to listen, really listen, to this Word . . . It is as profoundly difficult as it is simple."[77] Franzmann believed that, "listening is a life-or-death matter for the church."[78] This necessitated creating "laws of good listening" that "we call hermeneutics. And listening according to these 'laws,' listening in a highly conscious, disciplined, and systematic way, that we call exegesis. 'Isagogics' is a special branch of exegesis, one step in the process of disciplined listening."[79]

Franzmann did not conceive of listening as an easy task. It was, "an art to be learned even under the most favorable conditions."[80] "We know how hard it is to understand people on their terms, how easy it is to half-listen, to read one's own thoughts into another's words; how we readily misunderstand."[81] There are barriers to listening that make it difficult. Listening can be challenging even when people speak the same language, have a shared history, or have the same level of education. Martin understood how much more strenuous it was when distance played a factor, e.g., the difference between speaking with someone in the same room and speaking over a telephone. "But it grows increasingly difficult as there is less and less common ground (of language, culture, history) between the speaker and the hearer."[82] Listening is a complex art even in the most convenient of circumstances. It is made even more complex when one considers that the circumstances between the speaker and hearer of the scriptures are anything but convenient.

Franzmann asserted that for the would-be hearer of the "voice of the Good Shepherd in the Old and New Testaments there are three barriers to listening."[83] First, the barrier of language exists because of the Greek, Hebrew, and Aramaic languages used in the composition of the texts of scripture. Second, the barrier of history exists because of the gap in time and culture from their composition to the present. Finally, the

---

77. Franzmann, "Hear Ye Him: Training the Pastor in the Holy Scriptures," 82.
78. Franzmann, "Hear Ye Him: Training the Pastor in the Holy Scriptures," 82.
79. Franzmann, "Hear Ye Him: Training the Pastor in the Holy Scriptures," 82–83.
80. Franzmann, "Hear Ye Him: Training the Pastor in the Holy Scriptures," 83.
81. Franzmann, "Hear Ye Him: Training the Pastor in the Holy Scriptures," 82.
82. Franzmann, "Hear Ye Him: Training the Pastor in the Holy Scriptures," 82.
83. Franzmann, "Hear Ye Him: Training the Pastor in the Holy Scriptures," 82.

barrier of the flesh exists because "we hear the voice of God in this Book, and since Adam's fall we are all like Adam. We want to run and hide at the sound of God's voice."[84] These barriers are by no means insurmountable. If they exist because "time has built fences to keep us out, God has built stiles to get us over fences."[85]

When it comes to the barrier of language, Franzmann notes that there are more and better grammars, dictionaries, and other resources at the disposal of the church than ever before.[86] That barrier can be overcome through diligent study of the languages that teach people "to know how and where and in what setting a thing is said [because] . . . Where and how a thing is said in the Bible can be just as important as the fact that it is said."[87] This task of learning the languages produces a rhythm that leads a person "to look at each part as part of the whole, at the whole as made up of these parts, circling from the part to the whole and the whole to part until [a person] can see what each part means *in its place* as part of the whole."[88] Franzmann did not disparage using vernacular translations in overcoming this barrier of language. "We thank God for the good translations that He has given us . . . We cannot all learn the Biblical languages, and it is not necessary that we should."[89] This did not mean, however, that Franzmann believed only vernacular translations can or should suffice.

> But for those who can [learn the languages]—and most people can; they are not at all so difficult as many people think—it would be sheer nonsense not to learn them, nonsense and ingratitude to God.

---

84. Franzmann, "Hear Ye Him: Training the Pastor in the Holy Scriptures," 83. In this quote particularly one hears echoes of the hymn quoted in chapter one, "In Adam We Have All Been One." "In Adam we have all been one, One huge rebellious man; We all have fled that Evening Voice That sought us as we ran" (Franzmann, *Lutheran Service Book*, 569). Franzmann cites as a barrier to listening a perceived common desire of humankind to flee from God as Adam did in the Genesis 3 narrative. It should be noted that the hymn which clearly reflects this notion was written five years later. In other words, that hymn sprang in part from his hermeneutical presupposition.

85. Franzmann, "Hear Ye Him: Training the Pastor in the Holy Scriptures," 83.

86. Franzmann, "Hear Ye Him: Training the Pastor in the Holy Scriptures," 84

87. Franzmann, "Hear Ye Him: Training the Pastor in the Holy Scriptures," 84–85.

88. Franzmann, "Hear Ye Him: Training the Pastor in the Holy Scriptures," 85. Emphasis original.

89. Franzmann, "Hear Ye Him: Training the Pastor in the Holy Scriptures," 85.

> To be able, with a little effort, to move one step closer to the Good Shepherd, and not take that step? To be able, with a little effort, to hear the voice of the Good Shepherd more distinctly and more fully, and not make effort? That is nonsense: and for the one who is to be a shepherd of the flock of God, to feed the sheep of Christ—for a man with that privilege and that responsibility not to take the trouble to hear the Chief Shepherd in His own tongue—what shall we call it but ingratitude to the God who has given us both the languages and the means of mastering them? The languages are not a burden; they are a gift and a privilege.[90]

In today's theological education landscape it is clear that Franzmann has a word to say to those who would lessen the role of the languages in pastoral formation. His conviction demonstrates his commitment to letting the text dictate its own meaning.

The barrier of history is also not insurmountable. "Again the God of history has given us materials to build stiles across the fence; we can get close to Him still."[91] Franzmann believed that, "in order to hear what the voice of God means for us here and now, we must go back through history and listen to what that voice meant for men then and there."[92] This means that it is necessary to spend as much time and energy as is possible to "reconstruct the history of a Biblical book in order to see what situation in the people of God" necessitated the writing of the book.[93] Using the example of the Galatians, he notes that Paul could write with such ferocity concerning who should be accursed for giving another gospel and still speak tenderly about how he yearned to be with them.[94] "Unless we take the trouble to cross the barrier of history into the situation then and there, we shall not hear fully or understand clearly the voice of the Good Shepherd speaking to us here and now with a love that cares so much it must be stern."[95] The value of history in the exegetical task is foundational for Franzmann. What the text meant in its own time gives the basis for what it means in the ears of the hearer today. History aids in the ascertaining of that meaning. While this is certainly a foundational

---

90. Franzmann, "Hear Ye Him: Training the Pastor in the Holy Scriptures," 85.
91. Franzmann, "Hear Ye Him: Training the Pastor in the Holy Scriptures," 86.
92. Franzmann, "Hear Ye Him: Training the Pastor in the Holy Scriptures," 86.
93. Franzmann, "Hear Ye Him: Training the Pastor in the Holy Scriptures," 86.
94. Galatians 1:8–9; 4:19–20.
95. Franzmann, "Hear Ye Him: Training the Pastor in the Holy Scriptures," 86.

aspect of historical-critical methodology as it developed in the twentieth century, Franzmann did not understand himself as embarking on the same journey as historical-critical scholars. History was a tool to be used in service of the faith and life of the exegete and the hearer.

"The third barrier is the most formidable of all, the barrier of the flesh. No man, no son of Adam, *wants* to hear the voice of God; he wants to run away."[96] Martin understands this to be so because a person can readily overcome the first two barriers through aids like grammars or histories. The overcoming of this barrier cannot be taught as the overcoming of the other two can.[97]

> Skilled in the languages, at home in history, they know the sound and the feel of Holy Scriptures and can reproduce them with uncanny skill. But they have never felt the force of the Holy Scriptures; they have not heard the Good Shepherd speaking in the Scriptures *to them*. They have not been brought low by God's Law, and they have not been raised up by the Gospel of God. They remain, for all their wisdom and eloquence, a sounding brass and tinkling cymbal.
>
> The way across this barrier cannot, strictly speaking, be taught. We can teach men languages, and we can teach them history; we can give them grades, advance them if they do well, and fail them if they fail to do well. But we cannot "teach" them to deny themselves and follow the Good Shepherd wherever He leads and to remain always within the sound of His voice; we cannot "teach" them repentance and faith—and love. Not that we despair when we reach this barrier; on the contrary, this is when we are most confident. For here God Himself must take over, and He does take over.[98]

These paragraphs are integral for understanding Franzmann's perspective on hermeneutics and the exegetical task. That this barrier can only be overcome by the work of God, and that this is something in which one should be confident, bears repeating. All of the linguistic and historical skills, necessary as they are, pale in comparison to the fact that in them, the voice of God is clearly calling out to the world. The exegete, or

---

96. Franzmann, "Hear Ye Him: Training the Pastor in the Holy Scriptures," 87.
97. Franzmann, "Hear Ye Him: Training the Pastor in the Holy Scriptures," 87–88.
98. Franzmann, "Hear Ye Him: Training the Pastor in the Holy Scriptures," 88.

professor of exegesis, then, "cannot teach here, we can proclaim; we can bear witness."[99]

In passing the final barrier, the hearer of the scriptures, on account of the work of God, becomes a preacher.[100] That person can speak about what God has done. That person can bear witness about what the voice of God calls out to humankind. And this is the goal, that one become a preacher. "Unless our preacher and pastor, by the powerful grace of God, passes the barrier of the flesh, his skills in language and his knowledge of history are nothing and worse than nothing; they feed his pride and inflate his ego."[101] The barriers of listening, even if overcome in part, can still be barriers of a different sort. Linguistic and analytic skills can serve ego rather than the church. And if this is the case, then the hearer has not overcome the final barrier and the value of the "stiles" used to overcome the barriers changes dramatically. Only in the denying of self do those skills become "precious things indeed."[102] It is important to understand that the advocacy of historic and linguistic skills in the interpretation of the scriptures are foundational in historical-critical methodology as well as being Franzmann's own perspective. Throughout his career, however, when he argued against historical-critical methods he did not do it only on the basis of the role of language and history in the exegetical task. He did it on precisely this point, that in the scriptures God makes a specific address to humankind where the role of humankind is that of listener to God first and foremost. Franzmann made no distinction between the voice of God and the words on the page. The text is the voice writ large.

This work of overcoming barriers, to which Franzmann dedicated himself as both student and professor, is not something to bemoan or lament, however intense it may sound. "One gets the impression that many people feel a bit sorry for the young man who is preparing for the holy ministry; even parents and kindly aunts and uncles tend to cluck a bit over the struggling young theologian to say nothing of those friends of

---

99. Franzmann, "Hear Ye Him: Training the Pastor in the Holy Scriptures," 88.

100. This is not to be understood in the sense that any hearer of the text is called to the Office of the Holy Ministry as defined in The Lutheran Church—Missouri Synod. Franzmann is clearly writing about those studying to serve as pastors in his church body. It would be a different discussion to ascertain how he understood the role of any hearer of the text regardless of office. In his *Art of Exegesis* lectures, he explores that to a minimal degree.

101. Franzmann, "Hear Ye Him: Training the Pastor in the Holy Scriptures," 89.

102. Franzmann, "Hear Ye Him: Training the Pastor in the Holy Scriptures," 89.

his who are embarking on more 'successful careers.' They should save their sympathy for men who need it."[103]

BEGGARS BEFORE GOD

Earlier in his career at Concordia Seminary, Martin chose to use the concept of beggar to explain the relationship of the interpreter to the scriptures.[104] "Blessed are the poor in spirit, for theirs is the kingdom of heaven."[105] This familiar beatitude forms the backdrop for the discussion. One sees in the article his understanding of the language and history as he noted different usages, variations, and meanings of the word found in Matthew's Gospel, πτωχοι (ptōchoi),[106] in other biblical and classical instances. In doing so, he demonstrated what he would later refer to as the overcoming of the barriers of both language and history by speaking about what the word meant in the past in order to explain what it meant for Franzmann's present audience. His interpretation of what it means to be poor in spirit is ultimately one that is best understood as beggary because of what those who are poor in spirit receive, namely, the kingdom of God.[107] "For if there is one thing sure of the kingdom of God, it is this, that man receives it as God's gift."[108] In other words, it is not something earned but something bestowed to those who cannot grasp it of their own accord. The remaining beatitudes, then, flesh out "a basic attitude toward God, the Christian attitude."[109] "To be a πτωχός[110] is to join that procession of suppliant men and women whose faith Jesus recognized and praised; such men as the paralytic and his bearers, who brought, climbed, dug, let down (insistent beggary), simply to present their need

---

103. Franzmann, "Hear Ye Him: Training the Pastor in the Holy Scriptures," 89–90.

104. Franzmann, "Beggars Before God: The First Beatitude," 889–99.

105. Matthew 5:3 (NRSV).

106. The root of this is πτωχός (ptōchos), Franzmann will explicate his suggestion of the interpreter being a beggar using the root form in later paragraphs.

107. Franzmann, "Beggars Before God: The First Beatitude," 895.

108. Franzmann, "Beggars Before God: The First Beatitude," 895.

109. Franzmann, "Beggars Before God: The First Beatitude," 895.

110. Typically translated as "poor," as in the case of "poor in spirit above," but in Franzmann's estimation it has the ring of "beggar" to it (Cf. the aforementioned article, 890–94). BDAG allows for such a translation as it notes that it has the sense of being "economically disadvantaged," and "dependent on others for support." Cf. BDAG 896 s.v. "πτωχός."

to Jesus."[111] This is "akin to that fear of the Lord which is the beginning of all wisdom."[112] It means that "we are proud only of being δοῦλοι[113] of God and of Jesus Christ; all other pride is forever gone."[114] The conclusion of his essay is most illuminating.

> The Christian interpreter must remain a beggar if he would be a true interpreter of God's Word, remembering that it is *given* to men to know the mysteries of the kingdom of heaven. He will find his feelings towards Scripture classically expressed in Luther's last words: "Versuche nicht diese goettliche Aeneis, sondern neige dich tief anbetend vor ihren Spuren! Wir sind Bettler—das ist wahr."[115]

This is clearly a reference to Luther's last words and writing found in the room where he died. The full context of the quote Franzmann used is,

> Nobody can understand Vergil in his *Bucolics* and *Georgics* unless he has first been a shepherd or a farmer for five years. Nobody understands Cicero in his letters unless he has been engaged in public affairs of some consequence for twenty years. Let nobody suppose that he has tasted the Holy Scriptures sufficiently unless he has ruled over the churches with the prophets for a hundred years. Therefore there is something wonderful, first, about John the Baptist; second, about Christ; third, about the apostles.[116]

However, Franzmann only quotes the last bit, "Lay not your hand on this divine Aeneid, but bow before it, adore its every trace.' We are beggars. That is true."[117] The point He is making in using such a reference is clear. In all things, the interpreter is a beggar. He goes on:

> For none can interpret that does not adore. And the Christian preacher remains ever a beggar before God, and all pretentious

---

111. Franzmann, "Beggars Before God: The First Beatitude," 896.

112. Franzmann, "Beggars Before God: The First Beatitude," 897.

113. Typically translated as "slaves." For a full discussion see BDAG, 259–60, s.v. "δοῦλος."

114. Franzmann, "Beggars Before God: The First Beatitude," 898.

115. Franzmann, "Beggars Before God: The First Beatitude," 898. Precisely from which edition of Luther's works Franzmann quoted is difficult to ascertain as there is no footnote in the original document. It is likely that this is from the St. Louis German Edition of Luther's Works published by Concordia Publishing House between 1885–1910.

116. *Luther's Works*, AE 54:476.

117. Franzmann, "Beggars Before God: The First Beatitude," 898.

tinsel of "pulpit oratory" must be swept away by the beggarly simplicity of: "Lord, open *Thou* my lips that my mouth may show forth Thy praise." And the health and life of the Church depends upon her beggary, on her remaining conscious of the *sola gratia, sola fide.* For this beggary, though it leaves no room for personal pride and no room for personal glory, does leave full room for God and for His kingdom, for His sovereignly redemptive sway, and so leaves room for a glory that surpasseth.[118]

While the metaphor, that of beggar, in this 1947 essay may have been different than the metaphor of listener in the piece discussed above, the point is exactly the same. The posture of the interpreter is one that receives from God what God has to say. This address to humankind is the point. All exegetical work and effort are bent not toward making the preacher sound educated or eloquent, but toward those who need to hear what God has to say to them. It is God who opens the lips of the interpreter to speak in the here and now the words God originally spoke there and then. Anachronistically speaking, the barriers of language and history were overcome by Franzmann in this article, so too was the barrier of the flesh. This is so because the beatitude was discussed in its full understanding in terms of language and history but also because it renders its verdict on the interpreter's task.

It does not take much to see the influence of Wauwatosa on Franzmann's hermeneutical perspective. The focus of exegesis for the sake of the life and faith of the hearer is clear. The commitment to the linguistic and historic elements of the text is also clear. For now, it is enough to see that Franzmann was clearly shaped by the events of Northwestern College and the Wauwatosa theologians of the 1920s. His interest in education, the field he chose, and his subsequent career all bear the marks of those early days. It should not be assumed, however, that he was merely the Wauwatosa voice in Missouri. In fact, when Koehler died in 1951, it was Jaroslav Pelikan, and not Martin Franzmann, who wrote an encomium about him.[119] Although Martin certainly seemed to have taken cues from that perspective, he understood his life as a teacher and interpreter in a different way; as a listener who teaches others to listen. As a beggar who teaches others about the value of such beggary. For Franzmann, there is no distinction between the spirit and letter of the text. The words on the page, not what someone says those words mean, are the things to

---

118. Franzmann, "Beggars Before God," 898. Emphasis original.
119. Jaroslav Pelikan, "John Philipp Koehler (1859–1951)," 50–51.

which the beggar is beholden. He is not advocating for Wauwatosa, he is advocating for the text, the words on the page, and in doing so for the one who speaks in the text, the one who speaks the word.

3

The Posture of the Interpreter

PSHA!

WILLIAM F. ARNDT JOINED the faculty of Concordia Seminary in 1921 as professor of New Testament exegesis and literature.[1] Arndt is perhaps best known for his collaboration with F. Wilbur Gingrich on the English translation of Bauer's Lexicon. Affectionately known today as BDAG (Bauer-Danker-Arndt-Gingrich), *A Greek-English Lexicon of the New Testament and Other Early Christian Literature* is now in its third edition. It is a, if not the, standard lexical work. Those within The Lutheran Church—Missouri Synod, however, regard him for more than just his lexical exploits. He was a pastor, professor, publisher, and person who influenced the synod which he served.[2] Upon his retirement from Concordia Seminary in 1951, the faculty honored their colleague with the publication of a *festschrift*. It was fitting that the faculty did so not by publishing a separate volume, but by using the December issue of *Concordia Theological Monthly*, an academic journal with which Arndt was intimately linked.[3]

1. Paul M. Bretscher, "William Frederick Arndt: 1880–1957," 402.

2. See the article mentioned in the footnote above for a brief yet full recounting of his life and work.

3. Bretscher, "William Frederick Arndt: 1880–1957," 403. This particular one had some unique features. A resolution from the faculty, signed by all on May 25, 1951, adorned the dedication page. It read in part, "WHEREAS, as a scholar, a theologian,

For the *festschrift*, Martin Franzmann, who would become chair of the Exegetical Department a few years after Arndt's retirement, penned an essay titled "The Apostolic Psha!" In it, Franzmann utilizes a lesson he attributes to Hilaire Belloc.[4] That lesson is simply, there are things not worth a person's time; as such one must be willing to dismiss those things. Reimagining that lesson in terms of a relationship with God he writes:

> Now, if we are His, as we confess ourselves to be by His grace, the Psha! must inevitably follow: if we are His, there will be things that we shall have no time for; there will be attitudes and actions that we cannot stoop to; there will be a point at which a God-given impatience sets in, where we shall have to utter an Apostolic Psha! and proceed to more important matters.[5]

He calls this attitude "apostolic impatience."[6] Franzmann cites what he thinks is the best example of such impatience, Peter in the book of Acts. When charged with being drunk in public, Peter dismisses the claim out of hand. Time is too precious to waste on fruitless arguments. Franzmann goes on to say:

> We must not be too diligent about erasing every scrawl that appears on the wall ecclesiastical. We need not rise with anguished yelp and energy-consuming indignation at every mangy screed, for instance, that defames Luther or the Lutherans. The time is short; there is not always time for the hard-breathing and heavy-handed rebuttal, with footnotes. A sentence or two, a brace of facts—and let the rest be silence. Our Lord was silent, dreadfully

---

and a teacher, he has been of singular benefit to the entire church in the training of her ministry; and WHEREAS, in the interest of the church and in keeping with the precepts and teachings of the Word of God, he has helped to advance the cause of ecumenicity and of God-pleasing church union successfully and with due foresight, courage, patience, and discretion; and WHEREAS, in his labors as a colleague he has been consistently kind, considerate, understanding, and helpful, always bearing in mind his obligations as a servant of Jesus Christ and of the church; therefore be it Resolved, That the faculty, at this time of his retirement from our midst, express its appreciation for the valuable service he has rendered to Concordia Seminary and to the church at large; and be it furthermore Resolved, That the faculty assure him of its prayers for continued health, strength, joy, and blessing." "Tribute to William F. Arndt," *Concordia Theological Monthly* 22, no. 12 (December 1951).

4. Belloc was a late nineteenth early twentieth century poet, author, and activist. He is also well known for speaking from a Roman Catholic perspective.

5. Franzmann, "The Apostolic Psha!" 908.

6. Franzmann, "The Apostolic Psha!" 908.

> silent, sometimes too, and there were questions that He would not answer. And we shall do well to remember that He is building His Church, on a rock, and of such stuff that it shall prevail against graver thrusts than any that these small, unsavory assailants can deliver. The Church is an anvil that has worn out many hammers, and we ought not expend too much energy on puny smithikins that with contemptible hammerlets pelt its brazen solidity. No Church, not even one with a most amply-staffed department of public relations, has time for spiritual calisthenics; we have real battles to fight and satanically ineluctable struggles to engage in each day. These little slingers and darters are part of His Majesty the Devil's forces, no doubt; but they can succeed only by creating a diversion, in the military sense. Where they are ignored, they fail.[7]

The "energetic impatience" and "noble disdain"[8] that Franzmann is advocating for in this document needs an example or two to be understood rightly. He is not advocating for silence on all matters, but rather, for a dismissal of those things not worth the time and attention befitting a theologian. He concludes:

> So, by way of example, a Psha! to thin-blooded and rheumy-eyed philosophy; and a Psha! to prestige in all its forms—we count it dung; a Psha! to great men who say nice things about the Bible, deeming it a great source of ethical inspiration, valuable for the maintenance of good government and a free society, and a fine thing all around; a Psha! to all publicity that makes the Church look like a huckster selling a competitive product, like soap; a Psha! to theological gobbledegook that sicklies o'er the Good News with the pale cast of thought; and a stout Isaianic Psha! to all idols, including all our own twentieth-century varieties, the respectable ones.[9]

Here one sees the gauntlet laid down. No time for attitudes and perspectives that cheapen the biblical text into a set of "ethical inspiration[s]."[10] No time for things that cheapen what the church has to offer. No time for idols. Rather, time should be spent on the things that see the biblical text as life-giving. Time should be spent on those things that deepen the gifts the church has to share. Time immeasurable for the God and the gos-

---

7. Franzmann, "The Apostolic Psha!" 908–09.
8. Franzmann, "The Apostolic Psha!" 909.
9. Franzmann, "The Apostolic Psha!" 911.
10. Franzmann, "The Apostolic Psha!" 911.

pel. This chapter seeks to explore in part how Martin Franzmann spent his time as chair of the Exegetical department at Concordia Seminary. To that end, a deeper investigation of his hermeneutical perspective, as well as his exegetical work, and the reception of his scholarly work both among the faculty and outside the walls of Concordia Seminary is necessary. Not only did Martin remain consistent in his hermeneutical approach throughout his career, his perspective was not revolutionary. Rather, Franzmann's approach was a consistently conservative one which his contemporaries recognized.

ESSAYS IN HERMENEUTICS

Early in his career at Concordia Seminary Franzmann would write three consecutive essays focusing on hermeneutics that he defines as "that branch of theology which sets forth the principles that are to guide us in the interpretation of Scripture."[11] The purpose of these essays was spelled out in a brief note before the first essay began. Simply put, they were "designed to serve as guidelines for the writer's course in Hermeneutics at Concordia Seminary," and were "the first steps toward a textbook on Hermeneutics."[12] The interpreter's complete resignation and submission to what God said in the texts of scripture formed the central hermeneutical presupposition for Franzmann. While one might wonder why this would need to be the case, for Franzmann the answer was clear. "For the Lutheran theologian hermeneutical questions are anything but academic questions. Our life as Christians and as a Church depends on the Word; and since the Word is the ultimate authority, the Church of the *sola Scriptura* dare not be indifferent to the manner of its interpretation."[13] The interpreter is beholden to the Word, for from it all Christians and the entire church receives life.

---

11. Franzmann, "Essays in Hermeneutics," 595.

12. Franzmann, "Essays in Hermeneutics," 595. The essays were published consecutively in August, September, and October of 1948 under the same title, "Essays in Hermeneutics." The importance of the essays in ascertaining Franzmann's hermeneutical perspective cannot be overstated. These essays, along with two others, would become a kind of hermeneutical textbook for Concordia Theological Seminary in Springfield, IL. The content of them is also used by Franzmann in his efforts to train church workers who are not training to be pastors in interpreting the scriptures. All of this will be further explored in this chapter.

13. Franzmann, "Essays in Hermeneutics," 595. Emphasis original.

Franzmann began the first essay by defining the purpose of hermeneutics in broad terms. "It is the sole business of Hermeneutics to see to it that we really have the Word that spells our life. Positively, Hermeneutics is to lead us into Scripture in such a way that its perpetually fresh and infinite life may be constantly open to us and in progressive abundance ours."[14] Hermeneutics, then, is concerned with ensuring the place and delivery of the life-giving word to the church. It is also, however, concerned with defending the church. "Negatively, Hermeneutics can provide a defense against the two gravest dangers that ever threaten the Church of the Word; satiety and the perversion of Scripture."[15] By "satiety" Franzmann meant that hermeneutics defends the church against an abusive dogmatics. This can happen when "Exegesis is permitted to degenerate into a sort of Dogmatics in reverse, a procedure that does disservice to both Dogmatics and to Exegesis; for the pleasant and salubrious pools of Systematic theology cease to be so when they cease to be fed by the living waters of Exegesis."[16] In other words, when sound exegesis fails to be the living source for systematic or dogmatic theology the latter becomes, at best, stale, and the former becomes nearly unrecognizable. By "the perversion of scripture" Franzmann meant that hermeneutics defends the church against "error and falsification."[17] Hermeneutics "can make us critical of men's interpretations of Scripture and will constantly drive us back into Scripture and so place us, again and again, under the influence of the Spirit, who leads into all truth." Because the Word gives life, hermeneutics as a discipline provides a check on those things that might turn life into death. Both of the dangers are avoided because "a sound Hermeneutics keeps us with, and so under, the Word."[18] This is the key point, repeated over and over again throughout Franzmann's work, the interpreter, indeed the entire church, lives under, not over the word.

Requisite of any discussion on hermeneutics as it relates to scripture is a discussion of the nature of scripture. "The principles that are to guide us in the interpretation of Scripture must be derived from the nature of Scripture itself."[19] While it is clear by now that Franzmann saw the

---

14. Franzmann, "Essays in Hermeneutics," 596–97.
15. Franzmann, "Essays in Hermeneutics," 597.
16. Franzmann, "Essays in Hermeneutics," 597.
17. Franzmann, "Essays in Hermeneutics," 597.
18. Franzmann, "Essays in Hermeneutics," 597.
19. Franzmann, "Essays in Hermeneutics," 597.

scriptures of the Old and New Testament as the Word of God, it remains to be seen whether, or in what way, Franzmann dealt with the role of humankind in the production of scripture. He made that clear:

> The oracles of God are not a book fallen from heaven; rather, God spoke through men at a certain time, in a certain place, and in certain language. "*Men spake*"—that is one aspect of Scripture, the aspect that it shares with every other document ever written. The other aspect lies in the fact that here *God* spoke through men, and in this aspect Scripture is unique. We have in Scripture God speaking *once*, at a certain point in history, by men; and God speaking *once and for all*.[20]

It is this understanding of scripture that forms the basis for his hermeneutics.

> We might, then, picture the interpreter approaching the sacred text through three concentric circles: the circle of language, the circle of history, and the circle of theology or of Scripture. The first two of these circles are a recognition of the act that in Scripture God spoke once in the tongues of men at a certain point in history. The third circle is a recognition of the fact that in thus speaking God has spoken once and for all; that Scripture is a unity by virtue of the one Spirit that inspired all the books of the canon. It is a recognition also of the implications of Scripture for us, of the fact that that Scripture is "*profitable* for doctrine, for reproof, for correction, for instruction in righteousness; that the man of God may be perfect, throughly [sic] furnished unto all good works."[21]

Because Franzmann saw the documents that form the scriptures as produced through humans by God he saw both a divine and human aspect of them. This being the case, one must take into account both aspects when interpreting the text. The circle of language, circle of history, and circle of Scripture are not strictly separated. "These three circles are distinct in analysis only and must inevitably interlink and interlock in practice."[22] In practice, the use of linguistic and historical analysis are done as needed. If one circle governs the process, it is the circle of scripture. Linguistic and historical analyses are always done in service of the text that conveys the voice of God.

20. Franzmann, "Essays in Hermeneutics," 598. Emphasis original.
21. Franzmann, "Essays in Hermeneutics," 598.
22. Franzmann, "Essays in Hermeneutics," 598.

The remainder of the first essay in hermeneutics deals with the circle of language. This circle of language is quite obviously related to the barrier of language discussed above. A benefit of exploring this set of essays is that Franzmann explicated more fully and demonstrated practically what he meant by the role of language, and subsequently history and scripture. His exploration of the circle of language began with a Matthew Arnold reference, "A man who knows only his Bible will not even know that well." The point is clear. "One does not learn the full potentialities of a language from one book; and without a feeling for the potentialities of a language, its tones and overtones, the one book is not fully grasped either; the mind's hold remains slippery and partial."[23] Thus, it takes an exploration of the language itself, e.g., Koine Greek in the case of the New Testament, to begin to understand what text can or cannot, is or is not saying. "Within the circle of language, we may treat, first, words in isolation (etymology and usage), and then words in relation to one another (grammar, context, figurative language)."[24]

In a majority of cases etymology is "an excellent starting point in the study of a word, but usually no more than that. Exegesis of the word-picture variety usually sins in the direction of overreliance on etymology."[25] While words have a history, that history does not determine meaning in all instances. Usage matters. Franzmann unpacks how different the Greek of the New Testament is by stating upfront that it is "non-literary Greek, the spoken language of a people." This did not mean it is "vulgar" or "illiterate" as "the documents of non-literary Greek, the papyri, ostraka, and inscriptions," i.e., the particular instantiations of the language, demonstrate an understanding of what words meant and are thus "invaluable for establishing the connotations that New Testament words had for their first readers."[26] Usage also takes into account outside influence, particularly Semitic influence, since the authors of the New Testament were probably bilingual and because of the widespread use of the Septuagint. For example, "the Greek εἰρήνη has, by way of the Septuagint, taken on the richer and more inclusive sense of the Hebrew *shalom*."[27] This means that "context, especially the immediate context, will also play an

---

23. Franzmann, "Essays in Hermeneutics," 598.
24. Franzmann, "Essays in Hermeneutics," 599.
25. Franzmann, "Essays in Hermeneutics," 599.
26. Franzmann, "Essays in Hermeneutics," 599.
27. Franzmann, "Essays in Hermeneutics," 600.

important role in the determination of usage. Any great new event brings with it new words and fills old words with new meanings."[28] Usage can work in various ways: deepening, revaluating, appreciating, completely changing, or by concretizing a new application of older established terminology.[29] One must also "distinguish between general and particular usage, between general *koine* usage and that of the New Testament; and within the New Testament, between general New Testament usage and that of a St. John or a St. Paul. The immediate context and particular usage is decisive in any given case."[30] This works itself out practically for the interpreter, e.g., "in using a concordance, in the case of Pauline usage, the Pauline parallels receive primary consideration."[31] A dictionary or concordance may be "a good map for the way; but each must go the way himself if he would really interpret that is, meet the text and receive its impact first hand. . . . The concordance and the dictionary are indispensable aids to firsthand acquaintance but not a surrogate for it."[32] All of this is to say that for Franzmann, the meaning of the word was not always self-evident. There are varying usages, differing origins, and particular moments in time when a word meant a specific thing. The dictionary and concordance are useful because they can provide the means to understand those variations. That does not mean, however, that the interpreter merely opens a dictionary and selects a definition. This is the point behind noting that εἰρήνη can, and possibly should, be understood in connection with the Hebrew shalom and not apart from it. Familiarity with the language, and with the words themselves, will aid the interpreter in deriving what the word means in a particular instance, not what it meant once and for all time.

Grammar, context, and figurative language also have a place in the circle of language. "New Testament Greek is, after all, Greek, popular Greek, which has transcended the dialectical boundaries of the earlier periods and has relaxed, not abrogated, the strict regularity of the classical literary Greek."[33] Thus, it is necessary to understand the ways in which the grammar of a text is like or unlike other instantiations of the lan-

---

28. Franzmann, "Essays in Hermeneutics," 600.
29. Franzmann, "Essays in Hermeneutics," 600–01.
30. Franzmann, "Essays in Hermeneutics," 601.
31. Franzmann, "Essays in Hermeneutics," 601.
32. Franzmann, "Essays in Hermeneutics," 601.
33. Franzmann, "Essays in Hermeneutics," 602.

guage. The rules of the language, and how those rules may be employed or ignored, affects the way in which meaning is derived. "Consideration for the connection in which a word or group of words occurs is among the most elementary rules for the interpretation of any text."[34] Context is important not only because of what it aids the interpreter in understanding, but also because of the limits it places on the interpreter. Franzmann noted that such consideration for the connection "is easily forgotten especially when we have hit upon a bright idea, homiletically valuable, which we should like to 'get out' of the text. It is indicative that so many exegetical questions take the form, '*Can* this text mean so and so?'"[35] Rather than being concerned with what the preacher is trying to force a text to mean, Franzmann was adamant that the immediate and more remote contexts of a passage dictate the answers of, as well as the question posed to, the text. Context is at bottom a "connection of thought," which may be historical, chronological, dogmatical, logical, or psychological.

> To sum up, in the case of a passage not immediately clear we look to the immediate context, then to the remoter context of the work in which the passage occurs, then to the whole body of works by the same author, then to the whole New Testament, and then to the whole Bible. Here again, as in the case of usage, we let Scripture interpret Scripture.[36]

An example of this kind of passage is Romans 16:17. While this appears to be an "isolated passage" that is part of a "loosely joined series of exhortations," it should be read in terms of other works by Paul. If it were not possible to understand Romans 16:17 on the basis of Romans alone, it would be possible to get an idea of what Paul is getting at by examining the "larger context of St. Paul's treatment of error and errorists in *Galatians, Colossians,* and 1 and 2 *Corinthians,* with its drastic rejection of the misleaders and its tender concern for the misled."[37] This "would cast much light on the scope and meaning of the passage in Romans, which breaks in so unexpectedly into the chapter of greetings."[38]

One must also determine when the language used is figurative, and at times context can aid in that determination. This is important for the

---

34. Franzmann, "Essays in Hermeneutics," 602.
35. Franzmann, "Essays in Hermeneutics," 602.
36. Franzmann, "Essays in Hermeneutics," 603.
37. Franzmann, "Essays in Hermeneutics," 603. Emphasis original.
38. Franzmann, "Essays in Hermeneutics," 603.

interpreter because figurative language "addresses itself not only to the intellect but also the will and to the emotions of men. It *moves* men, in the manner as well as in the substance of its speaking."[39] Franzmann saw the purpose of figurative language "to illuminate a relationship or state in one domain by means of a comparable relationship in another."[40] This means one must "discern carefully that quality of the figure which the author evidently wishes to denote as explanatory to the idea."[41] Figurative language is necessary because sometimes no other way exists of expressing truth. This does not mean it is expressing something unreal. "The ultimate beauty of music is such that it can be expressed in no other terms than music; yet no one questions the reality of that beauty just because it cannot be reduced to a literally conceptual statement."[42] It is important to discern what is and is not figurative because of how that term can be misapplied to those texts that are literal and because of how the figurative texts can be misread as literal.

> The golden mean in interpretation lies somewhere between the extremes of an intellectual exegesis, on the one hand, which rationalizes away the flesh and blood of Scriptural expression and leaves only the bare bones of an abstract thought; and a false sort of literalism, on the other hand, which makes the inspired writers subject to all the "primitive" and naïve notions that first-century flesh was heir to.[43]

It is also in working through figurative language that "the circle of history interlocks with the circle of language," because "figures are drawn from manifold aspects of contemporary life," and because, "language is inseparable from life."[44] If the circle of language is concerned with the words and phrases used in the original documents, the circle of history is concerned with the situation that gave rise to the documents. It is concerned with "the world in which and for which the Scriptures were originally written."[45] For Franzmann, one cannot deny or downplay that "the very fact that a man is born of parents [means] he is irrevocably linked with

---

39. Franzmann, "Essays in Hermeneutics," 604.
40. Franzmann, "Essays in Hermeneutics," 604.
41. Franzmann, "Essays in Hermeneutics," 604.
42. Franzmann, "Essays in Hermeneutics," 605.
43. Franzmann, "Essays in Hermeneutics," 605.
44. Franzmann, "Essays in Hermeneutics," 604.
45. Franzmann, "Essays in Hermeneutics," 641.

the past and comes into the world with history upon him."[46] History, however, for the church is "not strictly past at all, but an ever-present continually effective actuality."[47] The New Testament itself bears this out. "When the Magi arrived in Jerusalem, Micah was no dim historical figure, but a present voice; and at Pentecost the voice of Joel, in the mouth of St. Peter, was a living, and for those who would hear, a decisive tongue."[48] This means then, that for the interpreter there needs to be an intimate knowledge of the culture in which texts were produced. Speaking specifically of Semitic of Palestine and Graeco-Roman culture of the Mediterranean Franzmann wrote, "The deeper and more comprehensive the interpreter's knowledge of those two cultures is, the more immediate will his contact with the sacred text be; his understanding and appreciation of the text will be correspondingly more vital and rich."[49] This is the wider sense of the circle of history. The broad understanding of the culture of the ancient world is indispensable. Familiarity with the ancient world can happen through the use of secondhand sources such as commentaries, dictionaries, and encyclopedias. Firsthand knowledge comes by means of interaction with documents from the time period or by visiting areas that have been preserved. Both are necessary for the exploration of the wider circle of history.

There is also a narrower sense of the circle of history. This narrow sense "includes the specific occasion that called forth a literary production, the circumstances under which it was written and received, the persons addressed, and so forth."[50] Its focus is a testament to the fact that "[e]very book of the New Testament is written for the times." Thus, "if we are to get the meaning which these books have for all time, we must first get at the meaning they had for the first time."[51] In arguing for this

---

46. Franzmann, "Essays in Hermeneutics," 641.
47. Franzmann, "Essays in Hermeneutics," 641.
48. Franzmann, "Essays in Hermeneutics," 641.
49. Franzmann, "Essays in Hermeneutics," 642.
50. Franzmann, "Essays in Hermeneutics," 642.
51. Franzmann, "Essays in Hermeneutics," 642–43. The push for the historical appreciation of the text was not a new one, but at the time historical-critical methods were starting to gain a hearing in conservative circles like Concordia Seminary. This will be dealt more fully with in the next section. For the sake of understanding the circle of history, it is enough to know that Franzmann not only sees it as integral to the task of interpretation, but that it is not a new or novel concept.

narrow context, Franzmann also addressed trends in biblical scholarship and how that applies to the circle.

> God makes all things serve the good of His Church: the vagaries and impieties of the elder Higher Criticism have, under His providence, had a beneficent by-product; they have recalled Biblical scholarship to a more sanely historical approach to scripture. We have been forced to study the live realities of its historical setting, and the result can only be beneficial. Common sense should have taught us this much: no man can be understood in a vacuum; he comes into the world with ties ready-fashioned that bind him to his family, his people, his cultural setting. He must be understood, if he is to be understood at all, in relation to his contemporaries and his ancestors . . . The Holy Spirit took men as they were, historically situated and historically conditioned, and used them so. . . . [sic] There is nothing novel in this renewed emphasis on the historical side in interpretation.[52]

He then spent the remainder of the essay, just over eight pages, unpacking how historical study impacts a reading of First Thessalonians. In doing so he demonstrated, practically and theologically, the necessary influence of the circle of history, noting "that the circle of history always includes the sacred past as well as the contemporary world."[53] Franzmann concluded his essay with a warning. "Only, we must not forget: history is a means, not an end. The historical approach is not the historian's approach. We do not aim to write the history of the primitive Church, neither do we seek the 'historical Jesus.' Theology is a *habitus practicus* still; and we enter the circle of history in order to hear the words that spelled, and spell, eternal life."[54]

Whereas the circles of language and history concentrate on the humanness of the scriptures, "on the fact that God the Holy Ghost spoke in tongues in definite moments in history," the circle of scripture, which is the emphasis of the final essay, concentrates on the divine nature of the scriptures, "on the fact that God the Holy Ghost spoke."[55] A longer quote reveals the depths of this for Franzmann.

> In the circle of Scripture we pass from skills and techniques to what is rather an attitude, a gift of God, a *charisma* to be prayed

---

52. Franzmann, "Essays in Hermeneutics," 643.
53. Franzmann, "Essays in Hermeneutics," 652.
54. Franzmann, "Essays in Hermeneutics," 652. Emphasis original.
55. Franzmann, "Essays in Hermeneutics," 738.

> for. For we are now concerned with that aspect of the Bible which makes it different from all other texts, however much it may, linguistically and historically considered, have in common with them; upon the fact that that it is the Word of God, not only the record of God's revelation of Himself, but the continuation of it; that here God not only spoke through men, but speaks.[56]

Scripture itself reveals God, not just in a past sense, but in a present one. It is not merely a record, it is revelation itself. At the outset, then, the interpreter is "confronted immediately with the same sharp either-or that is involved in every contact with God."[57] Here Franzmann is relying on German Lutheran Werner Elert, who says, "in our relationship to God there is no such thing as neutrality."[58] Franzmann referenced what he called "Luther's constant insistence on what must be the first axiom in theological interpretation, namely, that we be *under*, subject to, Scripture."[59] In rapid succession he then elucidated what that means using several Luther references and explaining them by saying:

> God is king, and His word is supreme; we are bound to it . . . God's Word is not a force that we can guide or control; it guides and controls us . . . Against its authority, reason has no claim . . . Neither has our feeling, our experience, anything to say over against this authority; especially is this so in times of trial when our feelings so readily run counter to revelation . . . Only so can scripture be grasped . . . We not only suspend judgment until we have heard the Word of God; we renounce our judgment when we hear it; we must learn not to think above what

---

56. Franzmann, "Essays in Hermeneutics," 738. Emphasis original.

57. Franzmann, "Essays in Hermeneutics," 738. Following this quote, Franzmann quotes German Lutheran Werner Elert in defense saying, "In our relationship to God there is no such thing as neutrality. Whether we obey His Law or not, whether we believe His Gospel or not, whether we love Him or not, fear Him or not—always we can do only the one or the other. No third attitude is possible. Disobedience is not defective obedience, but an active decision against God; likewise, unbelief; likewise, not fearing Him. That is to say that for which we decide when we decide against God is not a blank, a non-entity, but is an act that absolutely determines our existence. In unbelief and in disobedience we have consigned ourselves, whether we know it or not, whether we want it so or not, to that other which is absolutely antagonistic to God." Franzmann does not note where in Elert this passage is found, and whether or not the translation is his own.

58. Franzmann, "Essays in Hermeneutics," 738. While it is clear that Franzmann quotes Elert, he does not say where in Elert the passage is found, and whether or not the translation is his own.

59. Franzmann, "Essays in Hermeneutics," 738–39. Emphasis original.

> is written ... To render the word anything less than absolute obedience is to add to it something of our own, and the Word of God cannot tolerate adulteration ... Such an attitude of unconditional obedience will not be offended at the servant's form of the Word either, its apparent weakness with which God's revelation of Himself begins ... Interpretation is, therefore, finally a gift, not a skill or an achievement ... It is a gift of Christ ... It is a gift of the Holy Ghost who makes us spiritual.[60]

One sees here how foundational submission to the text is for Franzmann. The entire essay that deals with the circle of scripture rests on that point.

He did not, however, make such statements without exploring whether or not it is a reasonable endeavor. Franzmann sensed that there is often a demand that an interpreter remains open-minded and does not approach a text with any preconceived notions or ideas concerning it. This demand is often put in terms of being the ideal approach. But as Franzmann cannot and did not conceive of the scriptures in any way that does not consider them to be God's address to humankind that brings life, such an ideal approach is dispensed with. Because the scriptures grant life, the student of them must give them their due, the interpreter must maintain a posture of reverence.

> Our attitude toward Christ can never be neutral or open-minded; we cannot even for the purpose of study assume an attitude of neutrality. The Christian interpreter might do well to write upon his desk what Luther used to write out before himself in hours of trial: "Baptismus Sum"—to remind him that Jesus Christ is his Lord and that the Word which testifies of Him is to be met with "Speak, Lord, for Thy servant heareth."[61]

In the face of this reverent attitude, an ideal position of open-mindedness "is both impossible and wrong."[62] It is not possible to divest oneself of all presuppositions and come to a text as a neutral party. It is also wrong, in Franzmann's estimation, not to let an author determine the mean-

---

60. Franzmann, "Essays in Hermeneutics," 740. He does not cite them specifically. Rather he quotes the German and then renders an explanation of the quotes' meaning but does not directly translate them. This is why the following quote is so broken up with ellipses, the explanations themselves demonstrate the point being made in the essay, but are themselves separated by quotations in German.

61. Franzmann, "Essays in Hermeneutics," 741. "I am baptized."

62. Franzmann, "Essays in Hermeneutics," 741. Franzmann is speaking here of the demand for open-mindedness in any field interpretation not just biblical interpretation.

ing. One cannot understand Homer, Milton, or Goethe "by remaining coolly above him."[63] True understanding necessitates a "fully and sympathetically" submission to the author.[64] Thus, submission to a text is not an unreasonable demand at all, rather, it is an integral part of proper understanding. There is, however, a difference between submitting to Homer, Milton, or Goethe and to the scriptures. For in submitting to the scriptures, the interpreter "will have been taken by a power and a love that will not let him go."[65]

Two of the great Reformation principles regarding proper exegesis flow from this submission to the love delivered by the text. The first is, *unus simplex sensus*, that there is one plain or simple sense of the scriptures. There is no need for the interpreter to allegorize everything or deny the allegory when it is found because the scriptures are inherently spiritual. One need not attempt to mine more than what is there as had been done in previous epochs of interpretive history.[66] The second principle is, *scriptura sacra sui ipsius interpres*, that scripture interprets itself. "Such an attitude toward Scripture precludes any interpretation by an alien or imported norm, whether that norm be tradition, the consensus of the church, 'the spirit,' enlightened reason, or the Christian consciousness, a moral norm, a dogmatic system, or an assumed entity such as the whole of Scripture."[67] This means that nothing other than scripture should be the thing that brings light and clarity to the areas darkened by confusion. "All the light that is needed, theologically, in Scripture is provided by Scripture itself."[68] Dogma is not allowed to usurp the authority of words on the page. It cannot, "rationalize away tensions that Scripture itself has left unresolved."[69] One sees here a concern that the text has full authority over all things. Franzmann concluded by speaking of how the whole of these two Reformation principles relate to the circle of scripture, and how the circles relate one to the other.

---

63. Franzmann, "Essays in Hermeneutics," 741.

64. Franzmann, "Essays in Hermeneutics," 741.

65. Franzmann, "Essays in Hermeneutics," 742.

66. Here Franzmann spends time dealing with Medieval practice specifically. Cf. the aforementioned essay, 742–44.

67. Franzmann, "Essays in Hermeneutics," 744.

68. Franzmann, "Essays in Hermeneutics," 745.

69. Franzmann, "Essays in Hermeneutics," 745.

True interpretation is better occupied. For in thus interpreting, always remaining under Scripture, we shall not only introduce no alien or imported norms; we shall also remain always under the influence of the same Spirit who first gave the Word to the Church. That Spirit is the Spirit of truth and will lead us to seek and find Christ as the whole content of Scripture. That does not mean that we allegorize and twist texts to find explicit references to our Lord where none such exists. It does mean that we view and treat Scripture as an organic whole, with one Author, all the parts of which are vitally related to the one central theme of God's redemptive work in Christ. It is Christ, our Redeemer, whom we seek and find.

Practically, all this means that the concordance is more valuable than the dictionary; that the large dictionary with its systematized parallels is more valuable than the small dictionary; that theological lexica of the order of Cremer and Kittel are more valuable than merely lexical works; that the best part of a good commentary is often the collections of parallels from Scripture; that the margins of the Nestle are better than a good many commentaries; that the best of all is to be your own concordance of words and ideas, to do as Luther did, who read through all Scriptures twice a year, "bis ich ein ziemlich guter Textualis wurde."[70]

These "Essays in Hermeneutics" were not simply written in 1948 and ignored in subsequent years. In February 1961 they were combined with two other essays and printed under the title *Scripture and Interpretation*. This product was intended for use in the other Missouri Synod seminary located in Springfield, Illinois, the one where Franzmann was not on the faculty.[71] L. M. Peterson of the exegetical department in Springfield wrote the "Acknowledgements" saying, "the collection represents the only statement of length in our own Lutheran circles since Fuerbringer's Hermeneutik."[72] Thus, the three essays discussed above, and two others, were understood, even by those outside of Martin's own seminary, to be

70. Franzmann, "Essays in Hermeneutics," 746. Translation of the last line could be rendered: "until I was a quite good textual critic." The term "Textualis" does not seem to appear in Luther outside of this instance. The idea is that one must become competent in the text itself if one is to going to interpret the text at all. Credit belongs to Brooks Schramm for the rendering of "Textualis" as well as the the investigation of its usage in Luther.

71. Though during the 1972–73 academic year Franzmann would serve there.

72. L. M. Peterson, "Acknowledgements," in Franzmann, *Scripture and Interpretation*.

a substantive expression of Lutheran hermeneutics. Franzmann himself stated that they are, "an attempt to sum up my reading and my experience in the field of biblical interpretation."[73] This means then, that the "Essays in Hermeneutics," only deal in part with his hermeneutical perspective.[74] Before engaging in a study of the other two essays, "Revelation—Scripture—Interpretation" and "The Posture of the Interpreter," it is helpful to see how the circles were used in Franzmann's own exegetical work. In doing so, one will be able to see Franzmann's place and perspective relative to his own faculty and to those outside it.

THE WORD OF THE LORD GROWS UNREST

Martin's teaching career at Concordia Seminary centered on the New Testament. Specifically, his work in Matthew's gospel, the books of Romans and Revelation, and his isagogic materials on the New Testament as a whole resulted from his work in the classroom. Classrooms are, like almost every other setting, rarely free from outside interference. Martin's tenure as head of the Exegetical department at Concordia Seminary was fraught with controversial moments relating to biblical interpretation. Kurt Marquart, a conservative Lutheran figure who ended up as a professor at Concordia Theological Seminary in Ft. Wayne, suggested that, "the first public symptoms that the neo-Lutheran, historical-critical contagion had reached the Missouri Synod was the publication in 1950, and by the Synod's own Concordia Publishing House, of *From Luther to Kierkegaard*, written by the young intellectual Jaroslav Pelikan."[75] Marquart's assessment of the book is less than charitable. "With supreme confidence in the prevailing winds of doctrine, the book announced that the Lutheran Church had been set on the wrong philosophical track."[76] He goes on to accuse the book of something far worse. "Such glib 'trendiness' came now to dominate a new breed of Missouri Synod scholarship which stressed breadth rather than depth. Lutheranism's stately and venerable old doctrinal edifice was no longer seen from within, but only from the

---

73. Franzmann, *Scripture and Interpretation*.

74. The two other essays that warrant consideration will be dealt with only in terms of their unique contribution to the discussion as some of the content overlaps with the "Essays on Hermeneutics."

75. Marquart, *Anatomy of an Explosion: Missouri in Lutheran Perspective*, 108.

76. Marquart, *Anatomy of an Explosion: Missouri in Lutheran Perspective*, 108.

perspectives of its avowed enemies."⁷⁷ The judgment Marquart renders is not simply that he disagrees with Pelikan's assessment, but that he sees in Pelikan someone who opened a door that could have destroyed a "stately and venerable old doctrinal edifice."⁷⁸ Thus Marquart reveals something about himself, that he has a deep affinity for the old perspective. This is important to understand because his voice is not just a conservative one but one that was clearly not shy about speaking loudly while wagging an accusatory finger.

Pelikan left the Concordia Seminary in 1953. Marquart notes that "it may or may not be a coincidence that student unrest about verbal inspiration came to a head in the 1953–54 school year."⁷⁹ The students wanted to know how to understand the idea that the scriptures were "verbally inspired" by God.⁸⁰ That is to say, they were interested in understanding how God worked through authors to render the texts known as the scriptures. They wanted to know how the scriptures spoke about the doctrine and how the Lutheran Confessions addressed it.⁸¹ Led by F. E. Mayer, professors Arthur Carl Piepkorn, Walter Roehrs, and Martin Franzmann prepared a set of essays as a response to the students' inquiry. Franzmann's contribution to the essays began with the following statement:

> "Verbal Inspiration" may not be the best conceivable formulation of the doctrine of Scriptures, being subject, like all dogmatic formulations, to incrustation and misunderstanding. All dogmatic formulations, "Verbal Inspiration" included, suffer by comparison with the bright, plastic, vivid, and dynamic word of the Bible itself. But, it should be also noted, the doctrine of the verbal inspiration of the Scriptures is, like any other true doctrine of the Church, an act of thanksgiving and adoration. The fact that this doctrine, like every other doctrine, has at times received a dry and overintellectual formulation does not call into question its basically doxological character. (The fact that men have made swine of themselves on the fruit of the vine does not cancel or call into question the fact that the good Creator, God, gave wine to make glad the heart of man or the fact that Our Lord will drink it with us "new" in His Father's kingdom.)

77. Marquart, *Anatomy of an Explosion: Missouri in Lutheran Perspective*, 108.
78. Marquart, *Anatomy of an Explosion: Missouri in Lutheran Perspective*, 108.
79. Marquart, *Anatomy of an Explosion: Missouri in Lutheran Perspective*, 108.
80. Caemmerer, "Essays on the Interpretation of Scripture," 738.
81. Caemmerer, "Essays on the Interpretation of Scripture," 738.

> Verbal Inspiration is the Church of God's response to the condescending God, who has by His Holy Spirit revealed Himself to man, i.e., has offered Himself in Christ Jesus for personal communion with man—and personal communion with man involves verba, words.[82]

Franzmann clearly affirmed verbal inspiration but suggested that as a doctrine, it has been misused and perhaps even abused. For this statement Franzmann received no condemnation from Marquart. In fact, Marquart affirmed that Franzmann's essay is one among the others that attempts to "hold the line."[83] It does not matter if Marquart was right in accusing Pelikan of instigating trouble on the campus of Concordia Seminary. What is important is the fact that one of the staunchest supporters of the "old doctrinal edifice" saw in Martin Franzmann's essay an attempt to hold the line. If there was trouble on the campus, Franzmann was not to blame.

Unfortunately for Franzmann, the student unrest over the doctrine of verbal inspiration was not the only blip on the radar during his tenure on the faculty or as the eventual chair of the department. Another blip involved Martin Henry Scharlemann, a faculty member who arrived at the seminary in 1952. Scharlemann, a former United States Air Force chaplain, had trained for pastoral ministry at Concordia Seminary in St. Louis, did graduate study at Washington University in St. Louis, and postgraduate study at Union Theological Seminary in New York. In a 1980 interview Scharlemann said of himself:

> When I came to the seminary, '52, our theology was pretty frozen. No new question had been asked for decades . . . because there was a kind of assumption that all the questions had been answered, when in fact new questions arise in theology all the time, and this was a very, very unwholesome atmosphere in which to live. So I began to write some of those essays. . . . I took up the question of inerrancy. . . . My own idea was that we ought not even use the word because it had a Reformed background and usually misleads people when they read it. In fact, it often keeps people from reading the Bible because they're scared to run into some problem, since inerrancy suggests that everything is in neat order, which of course it isn't, in Scripture. Well, of

---

82. Franzmann, "The New Testament View of Inspiration," 743.

83. Marquart, *Anatomy of an Explosion*, 109.

course as soon as you start tinkering with the word "inerrancy" you get into trouble.[84]

Scharlemann admitted that he was the one who started asking questions about inerrancy. In short, inerrancy is the belief that the bible contains no errors of any sort, factual or spiritual. That is to say, on matters of history as well as matters of faith, the scriptures speak truth. If there is a contradiction with secular history, then secular history must be in the wrong. The questions he raised concerning inerrancy were initially meant only for discussion among the faculty. The paper presented to the faculty in 1958 titled "The Inerrancy of Scripture" was eventually leaked to the public.[85] Scharlemann sought "to defend the paradox that the Book of God's Truth contained 'errors.'"[86] After the paper had been made public Scharlemann presented three more controversial papers on the nature of inerrancy and the scriptures. This ignited a firestorm throughout The Lutheran Church—Missouri Synod. It eventuated into a public rebuke of Martin Scharlemann at the 1962 Synod Convention in Cleveland. "Resolution 3-10 called for the removal of Dr. Martin Scharlemann . . . for having 'publicly expressed teachings contrary to the clear doctrine of Scripture,' and for failure to make a 'clear-cut and decisive correction of these errors.'"[87] Faced with his removal, Scharlemann confessed his error, recanted his remarks, and pleaded for forgiveness. The convention affirmed Scharlemann "by a standing vote of 650–20."[88]

What does any of this have to do with Martin Franzmann? By Sharlemann's own admission, problems at Concordia Seminary over the nature of inerrancy did not develop because of some innovation brought on by Martin Franzmann, but because of Scharlemann's own interest in asking new questions. Verbal inspiration and inerrancy as defined above are

84. Martin H. Scharlemann, Interview transcript (Archives of Cooperative Lutheranism ALC-AELC-LCA Oral History Collection, ELCA Archives, Chicago, 1980), 34–35. Quoted in Todd, *Authority Vested: A Story of Identity and Change in the Lutheran Church—Missouri*, 180.

85. Todd, *Authority Vested: A Story of Identity and Change in the Lutheran Church—Missouri Synod*, 179.

86. Scharlemann, "The Inerrancy of Scripture," unpublished manuscript. Quoted in Todd, *Authority Vested: A Story of Identity and Change in the Lutheran Church—Missouri Synod*, 178.

87. The Board of Control of Concordia Seminary, St. Louis, Missouri, *Exodus from Concordia: A Report on the 1974 Walkout*, 5.

88. The Board of Control of Concordia Seminary, St. Louis, Missouri, *Exodus from Concordia: A Report on the 1974 Walkout*, 5.

important concepts for the Missouri Synod. At no point during his tenure was Franzmann accused of bringing innovation or revolution. A conservative voice blames Pelikan for the inspiration controversy, another voice blames himself for the inerrancy one. No voice accuses Franzmann. This is further supported by reviews of Franzmann's scholarly work involving his commentary on Matthew, Romans, and his New Testament isagogics text. Each of those in turn will be explored in brief. Such an exploration will demonstrate Franzmann's clearly consistent conservative approach to the scriptures.

STUDIES IN DISCIPLESHIP

The commentaries on Matthew, Romans, and Revelation, as well as his book regarding New Testament origins are coterminous with Martin's work in the classroom. Residential and correspondence course guides extant today show this to be true. One correspondence course titled "Introduction to the New Testament" required the purchase of Franzmann's own *The Word of the Lord Grows*.[89] It is clear, then, that the course guide was produced after the publication of the book. Both the correspondence course guide and the work itself, however, mimic an undated workbook entitled "Introducing the New Testament."[90] The workbook, course guide, and published work dealing with New Testament isagogical material follow similar, if not at times identical patterns. The workbook is most revealing in terms of whom Franzmann saw as capable and reputable authorities to which he could point his students. After a brief page describing the aim of the course, namely that it would be focused on the historical aspects of each book in the New Testament in their historical order, there is a footnote that offers a resource for those who wish to learn more about the historical discipline involved. That footnote points to Henry C. Thiessen and his 1943 work *Introduction to the New Testament*.[91] Thiessen, a professor at Wheaton College, is also well known for his *Lectures on Systematic Theology*. While this does not solve the mystery of when Franzmann's course workbook was produced, it does

---

89. *EN-101 Introduction to the New Testament*, (Concordia Seminary Correspondence Course, 1965).

90. This workbook is currently in the possession of the library on the campus of Concordia Seminary in St. Louis, MO. Even the library catalog information does not have a specific year for the workbook. The record only indicates the twentieth century.

91. Franzmann, *Introducing the New Testament*, 2.

show that Franzmann approved, at least in part, of Thiessen's conservative scholarship.

The Word of the Lord Grows, Franzmann's New Testament isagogics text, was published in 1961. Even after the events of Franzmann's tenure as chair of the Exegetical department, his colleagues recognized his work as conservative. Herbert T. Mayer wrote the review of Franzmann's work for *Concordia Theological Monthly*, the publishing arm of Concordia Seminary.

> The book has many features which will guarantee it wide use. Outstanding is the note of reverent humility and enthusiastic submission which marks every observation. Each book is set vividly against the historical background which called it into being ... For a work of this short compass, it is remarkably comprehensive. Almost every significant isagogical aspect is covered, or at least the reader is alerted to its existence and nature. To this reviewer, the real heart of the book lies in the content outlines, which in most cases are original. These outlines, combined with other comments, turn the book into a good condensed theology of the New Testament.[92]

Mayer's assessment is paralleled in *The Springfielder*, the publishing arm of Concordia Theological Seminary in Springfield, Illinois.[93]

> Dollar for dollar this may well be the best book bargain on the market today—excellent binding, superior content, and a price that is astonishingly reasonable. If the readership of *The Springfielder* numbers about six thousand, we sincerely hope that some six thousand orders for this superb introduction to the New Testament will be addressed to the publisher forthwith. Here is Biblical scholarship at its best, yielding nothing to intellectualism on the one hand, nor to obscurantism on the other.[94]

Effusive praise aside, one can clearly see that Franzmann's work is publicly affirmed by both publishing arms of the two seminaries within The Lutheran Church—Missouri Synod. The commentary itself reflects Franzmann's commitment to understanding the documents of the New Testament in terms of their historical situation so that one would then

---

92. Mayer, Review of *The Word of the Lord Grows*, 49.

93. This seminary eventually moved to Fort Wayne, Indiana. Concordia Seminary in St. Louis and Concordia Theological Seminary in Fort Wayne are the only two seminaries for The Lutheran Church—Missouri Synod.

94. Jungkuntz, Review of *The Word of the Lord Grows*, 37.

be able to understand what those documents might mean for the present day. Not everyone, however, was convinced that his work represented the best in scholarship. N. Leroy Norquist wrote the review for *The Lutheran Quarterly*. His review is short enough to read in its entirety.

> This book is an introduction to the literature of the New Testament. The author makes a serious attempt to show the historical setting, author, date, purpose, and content for each of the New Testament writings.
>
> The avowed aim of the author is "to produce a book which would leave the student, for the first, alone with his New Testament" (Preface). Apparently this means that he wishes to make it possible for the student to be able to read his New Testament sensibly without the aid of a commentary. The aim is good, but it is questionable whether the present-day student will develop the habit of reading his New Testament at all simply by reading a book about it.
>
> The author's position on questions of dating and authorship is generally conservative. He rejects the two-source theory for the Synoptics, accepts the very early date for Matthew, and believes that all the twenty-seven books of the New Testament were composed before A. D. 100. Unfortunately, the author's conclusions are stated without documentation either for or against. For this reason the book seems to be unsatisfactory for seminary students. Perhaps the layman might begin with this book, but certainly he, too, has the right to know about opposing views.[95]

Nordquist was not satisfied with Franzmann's work, but did admit that the work generally follows conservative opinion on issues of dating and authorship. Nordquist went so far as to say that the book produced by a seminary professor, one that had its genesis in the seminary classroom, was "unsatisfactory for seminary students." Those outside and inside Martin Franzmann's circle agreed that his work was conservative, but not all shared the exuberance that it was a masterful work fit for a classroom. That opinion seemed to belong exclusively to his colleagues.

It is not surprising that Franzmann's commentaries on Matthew and Romans share a similar review. Victor Bartling, a colleague on the campus of Concordia Seminary in St. Louis, heaped praise upon *Follow Me: Discipleship According to Saint Matthew*. That commentary was

---

95. Nordquist, Review of *The Word of the Lord Grows*, 374.

Franzmann's first. It too seems to have developed in the classroom.[96] In fact, a former student has said that reading *Follow Me* is like being in Franzmann's class because it gives a sense of how he taught.[97] Bartling begins his review of *Follow Me* saying,

> This first full-length book from the facile pen of our colleague Franzmann is unique and, we predict, will have a long life as a theological classic. Librarians may find it difficult to classify. It is not a conventional commentary on the First Gospel; yet it introduces the reader into the whole Gospel more effectively than most commentaries and deserves to be read alongside of the very best technical commentaries.[98]

Not everyone shared Bartling's assessment. Eugene Tanner, a professor at the College of Wooster, wrote a brief review for the *Journal of Biblical Literature* that was dismissive of the work. While Tanner approved of some of the authors Franzmann references, e.g., Kittel and Friedrich, Ljungman, Strack, and Billerbeck, he concluded, "it is disappointing to find that the author has entered only the outer courts of the community of the great scholars he has read."[99]

The review produced by *The Springfielder* is of interest.

> A reviewer, one supposes, is seldom so fortunate as to have before him two reviews of entirely opposite viewpoints on a book which he himself is reviewing. Victor Bartling's encomium (*Concordia Theological Monthly*, XXXIII (January, 1962), pp. 45–46) leaves little unsaid for anyone who knows the author personally and counts him as a friend. To Eugene S. Tanner (*Journal of Biblical Literature*, LXXX (December, 1961), p. 398), the book represents only an uncritical and unscholarly approach which fails to come to grips with this particular Biblical document.
>
> This reviewer is grateful that the author, contrary to Mr. Tanner's standards, does not operate within the critical-historical

---

96. There is a correspondence course guide for a course entitled *EN-561c Sermon on the Mount* as well as a workbook bearing the title *A Workbook in the New Testament Theology: Basileia Tou Theou* available in the library of Concordia Seminary in St. Louis. Although the commentary is more broad than the course guide or workbook, it is clear that there are shared ideas. It is also known that Franzmann taught courses on Matthew, Romans, and Revelation.

97. Interview James W. Voelz, July 25, 2017.

98. Bartling, Review of *Follow Me: Discipleship According to Saint Matthew*, 45.

99. Tanner, Review of *Follow Me: Discipleship According to Saint Matthew*, 398.

framework of a non-Matthean "Synoptic-solution" to the First Gospel.[100]

The review produced in the *Lutheran Quarterly* shared Moeller's assertion about the lack of a modern sensibility or affinity for any historical-critical methodologies. "There is no direct reference to the modern historico-critical school."[101] Despite that lack of reference, the reviewer sided with Bartling and Moeller in affirming the value of Franzmann's conservative scholarship for clergy and laity alike.[102]

Martin Franzmann's commentaries on Romans and Revelation were both produced relatively late in his career though there is no indication of any shift in his hermeneutical approach. They share similarities in their layout in that they unpack the text verse by verse. This was a change from the Matthew commentary, which is structured around the idea of discipleship and works broadly through sections. *Romans* was part of the Concordia Commentary series produced by Concordia Publishing House. At the time of the publication of *The Revelation to John*, Franzmann had retired from Concordia Seminary and was living overseas in Cambridge, England. If one were to quibble with the commentaries on Romans and Revelation, it would be that they are not technical commentaries, a similar charge to the one levied against *Follow Me*. The commentaries do not dwell on the finer points of grammar or untangle lexical knots. One might, by way of analogy, describe them in terms of the desire of math teachers. Franzmann gives the answer, but he does not always show his work. One review of the Romans commentary is most intriguing. Martin Scharlemann openly disagreed with Franzmann over the rendering of ἱλαστήριον (hilastêrion). Franzmann had rendered it "propitiation" in line with the King James Version. Scharlemann insisted that the word was less about avoiding God's wrath and more about God bestowing mercy.[103] The quibble was significant enough for Scharlemann to include it in what is generally a positive review of the commentary.

It is important to understand Franzmann in terms of his peers. Those who were his colleagues lauded his work. Those outside of his sphere

---

100. Moeller, Review of *Follow Me: Discipleship According to Saint Matthew*, 63–64.

101. Storaasli, Review of *Follow Me: Discipleship According to Saint Matthew*, 181–82.

102. Storaasli, Review of *Follow Me: Discipleship According to Saint Matthew*, 181–82.

103. Scharlemann, Review of *Romans*, 185.

saw it to be conservative. No one claimed he was innovating a new trend theologically or championing historical-critical methods. While serving the Exegetical department at Concordia Seminary, Martin Franzmann maintained fidelity to the scriptures, even if that meant poor reviews from outsiders. He affirmed beloved doctrines such as verbal inspiration and inerrancy even if he recognized the deficiency in those terms. About his career, and specifically about his time as chair of the department, one thing can be said, he was not to blame for change in exegetical methodology. The circles of language, history, and scripture were not mere ideas, they impacted his work significantly.

REVELATION—SCRIPTURE—INTERPRETATION

The October 18, 1960 issue of the *Lutheran Witness* published an article that sought to deliver the content of a recent conference to its readership.[104] The Counselors and Fiscal Conference, held at Valparaiso University in September of the same year, "in keeping with one of [the] Synod's wholesome traditions . . . devoted much time to doctrinal discussions."[105] Five professors, four from the St. Louis seminary and one from the Springfield seminary, delivered essays that sought to address relevant doctrinal issues. Martin Franzmann, one of those five professors, was assigned the topic "Scripture, with Due Attention to Current issues."[106] "But," he said, "if we are to deal profitably with the subject of the Scripture, we must begin with the subject of revelation."[107] His attempt "to deal profitably" was not limited to revelation only, it developed into a discussion about "Revelation—Scripture—Interpretation."[108]

104. This readership was predominantly a mix of clergy and laity of The Lutheran Church—Missouri Synod. The publication of the article suggests that the topics under consideration were of value to the wider the church body.

105. Friedrich, "They Studied Christian Doctrine," 538.

106. Franzmann, "Revelation—Scripture—Interpretation," in *A Symposium of Essays and Addresses Given at the Counselors Conference*, 44.

107. Franzmann, "Revelation—Scripture—Interpretation," 44.

108. All of the essays from the conference were published in full under the title *A Symposium of Essays and Addresses Given at the Counselors Conference*. That compendium was published by The Lutheran Church—Missouri Synod in 1960. Franzmann's essay is published in two places. First in that compendium, second in *Scripture and Interpretation* referenced above and there is no difference between the two. As the one published in 1960 predates the reprinting in February of 1961, all quotations from Franzmann's essay will be referenced to the 1960 publication.

Revelation "is God's act. God discloses Himself to man and deals with man personally."[109] Franzmann does not allow for any kind of revelation from or about God that originates in humanity. His opening salvo is in defense against "current theological literature [that] still speaks of prophets and apostles as great religious discoverers, as religious geniuses," because such an idea was, according to Martin, "wholly foreign to the Bible."[110] Revelation is also something unyielding. "No man escapes the Revealer."[111] It is because revelation is the action of God, not something generated in a human, that no one is able to escape it. When God speaks, reality has no choice but to listen. This constant action of God culminates in Christ. "The church lives and works under God's culminating revelation in His Son Jesus Christ . . . Jesus knows and declares Himself to be the Fulfiller of the Law and the prophets . . . His coming in the time of fulfillment, the day of the inbreaking of the reign of God."[112] That revelation is, then, both a fulfilment and a promise of greater and future fulfillment, which "does not cancel or annul God's previous revelation."[113] By this Franzmann asserted that the Gospel concerning Jesus does not "make void God's revelation of Himself in the Law."[114] In actuality, the Gospel makes the Law "count as it never counted before" because "no rabbi before Jesus and no moralist after Him ever took the Law so seriously as Jesus did."[115] The Law, then, is presupposed by the Gospel. Jesus comes in order to "rescue out of a desperate situation . . . men under the curse of the Law."[116] Franzmann notes how integral this understanding of the relationship between Law and Gospel is to any understanding of revelation.

> It is amazing to see how often this basic Law-Gospel fact of revelation is overlooked or slightly blurred in current discussions of revelation. One finds revelation described simply as "God's gracious activity." Our Lutheran Confessions have given us eyes for this double aspect of revelation, Law and Gospel, wrath and grace; we can see how the whole New Testament (to say nothing

109. Franzmann, "Revelation—Scripture—Interpretation," 44.
110. Franzmann, "Revelation—Scripture—Interpretation," 44.
111. Franzmann, "Revelation—Scripture—Interpretation," 46.
112. Franzmann, "Revelation—Scripture—Interpretation," 48–49.
113. Franzmann, "Revelation—Scripture—Interpretation," 49.
114. Franzmann, "Revelation—Scripture—Interpretation," 49.
115. Franzmann, "Revelation—Scripture—Interpretation," 49–50.
116. Franzmann, "Revelation—Scripture—Interpretation," 50.

of the Old), from John the Baptist to John the Seer on Patmos proclaims the Gospel against the stark unchanging background of the Law and wrath of God. And as we love the Gospel, we must proclaim the Law; for unless the Law is heard in all its rigor, men have no ears for the Gospel. Where the Law is unaccented, the Gospel has lost its real accent too.[117]

While it is clear that Franzmann is speaking as one might expect a Missouri Synod Lutheran to speak, it is important to note how he understands the scriptures to be the thing that reveals the "Law-Gospel fact."[118] The confessions have only "given us eyes" to see what is in "the whole New Testament."[119]

Yet, this does not conclude the section on revelation because of one of the current problems Franzmann was asked to address: "One-sided emphasis on *deeds* of God as instruments of revelation. False antithesis between truth as personal encounter with the Revealer and informational truth."[120] Franzmann saw that "in Biblical usage the line between word and deed, particularly the divine word and divine deed, is less sharp than in our usage."[121] Using the genealogy of Matthew and Paul's sermon at Pisidian Antioch as examples, Martin demonstrated that in the scriptures, the recitation of history, even if that recitation is formulaic, crystallizes the history. "These formulations present history in its once-for-all meaning or significance for us now. They are not less than the actual record of the revelatory deed and word but more; the recorded word and deed are pointed up, contoured, and directed toward us."[122] He saw this as akin to when someone claims his father was a good father. Such a statement "cannot be separated from history and cannot be put in antithesis to history."[123] His concern is the contemporary discussions that bifurcate the action from the word spoken about the action, e.g., the fact that God speaks in opposition to what God says. He asserted that "we need not concede that propositions are any less personal and powerful than the acts of God themselves. After all, is the I believe *that* of Luther's

---

117. Franzmann, "Revelation—Scripture—Interpretation," 50–51.
118. Franzmann, "Revelation—Scripture—Interpretation," 50.
119. Franzmann, "Revelation—Scripture—Interpretation," 50.
120. Franzmann, "Revelation—Scripture—Interpretation," 51. Emphasis original.
121. Franzmann, "Revelation—Scripture—Interpretation," 51.
122. Franzmann, "Revelation—Scripture—Interpretation," 52.
123. Franzmann, "Revelation—Scripture—Interpretation," 52.

explanation of the Creed any less personal than the I believe *in* of the Creed itself?"[124]

The relation of *in* to *that* in terms of belief frames Franzmann's discussion of the inerrancy of the scriptures. "Scripture is recital, the record of God's revelation."[125] Because he understands revelation to be "both encounter with the Revealer and the receiving of information from the Revealer," he is able to maintain an understanding of faith that "is both faith *in* and belief *that*, in organic unity."[126] By this he meant that, "faith in a Person is possible only on the basis of believing that the Person is a certain kind of person and has acted in a certain way."[127] Inerrancy hinges precisely on this point, "the value of a record is entirely dependent on its truth, its veracity, its factuality."[128]

> "I am the God of Abraham, Isaac, and Jacob" is recital, is crystallized history. Its value depends entirely on the truth of the fact that God is what the Old Testament proclaims Him to be, the living God, the Lord of history and manifested in history; it depends on the truth of the fact that God did deal effectually, graciously, and faithfully with the patriarchs. If he did not in fact thus deal with them, the record is worthless as a medium of revelation.[129]

It is abundantly clear that for Franzmann inerrancy was not a small matter, it was a foundational one without which revelation could not be trusted.

Saying inerrancy matters and demonstrating what inerrancy means are two different things. "We should beware lest we invade [God's freedom in self-disclosure] and attempt to determine a priori what God's inerrancy must be like."[130] Like other things, Franzmann believed that the way to determine a definition for inerrancy, to understand what it must be like, is to let the scriptures speak. "We can only accept what God has given us in faith, in the believing conviction that His idea of inerrancy is better than ours . . . we cannot even assume that there is one universally

---

124. Franzmann, "Revelation—Scripture—Interpretation," 54.
125. Franzmann, "Revelation—Scripture—Interpretation," 54.
126. Franzmann, "Revelation—Scripture—Interpretation," 54.
127. Franzmann, "Revelation—Scripture—Interpretation," 54.
128. Franzmann, "Revelation—Scripture—Interpretation," 54.
129. Franzmann, "Revelation—Scripture—Interpretation," 54–55.
130. Franzmann, "Revelation—Scripture—Interpretation," 55.

valid kind of inerrancy, a best kind which God must inevitably employ."[131] The multiplicity of gospels speaks to this variety the human mind dare not limit. The Gospels may not agree at every point, but faith recognizes them to be "Christologically inerrant."[132]

> Both the careful harmonizers of the Gospels and the confident critics of the Gospels forget this cardinal point, that of Christological inerrancy. Why is it that a harmony of the four Gospels, to say nothing of a critical reconstruction of the four Gospels, is always somehow less powerful than the individual gospel? Is it not because each Gospel is functionally, Christologically inerrant, is a power of God unto salvation on its own terms, in its own inerrant way? One marvels at the futility of these pious labors. It is as if the church had been given four luminous and speaking portraits of the Christ, and both the poor deluded harmonizer and the poor deluded critic think to improve on God's handiwork by somehow blending them or superimposing them on one another.[133]

Here Franzmann is asserting that each document should not only be understood on its own terms, in what it says about Jesus, but also in how what it says acts as a "power unto salvation." This does not mean that "historical or geographical matters [are] matters of indifference."[134] References to Pontius Pilate or August speak to Christ's actual walking on the earth, and are therefore extraordinarily important. It does, however, mean that in the last analysis, inerrancy "is a matter of faith,"[135] one that has no demonstrable character. "We shall never be able to prove the inerrancy of the Bible to any skeptic's satisfaction."[136]

Related to inerrancy is inspiration, however, "inerrancy is not the decisive aspect of inspiration. That aspect is power; the inerrancy of scripture is incidental to the power of the inspired Scripture."[137] Here one should keep in mind the circle of scripture, for the power of scripture is the voice of God that does not speak just to a specific time and place

---

131. Franzmann, "Revelation—Scripture—Interpretation," 54.
132. Franzmann, "Revelation—Scripture—Interpretation," 56–57.
133. Franzmann, "Revelation—Scripture—Interpretation," 57.
134. Franzmann, "Revelation—Scripture—Interpretation," 57.
135. Franzmann, "Revelation—Scripture—Interpretation," 56.
136. Franzmann, "Revelation—Scripture—Interpretation," 57.
137. Franzmann, "Revelation—Scripture—Interpretation," 58.

but still speaks today.[138] "Scripture is the record of God's revelation and is the continuation of it."[139] There can be no talk of revelation unrelated to scripture. Even when speaking of Jesus this is true, as the prophetic and apostolic texts that bear witness to him link him to the past and the present.[140] Here Franzmann stood in clear opposition to Karl Barth who he suggested is an example of modern attempts to "speak of Scripture as the human, fallible witness to revelation."[141] Verbal inspiration, for Franzmann, did not allow for the text to be bifurcated into its human and divine aspects. The words of the authors are the word of God. It also maintains that scripture is the personal communication of God to humanity. "If inspiration is not verbal, it fails at the very point where it is essential; for the prophets and apostles never received revelation for themselves alone but for the ministry to the people of God and to mankind."[142]

There has already been significant discussion concerning Franzmann's understanding of the role of language and history in the interpretive process, much of which is repeated in the concluding section of the current essay. Pertinent, however, is a brief quotation that highlights how he understood interpretation in relation to the "almost universally practiced historical-critical method."[143]

> We are to study our Bible linguistically and historically as we would study a profane document such as the works of Homer or Shakespeare. But this does not mean that the Bible ever becomes for us, in any stage of our study, another profane document.

138. Franzmann, "Revelation—Scripture—Interpretation," 58.
139. Franzmann, "Revelation—Scripture—Interpretation," 58.
140. Franzmann, "Revelation—Scripture—Interpretation," 58–60.
141. Franzmann, "Revelation—Scripture—Interpretation," 60. Franzmann, who is using Baillie as a foil throughout, quotes Barth's assertion that "Revelation has to do with Jesus Christ who was to come and who finally, when the time was fulfilled, did come—and so with the actual, literal Word spoken now really and directly by God Himself. Whereas in the Bible we have to do in all cases with human attempts to repeat and reproduce this Word of God in human thoughts and words with reference to particular human situations. . . . [sic] In one case *Deus dixit* but in the other *Paulus dixit*; and these are two different things." Franzmann in reply states, "It is difficult to see how such an attitude can be squared with our Lord's own attitude and that of His apostles toward the Old Testament, which is uniformly one of absolute submission to a divine authority." Franzmann, "Revelation—Scripture—Interpretation," 59–60. Emphasis original.
142. Franzmann, "Revelation—Scripture—Interpretation," 61.
143. Franzmann, "Revelation—Scripture—Interpretation," 63.

> Much of modern Biblical study from the eighteenth century onward is a terrifying example of what can happen when Biblical study becomes secularized.[144]

Franzmann's reticence to accept the methodology was not limited to the horrors he found in the demythologization of Bultmann, but was concerned also with conservative practitioners of it.[145] Faith sees the life of Jesus, as mediated through the scriptures, as a life unlike any other in history, thereby making any judgment of the historical probability of an event questionable at best.

> And history, for the Bible, far from running its course according to unalterable laws, is always in the hand of God, under the governance of God. It is the scene of his revelation and the medium of his revelation. The God of the Bible is the God of history, the living God who acts and reacts, who in the incarnation goes deep into the history and life of man. Bultmann has broken, not with the world picture of the Bible, but with the God of the Bible as He deals with man.[146]

The concern, then, and the problem with the methodology, is that it divorces the voice of God who embraces the history of the world with the words humans have used to relay such revelation. Interpretation, then, is a personal act that places the interpreter before the God of history. A God who is actively present in the life of the individual as much as God was actively present in the events of history. It is a personal revelation, a moment where God speaks to the person through the revelation of the scriptures.[147]

THE POSTURE OF THE INTERPRETER

The posture of an interpreter ultimately is one of imitation, of *mimesis*. Franzmann argued for this in his paper "The Posture of the Interpreter" which was delivered at a conference for Lutheran theologians in June of 1959, the theme of which was "Our Fellowship Under Scripture."[148] Much of that paper deals with things previously discussed in this chapter

---

144. Franzmann, "Revelation—Scripture—Interpretation," 63.
145. Franzmann, "Revelation—Scripture—Interpretation," 65–66.
146. Franzmann, "Revelation—Scripture—Interpretation," 66.
147. Franzmann, "Revelation—Scripture—Interpretation," 66–68.
148. Franzmann, "The Posture of the Interpreter," 149.

and we need not recapitulate them. This idea of *mimesis*, of imitating the apostles, is the dominant motif. "*Mimesis* of the apostle, in the New Testament sense, involves both the obedient recognition of apostolic authority on the part of those who are interpreting the apostolic Word and the will to continue the apostolic task under the power of the apostolic Word."[149] In this imitation, one is able to recognize, "the historically conditioned human Word as the fit and adequate vehicle of divine revelation."[150] As the apostolate is a uniqueness in history, "apostolic theology is essentially a theology of recital."[151] The interpreter is not one who slices the Word of God from the words of the apostle, but one who speaks only what has first been heard.[152]

> What, then, is the posture of the interpreter? It is the posture of the obedient hearer and the overawed beholder. He hears the verdict of the righteous God of the Law without evasion or attempts at self-defense; he hears with all defenses down. He looks upon the God of Grace as He reveals Himself in the face of His Son and says with Job: "Now mine eye seeth Thee; wherefore I abhor myself and repent in dust and ashes." (Job 42:5,6)
>
> If he abhors himself, he is set free for God, and his posture is the posture of adoration. His task of interpretation is a priestly ministration of the Word. He sees in the apostolate the vehicle by which God's last Word comes to him, the token and evidence of God's infinite condescension, a manifesting of God's impetus toward incarnation, and he glorifies the God who has given such authority to men.
>
> His heart burns within him as he hears the Word, as he hastens to tell his brethren. The vision that overawes him also sets him to work; like Paul, he is not disobedient to the heavenly vision. His posture is the posture of ministry.[153]

Martin Franzmann's posture was one of humility toward the text. Indeed, his hermeneutical perspective and exegetical method were akin to taking off his shoes because he knew the ground on which he was standing was holy ground. He had no time for those things that sullied the ground on which he stood. He made no compromises with attitudes of indifference.

---

149. Franzmann, "The Posture of the Interpreter," 153.
150. Franzmann, "The Posture of the Interpreter," 157.
151. Franzmann, "The Posture of the Interpreter," 147.
152. Franzmann, "The Posture of the Interpreter," 159.
153. Franzmann, "The Posture of the Interpreter," 164.

He spoke a *Psha!* to anything that put the interpreter over the text. Language, history, these things are integral to the exegetical task, but they are only a part. The text itself, the revelation of God via the marks on the page, that is something for which Franzmann had time. Something to which he never uttered *Psha!*

4

Words of Life

CHRISTIAN POETRY

IN 1946, JUST BEFORE he left Northwestern College to become a professor at Concordia Seminary in St. Louis, Martin Franzmann wrote a series of articles on the value of Christian poetry. These articles were not meant for scholars; they were meant for the church. It was not an academic journal that published the four articles but the magazine *Northwestern Lutheran*. This publication drew readership, primarily, though certainly not exclusively, within the Wisconsin Evangelical Lutheran Synod, from clergy and laity alike. The first article broke down two prejudices:

> The first prejudice is based on the feeling that poets are, somehow or other, "funny:" they, the poets, do not speak right out; they sneak around corners with pictures and suggestions instead of standing forth and delivering what they have to say in round, unvarnished fashion, "like a man." Poets are thought to be strange, not quite men, not quite human. We distrust them or, what is worse, ignore them. . . . The second prejudice is held by readers and lovers of poetry in general against *Christian* verse in particular; it is crystalized in the saying: "The Devil has all the good tunes." . . . Too many pious and well-intentioned, but not, unfortunately, poetically gifted, people have written indifferent Christian verses, and too many easy-going people have printed them. Verse is not necessarily good poetry because it happens

to be about God; and we have—in church papers, devotional works, sermons, and hymnals—been treated to much that cannot qualify as poetry under even the laxest definition of that difficult term.[1]

Here Franzmann assessed two things: first, the distrust toward poets in general, and second, the disgust toward poets and lovers of poetry. He attempted to give his audience a wide enough berth to find themselves within one of the two categories so that he could then argue for the value of Christian poetry. The rhetorical effect of this attempt draws in as many readers as possible, those unsure or distrusting of poets and poetry and those who have a stake in the game. In one sense, it does not matter if Martin was successful in drawing in the vast array of readers. What matters is that one sees that he was attempting to write for a wide audience. He was seeking to argue for the value of something, not just for the lover or hater of poetry, not for scholar, clergy, or laity alone, but for something that he saw as valuable for people of any poetic persuasion, for scholar, clergy, and laity alike. His message is a message for all.

The articles on Christian poetry were only the beginning of Martin's effort to write for the church as a whole and not just for subgroups within it. Certainly Martin did write for particular audiences throughout his career. His contributions to *Concordia Theological Monthly* were clearly aimed at a more scholarly audience. Yet, he did not fail to continue through his career, even during his tenure as chair of the Exegetical department, to serve the church as a whole and not just the seminary at which he taught. The goal of this chapter is to investigate those literary contributions to the life of the church.[2] To that end his sermons, devotional material, and even published prayers will be assessed. Additionally, there will be interaction with material designed for lay consumption that is not specifically devotional, sermonic, or prayer, but material that presented his consistently conservative approach to the scriptures to the wider church. The poetic flair evident in so much of his writing overflows as he interacts with laity. His approach, more than being merely conservative, was doxological throughout. Martin Franzmann served not just the seminary, but the church. His work consistently made its way out of the ivory tower and into the homes and hearts of believers.

---

1. Franzmann, "Christian Poetry," 134.

2. This chapter will not include a focus on the writings concerning his ecumenical work. The succeeding chapter will address that work.

SO WE PREACH

One year, almost to the day, after Martin's first article on Christian poetry was published The Lutheran Church—Missouri Synod celebrated its centennial anniversary. *The Lutheran Witness*, the magazine of the LCMS, honored the occasion. One of the articles in that magazine entitled "So We Preach" was written by Martin Franzmann, who was still in his first year of teaching at Concordia Seminary in St. Louis. The focus of the article was the gospel. "And the whole meaning and the whole glory of our hundred years' history lies solely in the fact that we have preached that Gospel without additions, without abridgement, and without reservations."[3] It is interesting, though not surprising, that Franzmann would call it "our hundred years." He has not even been part of the Missouri Synod for one year but that does not stop him from identifying with the church body's entire history. Having done so, he then explicated the gospel and its implications for the life of the church in the next hundred years. The question is rightly asked, then, what is the gospel? Franzmann answers, "'The power of God unto salvation to everyone that believeth; to the Jew first, and also to the Greek;' that is the gospel."[4] Quoting from Paul's letter to the Romans is likely what his audience would expect as Missouri Synod Lutherans. That in no way, however, suggests that Franzmann was being disingenuous, he knew his audience. More importantly, though, he believed what he said. He threw his voice in with theirs. "The salvation we offer means life, life in its only real sense."[5] We offer it. It is life in the only real sense. These are not just words to ingratiate the newly-minted professor, they are an expression of a shared mindset.

It becomes clear that Franzmann was not merely parroting expressions he thought the audience would approve after he spent time speaking of life and salvation and its antithesis, death and perdition.

> And we offer this salvation to all mankind, to everyone that believeth, to all the world; that is to say, to all the guilty, for God's grace extends as far as His judgment. That is what we have been doing these hundred years, that is what we are doing now, we "exclusive" Lutherans that will not dip our feet into the stream of a unionistic ecumenicity, we narrowhearted Lutherans, we dogmatical hairsplitters, we that have bound ourselves hand and

3. Franzmann, "So We Preach," 132.
4. Franzmann, "So We Preach," 132.
5. Franzmann, "So We Preach," 132.

foot—yea, brain, will, desire, heart, soul, and all—to a Book that will not let us go. We offer salvation to all. We offer it more freely because we know it more truly.

In one fell swoop Franzmann affirmed the one-hundred-year history while at the same time challenged the stereotype that the Missouri Synod is "narrowhearted" and "dogmatical hairsplitters." He was not writing just to clergy or scholar, but to the church as a whole. It is as if he was saying, we have the gospel, we preach it for the world, even if we have some things to overcome. And why is Franzmann convinced they can overcome the stereotypes? Because of the book to which they are bound, because of the scriptures that grab ahold and will not let go. Franzmann had yet to write his "Essays in Hermeneutics" or present the "Posture of the Interpreter." He had yet to single out for his church body the finer points of his perspective and yet he has laid all of his cards on the table. The point is clear, if the synod is beholden to the text, the text will push the synod beyond its comfort zone. It will do so because the text is God's Word, and that word not only condemns but it also brings life. The scriptures are one of the means by which God speaks gospel to the world and so any church body that wishes to preach that same gospel takes their cue from God.

> We lay down no conditions. We ask none to take any man's word as authority over him or any man's power to dominate him. It is God's Word that we ask men to accept and God's power that we ask men to succumb to. There are no conditions; only believe. We demand no performance. We ask no one to climb laborious ladders to a probable heaven. We ask men to believe and to let God work. We place no bars, racial, political, or social. The Lutheran Church is not a German church, an English church, or a Chinese church; it is neither a white man's church nor a black man's church; neither a rich man's church nor a poor man's church. The gospel that we preach is a universal Gospel and the grace it offers is universal grace.[6]

Such an assertion needs to be understood in its historical context. The Missouri Synod had only recently made the change from speaking German exclusively to speaking English. Two world wars necessitated that change, but that did not mean the members of synod did so willingly. In arguing for the gospel that rests in God's power alone, Franzmann was

---

6. Franzmann, "So We Preach," 132.

demonstrating that the gospel, and so the church, is not beholden to any national, racial, lingual, or economical identity. It is bound only to God. He concludes:

> So we preach. We cannot do otherwise; our life principle is the Spirit of God; and if we live by the Spirit, we must also walk by the Spirit. In so preaching, whatever our shortcomings may have been, lies the glory of our past. In so preaching lies the only hope of our future. There is no conflict between conserving and going forward; for unless we conserve this, our life, we shall not go forward at all.[7]

The Spirit of God is the life of the church. That Spirit is intimately tied to the gospel proclamation Franzmann was lauding throughout the article. The Spirit's gospel orientation is the basis upon which the past was built and the basis upon which the future moves forward.

The above article was the first of Franzmann's published by the *Lutheran Witness* but it was certainly not the last. Whatever controversial language that might have been perceived within a church body, one with some of the strongest immigrant identities among American church bodies, did not prevent future articles of his from being published. The lack of outcry seems to suggest that Franzmann's words did not fall on deaf or intractable ears, but on ones willing to listen.

CHAPEL ADDRESSES

Although Martin was teaching at one of the two seminaries of The Lutheran Church—Missouri Synod, he was not an ordained clergyman. It is difficult to say if this fact insulated Franzmann from theological attacks. It is likely that the well-known fact concerning his lack of ordination played a lesser, if not nonexistent, role in the assessment of his theological output. People knew he was not ordained, but still put him in positions to teach and represent the church. In 1948 the *Lutheran Witness* published a "chapel address" of Martin Franzmann. It is not unreasonable to assume that the homily had to be titled as a "chapel address" due to his lack of ordination. Article XIV of the Augsburg Confession, a document to which the Missouri Synod pledges complete fidelity, prohibits anyone from teaching or preaching without a public call. This prohibition works itself out in the life of the church body by necessitating that those who

---

7. Franzmann, "So We Preach," 132.

"preach" must first be called to do so.[8] Normally "call" and "ordination" go hand in hand. Missouri maintains that the pastoral office, or office of the public ministry, is a divinely instituted office. The office is responsible for the preaching of the Gospel and the administration of the sacraments. Only those people who have been set aside for the public discharge of these duties are allowed to do so in the life of the church. Apart from those who are ordained into the office, no one can be called by a congregation, or church entity, to exercise the duties of the office.

In light of this, the chapel address of Martin Franzmann is somewhat puzzling. Martin had indeed completed the prescribed seminary instruction in the Wisconsin Evangelical Lutheran Synod. Upon graduation, however, he was not called to serve as a pastor, and thus, was not ordained. When he transferred into the Missouri Synod, there was apparently no thought given to ordaining him.[9] It would not be until his time in Cambridge, England, when his position as tutor necessitated ordination, that Martin was ordained. In his life of service to the Missouri Synod, however, he was not ordained. "He was deemed to be the Missouri Synod equivalent of Melanchthon. This kind of exception that proves the rule . . . He would preach in chapel and wear a cassock and surplice, but with no stole."[10] The lack of stole indicated that no one tried to hide this fact from those to whom Martin preached. This is no small point. Not only did Martin preach, but he represented the church body at several ecumenical gatherings.[11] If there was any thought that his vocal perspective was problematic, it is likely that he would not have had that kind of freedom and respect. But respect was clearly something he had. There was no attempt to hide his status, and there were several publications of his sermonic material. By calling them chapel addresses, no one

---

8. For a fuller discussion of the Missouri Synod perspective on call, ordination, and the pastoral office, see The Commission on Theology and Church Relations, *Theology and Practice of the Divine Call* (St. Louis: The Lutheran Church—Missouri Synod, 2003).

9. Richard Brinkley, in personal correspondence, has suggested that "sometimes genius is enough," to validate a person's work. While no documentation was discovered indicating why this was not thought to be an issue, it is likely that the relationship of the Synodical Conference, and the differing views on the Office of the Ministry between Missouri and Wisconsin, allowed Franzmann to pass through the ordination barrier unimpeded.

10. Interview with James W. Voelz, July 25, 2017.

11. His ecumenical work is the focus of the following chapter.

is trying to hide the fact that he was not ordained. The publishing of them indicated the status he attained early in his Missouri Synod career.

That first chapel address, published in 1948, was titled "Quick to Hear, James 1:19–21." Unsurprisingly, the sermon focused on the importance of hearing God through God's word, i.e., the Scriptures. Franzmann began by stressing the continued presence of the Spirit of God through the Word. "If we ask where Pentecost is to be found today—where that Spirit and the new fire is—the answer is: In the Word. It is, therefore, of critical importance how we hear that Word; whether we confront it with 'What shall we do?' or dismiss it with 'These men are full of new wine.'"[12] He continued by talking about the two stages theologians pass through. The first stage is when a young theologian gains enough insight and knowledge to see and express the deficiencies in the church.

> First, the young student sees that some of the tin gods whom he has worshipped from afar have feet of clay; that they can be petty and very unspiritual. He hears creakings and rumblings in the operation of ecclesiastical machinery that betoken that the oil of sweet charity is not reaching every valve and cog of its complex make-up. With a bleat of dismay he discovers that the Church is not perfect, and he begins to wonder whether the Church is good enough for *him*. He becomes exceeding [sic] swift to speak and swift to wrath, and in session after session he sits down with kindred souls and with considerable critical acumen and a vast lack of charity he proceeds to take the Church apart. The Church is out of joint, they find; and they deem it no very cursed spite that they were born to set it right.[13]

This stage is then set in opposition to the second one, where the theologian's wrath is directed away from the church onto the self.

> The second stage comes later, and the young theologian's second knowledge hits him harder. More slowly, and less vocally, he begins to discover that all is not well with himself. He begins to suspect that he is not good enough for the Church. That is a wholesome stage; we become more ready to hear than to speak. Our wrath has somehow spent itself. To this stage St. James can bring us; at this stage St. James can help us.[14]

---

12. Franzmann, "Quick to Hear, James 1:19–21," 191.
13. Franzmann, "Quick to Hear, James 1:19–21," 191. Emphasis original.
14. Franzmann, "Quick to Hear, James 1:19–21," 191.

The rhetorical point is clear. Swift and wrathful diagnosis of the problems of the church is the mark of an immature theologian. It is only the mature theologian who listens with charity before speaking in wrath. The developed theologian recognizes the deficiencies within, and does not blame the church for them. Listening is far better than speaking.

The listening, however, is not just a general listening to anyone who is speaking. No, for Franzmann, the first voice that must be heard is God's.

> We must first hear God. Now, this is a simple, unexciting, and singularly undramatic business: not half so exciting as starting a really bang-up Movement, with a capital M. Not half so exciting as running around, forming committees, and making hectic motions; nor has it the immediate grab-my-hand-and-call-me-comrade sense of shallow gregariousness that we all love so well (though in its own way, its divine way, and in its own time, it will found and foster the only comradeship worthy of the name). It means sitting down, on a chair, at a table, with books, principally with the Book. It means going to classes and all that—it means hearing, hearing, hearing, and hearing again.[15]

As a preacher Martin was trying to form the students of Concordia Seminary in a specific way. He was impressing upon them something he made clear in the classroom, that the first voice that should be heard is God's. The question is, though, why publish this? The value for a seminary campus is clear, but what good is this message for the wider church? Certainly at the base level it has the value of showing the wider church what is being taught at the seminary, at least what is preached in the chapel. The latter paragraphs of the sermon, which stress the value and central place of exegesis, speak to that point. The value for the church, however, is far greater than merely a dissemination of information.

> But the truth remains: only God at work can work the righteousness of God. Our angry impetuosity cannot do it; it can only impede and mar. Our filthiness—that is a strong word, but it fits exactly our dirty self-insistence and self-seeking and self-delight—can only hide the glory of His grace, can only becloud the Giver, God, with whom is no variableness neither shadow of turning. So, strip it off; let not our slogan be: "I am the man, and wisdom shall die with me!" but: "Thou, my Lord and my

---

15. Franzmann, "Quick to Hear, James 1:19–21," 191.

God, art He!" Face Him; be swift to hear; in meekness receive the engrafted Word, which is able to save your souls.[16]

Here one sees Franzmann doing what he did his entire career, teaching people to hear the voice of the God who saves them. It is not only individuals at seminary who can rise up with angry impetuosity. The church, clergy, and laity alike, have that "filthiness" about them. One sees a clear example of Franzmann poetic and vivid language, a hallmark of his doxological approach. It may have been a chapel address, but it was an address that had value for the church. Put away the anger. Hear one another. But in order to do that, first hear the voice that saves you through the Word.

HA! HA! AMONG THE TRUMPETS

The chapel address published in 1948 was not the only published bit of Franzmann's sermonic material.[17] Over the years four more sermon-like articles would be published by the *Lutheran Witness*.[18] These articles were eventually re-published along with eleven other Franzmann sermons in a 1966 book entitled *Ha! Ha! Among the Trumpets*. Each sermon was positioned in the table of contents relative to a specific time in the life of the church year. It is difficult to ascertain whether the aforementioned articles were turned into sermons or were sermons simply published instead of preached in a real context. In one instance, the article published under the title "Who Cares?"[19] is clearly expanded upon in the later published advent sermon "He Shall Be Great."[20] The preface provides insight into Franzmann's understanding of preaching. He openly admits, "I am not a preacher by profession: the church has called me to be a New Testament exegete, a professional interpreter of the New Testament."[21] Preaching is something he does "indirectly, through my students. To preach directly is a privilege which I only enjoy occasionally."[22] In admitting this, he was not laying claim to be a preacher by trade, nor was he trying to hide the

16. Franzmann, "Quick to Hear, James 1:19–21," 191.

17. As late as 1973 *The Springfielder* published one.

18. These are: "The Young Man Who Fled"; "If We Walk in the Light"; "Who Cares"; "The Resurrection of the Dead: The Beating Heart of All Our Hope."

19. Franzmann, "Who Cares?" 584–85.

20. Franzmann, "He Shall Be Great," 31–35.

21. Franzmann, *Ha! Ha! Among the Trumpets*, preface.

22. Franzmann, *Ha! Ha! Among the Trumpets*, preface.

fact that preaching is not the thing to which the church had called him. Yet he believed it to be a "salutary discipline" and a "good thing for the professional exegete"[23] to do. Why? "Preaching puts the exegete to the final test, the test of proclaiming the Good News to God's people in the last days, with the judgment seat of his Lord in full view."[24] Furthermore, what comes through in crystal clarity is a point emphasized by Franzmann in other places, namely, that preaching is about helping people to hear God's voice.

> In the pulpit the exegete can no longer argue his points; now he must *proclaim*—he must make *the* point, the life-or-death point. Now he cannot linger long over those marginal technical aspects of interpretation that are his intellectual delight; he is not now a professional but a man. Now he cannot fudge or hedge on the substance of his speaking; now he must confess. Now he must face his text in utter nakedness and let it speak, or better, let *Him* speak who is the sounding Voice in all those texts.[25]

It is worth noting Franzmann's consistency. In previous chapters, it was noted that Franzmann's hermeneutical framework, whether the metaphor was circles or barriers, ultimately included a provision for the text of scripture to speak into the life of the hearer. This is of the utmost importance because of the one who is speaking in the text of scripture, i.e., God. Preaching is the ultimate expression of exegesis. It is not about the "intellectual delight" but about the "life-or-death point."

Confessing is the place to which exegesis leads and it is a hard thing to do. This is part of the point Martin Franzmann made in a sermon first preached at the installation of an Old Testament faculty member at Concordia Seminary.[26] Using the beatitudes as a framework, Franzmann elucidated the value of being "poor in spirit." Not surprisingly he said that it is "more basic than virtue of humility. It means being a beggar before God."[27] He developed the idea that someone should do nothing

---

23. Franzmann, *Ha! Ha! Among the Trumpets*, preface.
24. Franzmann, *Ha! Ha! Among the Trumpets*, preface.
25. Franzmann, *Ha! Ha! Among the Trumpets*, preface. Emphasis original.
26. The installation was for Dr. Alfred von Rohr Sauer, professor of Old Testament. It was first published in *The Concordia Pulpit for 1950*, vol. XXI (St. Louis: Concordia Publishing House, 1949), 368–73.
27. Franzmann, *Ha! Ha! Among the Trumpets*, 79.

other than proclaim what God has done and what God has communicated through the scriptures. Late in the sermon he made the following statement.

> Blessed you shall be in your work. That is as sure as God is true. Happiness you may have, and we all pray that you will have a full measure of it. But I should hesitate to assure you of it, as a theologian. The work is not easy; the hours are long—or what is worse, there are no hours. The problems and responsibilities are grave. We shall find that the second Beatitude, which promises blessedness on them that mourn, was spoken to professors of theology too; grief is no rare vegetable in our diet. For we serve a church the glory of whose history is the fact that its course has always been a firm, determined confessional march; a church that has never had much taste for the mincing minuets of concession and compromise. Those mincing minuets are marvelous things to watch; they look so hard and yet they are so easy. But the hard thing is to march: to be good, not clever; to be faithful, not brilliant; to be honest, not urbane; to be the rough wool blanket that keeps the faithful people warm, not the flapping scarf of changeable silk that men admire. No one has promised us that confessing the truth will make us happy, but we shall be blessed—of this we may be sure.[28]

Franzmann's point was simply that confessing the truth is not always a happy endeavor, but it is one that bears fruit in the life of the church. That truth is Christ's redemptive work. Everything that an Old Testament professor would be doing was in service to the confessing of that truth. One can see the value of this message for the seminary community. But what is the value of this statement for the wider church? In other words, why publish this sermon? Simply, to communicate to the church a mindset. It is a mindset that seeks to be warmed by wool, not impressed by silk. Confessing is not easy, especially in a time such as when this sermon was re-published in the latter half of the 1960s. Societal issues aside, this was a time when Lutherans of all stripes, and whole church bodies in general, prompted also by Vatican II, were interested in, at most merging, or at least fostering stronger relationships. Franzmann's conservatism shone through in this paragraph as a means of assuring the church that confessing the truth, while it may not make people happy, is the thing to do in the face of "mincing minuets." Here again, however, his doxological

---

28. Franzmann, *Ha! Ha! Among the Trumpets*, 83–84.

perspective undergirded the conservative position. What appears to be a formulaic utterance, i.e., concession and compromise, are signals that indicate in an alliterative way the unchangeable path on which the Missouri Synod marches. He was affirming the synod's confessional conservative march while at the same time shaping what that march looks like.

Communicating mindsets is something that Franzmann did adeptly in his sermonic material. Consider the following example. In a sermon commemorating the Reformation Franzmann wrote on the value of hymnody. This sermon, which meditates on Colossians 3:16, begins with the famous axiom, "Theology is doxology. Theology must sing."[29] It then recounts the value of testing the hymnody of the past and present "to see whether its song is true, to see whether its doxology is theology."[30] He proceeded with a discussion of what it means that a song is spiritual, namely, that it is "wrought by the Holy Spirit."[31] "A spiritual song must therefore breathe the air of eternity, must have a scent of heaven about it. It must be the prelude and the beginning of that new song which the church triumphant shall one day sing in the New Jerusalem."[32] Hymns must reflect good theology or they are of no value for the church. A larger portion of the sermon needs to be reproduced to demonstrate the mindset Franzmann was trying to instill in his hearers.

> As we survey the hymnody of the Reformation we can but gratefully acknowledge that God has here given the church a song that is really spiritual. And as we survey all hymnody we must acknowledge that the Holy Spirit worked not only in the Reformation but in all times and in all places in the one Christian and apostolic church, that in the best of what Christian poets and Christian music makers have produced the church possess so vast a store of the absolutely excellent that it need never stoop to substitutes.
>
> And yet there has always been a terrible fascination in *Ersatz*[33], especially for a sick church, a church grown so languid that it cannot bear to live in the tension of the last days. And so we have, instead of the splendid picture of the church universal making a full-throated, joyful noise unto the Lord, the picture

---

29. Franzmann, *Ha! Ha! Among the Trumpets*, 92.
30. Franzmann, *Ha! Ha! Among the Trumpets*, 93.
31. Franzmann, *Ha! Ha! Among the Trumpets*, 93.
32. Franzmann, *Ha! Ha! Among the Trumpets*, 93.
33. "substitute." Here denoting a substitute of an inferior quality.

of the weary church sitting in a padded pew, weeping softly and elegantly into a lace handkerchief.[34]

The critique pits a full-throated voice against a weary weeping into a lace handkerchief. Such a reference, gendering the critique somewhat, indicates a preference for a strong masculinity as opposed to a weak femininity. To be sure, Franzmann was lifting up the value of hymnody throughout the church, not simply those from the pens of Lutherans. Yet, at the same time, he was criticizing the desire to substitute the best the church has to offer with something of lesser value, thereby attempting to prevent the emasculation of the church. The result of that substitution is not full-throated praise, but weary weeping. He goes on.

> And the amazing thing is how eloquent men can grow in defense of this shoddy *Ersatz* hymnody. They begin by criticizing the good hymns as "hard to sing." One might ask in return, Why must a hymn be easy? Who has ever said that it should be easy? Look at that woodcut of Albrecht Duerer's where he depicts that scene from the Apocalypse in which those that came from the great tribulation, who have washed their robes in the blood of the Lamb, sing their heavenly song. Look at those faces, their intensity of concentration, faces almost contorted with the energy of their devotion, if you would know what singing with grace in your hearts to the Lord really means.
>
> The fact that there is an amazing agreement on the part of hymnodists and musicians in the parts of the church as to what constitutes a good hymn counts for little with these critics. The hymnodist's passion for perfection is viewed with suspicion, as a sort of professional snobbery, and is usually countered with, "I don't know much about it but I know what I like." That really is the ultimate in snobbery. To pit my piping, squeaking, little ego against all the good gifts that God has given His church! It is worse than snobbery; it is ingratitude. It is as though God had led us out into His great, wide world and shown us ripe, waving fields of grain and said to us, "Here is bread, and all for you." It is as though God had shown us all the cattle on a thousand hills and said to us, "Here is milk and cheese and butter and meat for you" and we then replied: "No, thanks! It is not to my taste. I'd rather go to a messy, dusty, fly-infested county fair and eat cotton candy."[35]

---

34. Franzmann, *Ha! Ha! Among the Trumpets*, 94–95. Emphasis original.
35. Franzmann, *Ha! Ha! Among the Trumpets*, 95–96.

Franzmann was pulling no punches. He was comparing the substitute hymnody to snobbery and ingratitude of the worse kind. Good hymnody, hymnody that communicates good theology, may not be easy to sing, nevertheless, it should be sung in all its difficulty without complaint. Bread, meat, and cheese should not be traded for cotton candy. Franzmann spent two more paragraphs arguing this way. He did not chide production of contemporary hymnody, but sought to hold it to a high standard. And that standard does not disqualify on the basis of easy of singing. Good hymnody, for the present, includes the best hymns of the past regardless of their present difficulties. "The church must cherish the best, but its song should not be a mere repetition of the song in the past. . . . With our song we shall guide one another continually to the center and fountain of the Christian's life and thus really teach and admonish one another."[36] This is ultimately the point, that hymnody actually communicates something to the one who sings it and the one who hears it. If that something it not theologically good, then it is problematic. Easy or difficult matters less than doctrinal soundness. Why? Because hymnody impacts the life of the hearer. He concludes:

> We shall see then realized the ideal of all Christian song: the whole man with all his powers, with all the skills and gifts that God has bestowed on him wholly bent on giving utterance to the peace that rules within him, wholly given to the purpose of letting the Word of Christ that dwells in him richly become articulate and audible through him to the upbuilding of the church and the glory of God. Then shall our theology be doxology.[37]

The book initially published in 1966 was reprinted with a new preface in 1994. Ronald Feuerhahn, Franzmann's pastor in Cambridge, penned it. By all accounts, Martin Franzmann was a gentle preacher, not given to boisterous motion or voice. Feuerhahn addressed his oral style in a paragraph saying, "about his delivery one would not use that questionable expression that he 'preached with power.'"[38] The final paragraph of the preface begins, "The quality of writing shows when its effectiveness endures; Franzmann's delivery of the message is as fresh today as ever."[39] In this instance of "delivery," Feuerhahn does not mean Martin's actual

---

36. Franzmann, *Ha! Ha! Among the Trumpets*, 97.
37. Franzmann, *Ha! Ha! Among the Trumpets*, 97.
38. Feuerhahn, "Preface," in Franzmann, *Ha! Ha! Among the Trumpets*.
39. Feuerhahn, "Preface," in Franzmann, *Ha! Ha! Among the Trumpets*.

preaching style or dynamics. It means the content, the words on the page. Those words had a fresh message in 1994, but it was a message that was not new. The dust jacket of the 1966 original publication reads, "Author Franzmann marshals his expert exegetical stable to open up the vast brilliance of God's living word. . . . In these sermons the *then* of the written Word becomes the *now* of the proclaimed word."[40] In his preaching Franzmann sought to instill a mindset that bent everything to the Word of God. Whether it was at the installation of a seminary professor or the festival of the Reformation, the mindset was the same, God's Word, God's truth, so defined and realized in the person and work of Jesus Christ, so defined and explicated on the pages of the biblical text, are the means by which the church lives its life collectively and individually. This message permeated all aspects of his writing, whether the audience was clergy or laity.

PRAY FOR JOY

In the early 1960s, Concordia Publishing House, the publisher of The Lutheran Church—Missouri Synod, produced a set of four books designed for use in family devotional life. Each book within *The Family Worship Series* focused on a different audience, i.e., "families with small children," "families with children from 9 to 13," "families with teen-agers," and one "for adults."[41] It was hoped that these books would serve as resources to enable a family "to be priests of God to each other."[42] Martin Franzmann was asked to write the devotional for adults. He did not, however, have a choice in the content. He was asked specifically to write his devotions for adults on the basis of Colossians. This was a move outside of his comfort zone.

> Each of us no doubt has his favorite book or books in the New Testament, books that speak with especial directness and warmth to his heart. I confess that Paul's letter to the Colossians was not one of mine. I appreciated it and valued it as the very word of God to me, of course; I could not do otherwise as a baptized man. But I turned instinctively to other books in

---

40. The dust jacket of *Ha! Ha! Among the Trumpets* (1966).

41. Back cover advertisement for the series. Franzmann, *New Courage for Daily Living: Devotions for Adults*.

42. Back cover advertisement for the series. Franzmann, *New Courage for Daily Living: Devotions for Adults*.

the New Testament for answers to my questions and needs, to Paul's letter to the Romans, to the letter of James, to the Gospel According to Matthew. God has a way of making us enlarge our horizons; it was not until I was asked to write a series of devotions on the Letter to the Colossians that I became fully alive to the riches of the letter, riches of insight and knowledge, riches of inspiration and encouragement, riches of help and strength.[43]

Here one sees Martin acting as both teacher and servant of the church. While the broad scope of Franzmann's exegetical work included the entirety of the New Testament, he did not write a commentary on Colossians and admitted that it did not have pride of place in his own piety. But that did not stop him from answering the call. It is not as if Martin needed to publish another book to pad his academic profile. His commentary on Matthew and Introduction to the New Testament had recently been released and he was a regular contributor to *Concordia Theological Monthly* and in the *Lutheran Witness*. In other words, based on the common expression among academics today, Martin had published and was certainly in no position to perish. In taking on the task of writing the devotional Martin heeded the call to serve. He was asked to do something for the wider church, and he did it. It did not matter that the scope of the project was beyond his usual horizon.

In writing the devotional he used the opportunity as a platform to teach something not just about Colossians but about how God works. Consider again the following portion of the quote above: "I appreciated it and valued it as the very word of God to me, of course; I could not do otherwise as a baptized man." Here one sees his hermeneutical framework in full view. The scriptures are God's address to humanity. Colossians may have been written by a specific author, to a specific community, at a specific time in history, but it was for Martin, a letter to him. Stating such a thing does not negate the linguistic or historical features of the letter, but it shows how Franzmann understood the scriptures holistically. To be baptized means to be a hearer of the word of God to humanity. It may be that Colossians was not his favored letter, but Martin heard in that letter, before and after the devotional endeavor, the voice of God. To be sure this reflects piety as much as academic forethought. In fact, it is likely that Franzmann would prize the former over the latter. His hope for the devotional, in part, was that God would use it to widen the horizons of others as his own had been widened. He concluded his preface with the

---

43. Franzmann, *New Courage for Daily Living: Devotions for Adults*, 3.

following sentences. "If this little book helps others to a similar discovery, I shall feel that a gracious Lord has rewarded me richly. I hope, too, that others will be encouraged to look beyond their favorite books and go farther afield in God's green pastures than heretofore. I can assure them that they will be the better and braver for it."[44]

The devotions contained in the book are brief mediations on specific passages, or at times a single verse, each concluding with a prayer. The final devotion provides insight into what Franzmann was attempting to do, and perhaps hints at why the devotional was titled *New Courage for Daily Living*. Martin began by quoting Colossians 4:18, "I, Paul, write this greeting with my own hand. Remember my chains. Grace be with you."[45] The focus narrows to the last two sentences which Franzmann used as a means of talking about weakness and strength in the life of the church.

> We are all of us bound and fettered in one way or another; we all live and work within limitations. We are fettered by our frail humanity and by the strong sins that still cling to us; we are limited by physical disabilities, by our diffidence and shyness, by our lack of insight into other people's hopes and fears, by our lack of tact in approaching our fellowman, by the insufficiency of our knowledge, by our lack of skill in speech. Some of us are limited by the narrowness of our lives; we may have but small opportunity to mingle with men. None of us is so strong and great in Christ that he is sufficient to himself; even the strongest and greatest needs his fellow Christians' sympathy and their prayers, needs his brothers' word.[46]

Everyone is bound in some type of fetter. There are limitations for each person in some fashion. This means that people need one another. The point is obvious, the church, like the apostle, is in fetters. He continues:

> But none of us is so little, so weak, so fettered that he cannot be a vessel for the grace of God, that he cannot in some measure reflect upon others the light that has shined on him. God has willed it so; He has willed that "we have this treasure in earthen vessels, to show that the transcendent power belongs to God and not to us." We are all earthen vessels, cheap and fragile ware; but God pours oil into each bowl and lights a wick in it so that

---

44. Franzmann, *New Courage for Daily Living: Devotions for Adults*, 3.
45. Colossians 4:18 (NRSV)
46. Franzmann, *New Courage for Daily Living: Devotions for Adults*, 95.

even the cheapest and most fragile bowl can be a lamp to light up one corner of the world.[47]

People may have limitations, but they are still usable by God to light up the world. Franzmann's prefatory remarks sought to set the stage for God to enlarge the horizons of people who may not have given much thought to Colossians. The final devotion seeks to enlarge the horizons of people who may not have given much thought to themselves. His point is clear, broken does not mean useless. There is strength and courage from the one who pours the oil.

Franzmann would eventually write another devotional although it would not be focused on a specific New Testament book. As the title suggests, *Alive with the Spirit*, sought to unpack the role of the Holy Spirit in the life of the believer. It follows the familiar format of scripture quotation followed by explanation. Published during his retirement years, the twenty-nine devotions were in many ways a distillation of his life's work. The poetic flair, so common throughout his writing, is enshrined on every page, at one point calling stained glass something that, "turns daylight into doxologies."[48] His understanding of the word of God that makes present both the past and future, litters the text. "The Holy Spirit has the power to make vividly present what is long past and to move the distant future into the realm of our experience."[49] "Where the Spirit lets us hear the voice of the Good Shepherd who died for us and rose again, there we are safely at home with the Good Shepherd forever."[50]

It would be a mistake, however, to consider his devotional work only to be a quaint rehashing for lay consumption. Franzmann's work in this regard was focused on affecting the daily life of the believer, not in dumbing down his academic work to gain notoriety. One of the ways this comes through is in a book of published prayers. The prayers are not formulaic; rather, they reflect, stylistically, poetic verse. They were not intended to be put on display for admiration. "Publishing one's prayers comes dangerously close to praying at street corners to be seen by men. I hope the users of this book will put a more charitable construction on this publication and consider it an attempt to help others toward fulfilling the apostolic injunction to 'pray constantly' and to 'give thanks in

---

47. Franzmann, *New Courage for Daily Living: Devotions for Adults*, 95.
48. Franzmann, *Alive with the Spirit*, 30.
49. Franzmann, *Alive with the Spirit*, 31.
50. Franzmann, *Alive with the Spirit*, 78.

all circumstances,' even in some of the less likely and obvious ones."[51] There is no reason to think Franzmann is merely being humble for the sake of appearance. By all accounts, he genuinely was humble despite the brilliance that often accompanied his pen. Taking him at his word, and at the word others have repeatedly said about him, means taking seriously that he did not write for his own sake, but for the sake of the church.[52]

The published prayers of *Pray for Joy* reflect his concern for the church in all situations. A brief scan of the index shows as much. There are prayers for several different situations: "Praise for the Sureness of God's Gifts," "To Find Joy in Life's Trials," "Thanks for Harsh Medicine," "On a Rainy Day," "For the Consecration of Sex," "Thanksgiving for the Pure Pleasure of Motion," "In an Art Gallery," "For Busy People," "For Young People," "While Reading the News," "In a Democracy," "For Men in Protest," "For the Slob," and even "Over a Glass of Wine." The index contains several more situations, some of which might be of interest even to Christians today. One particular prayer shows how Martin tried to communicate some of himself into the life of the church. It is here reproduced as it appears in the text.

To Respect Language

O good creator,
O Judge of the world,
> You left us long reminders,
>> after the Fall,
>>> in the midst of the world's futility,
> of that far-off, that very good creation
>> which Your Word called out of chaos
>>> and adorned with marshaled loveliness
>>>> for our delight.

Even after Babel
> You left on human words
>> the imprint of Your will
that the family of man

---

51. Franzmann, *Pray for Joy*, 9.

52. All interviews conducted echoed this concerning him. Even published work that disagrees with him never attacks his personal qualities. He is by all accounts genuinely humble.

      should live in colloquy
      and one day speak Your name together.
You have put the promise of Pentecost
      on our speech.
And Your Son has put upon our every word,
          our every idle word,
      The accent of accountability.

O Judge of all our words,
wipe clean the slate,
wipe out the record
      of that fearful debt
          which idle words have written.
Teach us once more to speak,
        under the sky
            of Your forgiving love,
    as men made in Your image
        ought to speak,
    as men for whose redemption
            the Word went into death
        should speak,
    as men tongued with the Spirit's fire
        ought to speak,
treasuring the gift
      of articulateness,
      of lucid commerce
          with You, with men.

Strip from our words
      the trashy tinsel,
      the seductive streamers
          of our expert propaganda.
Quench the coruscations
      of our treasured wrath.
Put away the measured meanness
      of our contempt.
Silence the sodden measures
      of our cheap sentiments.

> Let our words be clean
>   and fresh
>   and strong
>   with paradisal innocence.
> Let them be human words again,
>   worthy of man,
>   worthy of You, O Son of Man,
>   who once shared with us,
>   familiarly, our speech.[53]

Here one sees the poet at work once again. Not just in his linguistic formulation, but in the formatting of the text that forces the reader to take time to read carefully. The alignment of certain phrases, the patterns and refrains, all beg for this to be prayed aloud. All the prayers in the book are formatted in similar fashion. It seems that part of the goal was not only to speak to the situation of the reader, but to allow the readers to speak audibly into their own situation. Of course, it is not necessary that these be read aloud. Indeed, one can garner a great deal from reading them silently and slowly. But the respect for language for which Franzmann prayed is a respect that goes beyond the person praying it. It is focused on using language rightly for the sake of humanity. The hope was that words would not divide but reflect the unity God showed in taking on humanity, in taking on human speech itself.

WORDS OF LIFE

"The Bible is not an opiate or an intoxicant. It is the voice of God saying, 'Come unto Me.'"[54] So wrote Martin Franzmann in a 1971. The context of this writing is an article about the nature of truth in the New Testament. Unsurprisingly, Franzmann argued that truth is more personal than propositional.[55] It is about Jesus not about ideas. In writing those words, Franzmann sought to address not an audience of pastors and theologians, but one of school teachers.[56] This was not the first time he

---

53. Franzmann, *Pray for Joy*, 44–46.
54. Franzmann, "What is Truth," 50.
55. Franzmann, "What is Truth," 44–50.
56. The Lutheran Church—Missouri Synod had, and in some ways still has, a very large number of congregations with private schools attached. The teachers Franzmann

would address such a crowd. Part of his work as a seminary professor was instructing not just his own seminary students, but the church as a whole. He had done something similar in 1964 with a number of other faculty members[57] on the subject of interpreting the bible. Again, the audience was not his students, but pastors, directors of education, and bible class leaders.[58] In other words, the audience was the wider church. Franzmann's contributions were on "Problems and Principles of Interpretation" and "The Apocalypse."[59] Much of what Franzmann lectured on concerning "The Apocalypse" would later be published in his commentary on the same. The content of "Problems and Principles of Interpretation" was in many ways a recapitulation of what he had published early in his career under the title "Essays in Hermeneutics." His lecture was subdivided into the familiar sounding section titles, "Meaning Through Language," "Meaning Through History," "Meaning Through Revelation," and "The Posture of the Interpreter."[60] He unashamedly announced, "In the Bible God is the Person who is speaking; and His Word counts as no other words does."[61] He affirmed both the need to be historical, that is, to understand the historical situation of the text, and the need to be critical, that is, to exercise "discernment or judgment."[62] But more than that, he asserted the need to live in tension.

> I think that we of The Lutheran Church—Missouri Synod have an especial responsibility, all of us, because God has given us a great gift. This great gift that God has given us in our church is this: our profound and resolute trust in His Word, our unbroken, unfractionated confidence that in this written Word we have the fountains of Israel, our trust, that if we will give this Word a hearing, it is powerful enough and clear enough to lead

---

is addressing are teachers at those schools, or even high schools, affiliated with The Lutheran Church—Missouri Synod.

57. Other lecturers were Frederick Danker, Walter Wegner, Alfred von Rohr Sauer, John Elliot, Lester Zeitler, and Oscar Feucht. It is Feucht who would serve to edit a compendium of the lectures. That compendium was designed to be "A Resource for Teachers of the Bible: Pastors, Directors of Education, Bible Class Leaders." It was sponsored by The Board of Parish Education of The Lutheran Church—Missouri Synod.

58. Feucht ed., *Interpreting and Teaching the Bible*, cover.
59. Feucht ed., *Interpreting and Teaching the Bible*, Table of Contents.
60. Franzmann, "Problems and Principles of Interpretation," 31–60.
61. Franzmann, "Problems and Principles of Interpretation," 37.
62. Franzmann, "Problems and Principles of Interpretation," 58.

> us ever and again to Him who is the Light of men. This is a grace that has been peculiarly our church's, and it is the source of our peculiar strength. Therefore we should not be too much discouraged if feelings grow rather high and tensions become rather strong over problems arising in the interpretation of it. The gift and tension go together; and the tension can be a fruitful tension. But we should also remember that the unused gift of God, the desecrated gift, is withdrawn. To him that hath shall be given, and from him that hath not even what he has shall be taken away.[63]

Here Franzmann was addressing the elephant in the room. In 1964 memories of the Cleveland convention, when Martin H. Scharlemann repented of embracing and advocating historical-critical methodologies, were indeed fresh. Franzmann took the opportunity in his lecture to speak about how the tension can be useful for the church, as long as it does not neglect the gift. He went on:

> In what sense can the methodology of the interpreter so oriented at these three points (in his baptism, in the church, and before the judgment) be historical and critical? I am sometimes accused of painting an overblack picture of historical-critical, and I am reminded that all of us are in one way or another both historical and critical. I'll concede that we all have to be. God goes the way of history. When our God walks, He treads upon the ground. That is His peculiar glory, that He comes down and condescends to us. What I have been saying is not a plea for an unhistorical or ahistorical apprehension of scripture. It is a plea for interpreting the Scripture on its own terms, in terms of history as the Bible itself sees it, history under the free dominion and the inescapable judgement of God. So much for "historical."
>
> What of "critical"? Critical means basically that the interpreter exercises discernment or judgment. Everyone of us finds that in reading Scripture, as in any dealing with language, we are called upon to perform a critical act. We must decide whether the word means this in this context or that, according the linguistic or historical context in which it appears. As soon as we are engaged with language, we are engaged in a critical act; and the Bible asks of us to perform critical actions.[64]

---

63. Franzmann, "Problems and Principles of Interpretation," 58.

64. Franzmann, "Problems and Principles of Interpretation," 58. Emphasis original.

Franzmann was affirming being historical and critical, but only in the way he explicated it. He was attempting to assuage concern, while maintaining the tension with the gift expressed earlier. Being historical and critical are inescapable for all interpreters, not just for academics. "In this sense and in this way we all can and we all must be historical-critical interpreters. That is our business. It is not our business to decide, by canons that our secularized century has decided, what could or could not have happened in the Life that is the life of men, the Life without analogies, the life of Jesus Christ our Lord."[65] Franzmann, in plain view of the entire synod, affirmed what it means to be, and in what way one can be, "historical-critical." It means taking the history as history, not determining what can or cannot be history on some outside basis. It is of necessity that all interpreters take this seriously, not just academics, because the life of the church hangs in the balance. Franzmann is eminently concerned with that life. He does not want to see the synod split unnecessarily. By framing "historical-critical" in such a way, he is offering a definition, and thereby creating space, for variety. But this variety is not unrestrained. The space is not so wide as to include all historical-critical methods, rather, Franzmann is defining the terms for both academic and laity. He is warning academics from overstepping while suggesting to the laity that being "historical-critical" is not necessarily problematic. As the events of the next decade would unfold, it seems he was right to be so concerned.[66]

Much more literature aimed at a wider audience than the academically oriented exists. Franzmann regularly published articles of a devotional or sermonic nature that appeared in the *Lutheran Witness*. Each time he would draw on his expertise in the field of the New Testament, whether that was to address the various translations of the biblical text, the meaning of Pentecost, or the value of the season of Advent for the life of the church.[67] In 1956, Martin would pen a recurring column in the *Lutheran Witness* titled *Words of Life*. Much of it was a distillation of his work in the gospel of Matthew. It sought to inculcate what it meant to be a disciple. Being a disciple "means being called and taken up into the movement of this gift—compassion of God; it means seeing in the need and agony of men the great harvest opportunity of the God of mercy . . . seeing the meaning of all history and all life, with all its opportuni-

65. Franzmann, "Problems and Principles of Interpretation," 60.
66. These events will be explored further in the final chapter.
67. See Franzmann, "Why So Many Bibles?" 134–35; "The Old Fire and the New," 207; "Sure—but not Complacent," 572–73.

ties for work and action in the fact that, as all men have sinned, so they are 'justified *freely* by his grace.'"[68] It highlighted and explicated the nature and function of "the kingdom of God" in Matthew's gospel. "'Kingdom of God' means primarily God in action, God the King reigning and exercising royal grace and power."[69] Despite the variety, it seems as though the column had a singular aim, outlined in the concluding paragraph of the first issue. "We must therefore learn to hear the Bible out on *its* terms. And it will be the purpose of this little column to attempt to tear the veil of familiarity away from some of the words which Scripture uses and to let us see them as the living words that they are, words filled with the life of the living, acting, saving God, the Father of our Lord Jesus Christ."[70]

Martin Franzmann served the church because of that uncompromising conviction. His work as a professor of exegetical theology was not concerned primarily or exclusively with the advancement of knowledge, but with the acclamation that in the scriptures God speaks to humanity. The life of the whole church is rooted in those words of life found on the pages of the biblical text. It did not matter where the church was to be found. It did not matter if it was in a seminary classroom, in a lecture hall filled with teachers of the bible, in the living room, or in the prayer closet. No matter where the church was found, there was Martin serving it, not because he had something special to offer, the beauty of his doxological offerings notwithstanding, but because of the word that offers everything, because of the word that brings life.

68. Franzmann, "Words of Life," 459.
69. Franzmann, "Words of Life," 95.
70. Franzmann, "Words of Life," 7.

5

Grace Under Pressure

REGRETFULLY

IN 1976, AFTER MARTIN Franzmann had passed away, Gerald Hoenecke, at the time a member of the faculty at Wisconsin Lutheran Seminary,[1] penned a brief column offering tribute to the deceased. "Dr. Franzmann," he said, "will be remembered by his contemporaries in our Synod for his scholarliness and originality, his rhetorical and poetical ability, but above all for his devotion to the Scriptures."[2] Such a tribute is hardly unique. What follows, however, is quite extraordinary. "He left our Synod to join The Lutheran Church—Missouri Synod in the midst of our confessional controversy with that church body, presumably in the hope of thus being in a better position to contribute something positive to the solution of the problem."[3] During the decades leading up to and including the 1950s relationships between the constituent bodies of the Evangelical Lutheran Synodical Conference of North America, most notably between the Missouri and Wisconsin Synods, deteriorated rapidly.[4] Once

---

1. Gerald O. Hoenecke served the faculty from 1952–1978.
2. Hoenecke, "Dr. Martin H. Franzmann," 226.
3. Hoenecke, "Dr. Martin H. Franzmann," 226.
4. This conference was made up at the time by four bodies: The Lutheran Church—Missouri Synod, the Wisconsin Evangelical Lutheran Synod, the Evangelical Lutheran Synod, and the Synod of Evangelical Lutheran Churches (formerly known as the Slovak Synod). It would dissolve officially in 1967 after the WELS and ELS bodies

proud confessional Lutheran voices were now suspicious of each other particularly in the areas of church fellowship. Hoenecke's tribute lauds Franzmann's efforts, noting that Martin was instrumental in the authorship of two documents, one a statement on Scripture and the other a statement on the Antichrist, both of which were useful in maintaining relationships within the troubled Synodical Conference. Hoenecke does not, in actuality, only heap praise.

> Regretfully, the hope of restoring full doctrinal unity in the Synodical Conference was not realized, partly at least because of a statement on fellowship, of which Dr. Franzmann was the chief author, which in 1960 led to an impasse in our joint discussions and subsequently to our Synod's resolution to suspend its highly cherished fellowship of 90 years with its former sister synod.[5]

The final sentence quoted above is the last sentence in Hoenecke's column remembering Dr. Franzmann. It appears, at the very least, that Hoenecke held Franzmann partially responsible for the break.

Martin Franzmann was an ecumenical figure. That is to say, that throughout his life, especially his life spent within The Lutheran Church—Missouri Synod, Martin served as an official representative, nationally and internationally, of his church body. Nationally he worked as the secretary of the Synodical Conference, was a member of the Commission on Theology and Church Relations of the LCMS, participated in dialogs with the National Lutheran Council, and its successor, the Lutheran Council in the USA. Internationally he attended the free conferences at Bad Boll and throughout Europe as participant and presenter and was one of the official observers sent by the LCMS to the meetings of the Lutheran World Federation (LWF) in Hanover. It is important to note that Franzmann understood the ecumenical task, as well as ecumenicity in general, in broad terms. "The church, if it lives in obedience to its Lord, is not 'also' ecumenical; it is ecumenical by definition since the Lord of the church is ecumenical—Lord of all that call upon His name."[6] Ecumenical work includes, then, interaction not only with church bodies of different confessions but also with those church bodies that claim the

---

removed themselves from the conference beginning in 1961. The SELC ended up merging with the LCMS upon the dissolution.

5. Hoenecke, "Dr. Martin H. Franzmann," 226.

6. Franzmann, "Meekness as the Basic Ecumenical Attitude," in Franzmann and Lueking, *Grace Under Pressure: Meekness in Ecumenical Relations*, 3.

same confession. In other words, it is Lutherans dialoging with American Evangelicals as well as Lutherans dialoging with other Lutherans. The Lutheran Church—Missouri Synod operates with a similarly broad definition as well, because it understands ecumenical work in terms of church fellowship. Fellowship, i.e., sharing altars and pulpits, is only possible on the basis of complete agreement in doctrine and practice. Martin Franzmann was a committed conservative Missouri Synod Lutheran. That meant, among other things, that he took the Lutheran Confessions seriously because they are expositions of scriptures. Yet, because of his work as a New Testament scholar, his perspective on ecumenicity reflects his fidelity to the scriptures, perhaps even more than it does his fidelity to the confessions. Moreover, that perspective was formed and shaped not just by the content of the scriptures, but by their very nature and function.

THEOLOGY OF FELLOWSHIP

The document that Hoenecke referenced in his tribute to Martin Franzmann is entitled "The Theology of Fellowship." In 1956, at a convention in St. Paul, Minnesota, The Lutheran Church—Missouri Synod passed a resolution requesting "a restudy of the question of 'fellowship, prayer fellowship, and unionism.'"[7] In reply to the request the seminaries each appointed faculty members to study the question at hand.[8] That Hoenecke identifies Franzmann as the primary author of the document is unsurprising. Not only had Martin been a member of the Wisconsin Synod, he was also the secretary of the Synodical Conference from 1952 until 1956. Additionally, he was the vice-chairman of the Committee on Doctrinal Unity for the LCMS from 1950 until 1962 when the committee was replaced by the Commission on Theology and Church Relations (CTCR). He served on the CTCR until his retirement from Concordia Seminary in 1969.

---

7. *Report of the Commission on Theology and Church Relations: Theology of Fellowship*, 2. See also "The Theology of Fellowship," in *Four Statements on Fellowship*, 15–16.

8. The document published in November of 1960 names Fred Kramer and Lorman Petersen of the LCMS seminary in Springfield and Erwin Lueker and Martin Franzmann of the seminary in St. Louis. The report published by the Commission on Theology and Church Relations in 1965 does not name the authors or contributors. Cf. "The Theology of Fellowship," 2.

The "Theology of Fellowship" document was published alongside three other documents, each from the constituent parts of the Synodical Conference, in a book entitled *Four Statements on Fellowship*. It was hoped that this document would "re-establish" the "true concord" that had existed in the Synodical Conference.[9] "The Theology of Fellowship," written by four professors representing both Missouri Synod seminaries, was approved by the faculties of both seminaries. This was done, however, at two different points in time. Part One, the part that Hoenecke references in his tribute, was the initial response to the Synod request to study fellowship.[10] It was completed in time for meetings in 1960 with the Joint Union Committees. Hoenecke is not the only one to suggest the role this document played in the dissolution of the Synodical Conference. To this day Wisconsin recognizes the impact of this document.

---

9. *Four Statements on Fellowship*, 3.

10. Part Two of the document in question need not be considered at this time. It consists of an appraisal of the "Principles Governing the Exercise of Fellowship," with specific attention directed at separatism and unionism, as well as a suggested application of those principles. This section of "The Theology of Fellowship" was not approved by the seminary faculties and disseminated to the church until October of 1960. The preface of *Four Statements on Fellowship* spells this out in detail.

With regard to the materials of The Lutheran Church—Missouri Synod it should be stated that "The Theology of Fellowship" was prepared and approved by the joint faculties of St. Louis and Springfield in 1958. Further materials dealing with Scriptural principles of fellowship and their application to specific circumstances were prepared by the joint faculties and were adopted on October 29, 1960. Discussion of these statements has not yet been completed by the Joint Doctrinal Committee of the Synodical Conference, nor have they officially been acted upon by a convention of The Lutheran Church—Missouri Synod. (*Four Statements on Fellowship*, 4.)

This means, then, that Part One is likely the document that caused concern in May of 1960. While it is possible that an early version may have existed for the meetings that brought concern in May of 1960, the preface suggests that the final version of Part Two was not approved until October, months after the WELS delegation recognized the impasse.

It should also be noted that in subsequent years Part Two was revised multiple times. The first major revision appeared in 1962 and the second appeared as an additional part to the document in 1965. The revisions, now known as Part II and Part III, exist in a final report from the Commission on Theology and Church Relations of The Lutheran Church—Missouri Synod which, along with the original Part One, were submitted to the 1965 Synod convention. Part II of that document investigates the historical instances of fellowship while examining the confessional basis. Part III is mainly a revision of Part II with special attention paid to scriptural references that form the basis of rejecting fellowship.

> In 1960, the Missouri men submitted their "Theology of Fellowship" to the Joint Union Committees... this document spoke of a "growing edge of fellowship" and contended that "in reaching out to those not yet in confessional fellowship with us there is the possibility of the beginning of the practice of fellowship." This was the start of what has become Missouri's position on "levels of fellowship." In the meetings in May 1960, after three days of discussions, the Wisconsin delegation recognized that the consideration of this subject had reached an impasse. The doctrine of church fellowship became the primary divisive issue that resulted in the 1961 Wisconsin Synod resolution suspending fellowship with the Missouri Synod.[11]

That Martin Franzmann would be associated with this kind of failure to preserve unity is somewhat intriguing. The question must be asked, why would the document, penned primarily, though not exclusively, by a son of the Wisconsin Synod, be inflammatory enough to be an instrumental piece in the severing of fellowship? An evaluation of Part One is necessary to answer that question. The document in question consists exclusively of scriptural passages referencing how God has worked in the world. One appraisal sums up Part One in a helpful and succinct fashion.

> The findings in Part I may be summed up briefly as follows: God created man for fellowship both with Himself and with his fellowmen. Man destroyed this fellowship by the fall into sin, by which he became an enemy of God and brought strife and enmity into the human family. However, God in His great mercy in Christ redeemed man from sin in order that He might restore him to fellowship with Himself and with his fellowmen in the Christian church. The Scripture, particularly the New Testament, abounds in passages which extol this fellowship. Therefore Christians should consider fellowship, also church fellowship, the normal thing in their relations with one another. They should desire such fellowship, and should constantly be concerned to extend the blessings of this fellowship to others.[12]

---

11. "Theses on Church Fellowship," Wisconsin Evangelical Lutheran Synod, https://wels.net/about-wels/what-we-believe/doctrinal-statements/church-fellowship/. Accessed April 5, 2018.

12. *Report of the Commission on Theology and Church Relations: Theology of Fellowship*, 35.

That is to say, a scriptural study led to the conclusion that Christians are not also ecumenical,[13] as if it were an add-on. Christians are by definition ecumenical because God is in the business of restoring severed relationships. Part One states this outright. "The call to faith is simultaneously the call into fellowship (1 Cor. 1:9)."[14] The document goes on to utter unequivocally that, "those who have fellowship with God through faith in Christ are also in fellowship with one another (1 John 1:3). As faith makes all men children of God, so it also makes them all brethren in Christ (Gal. 3:26 and 27)."[15] Moreover, "this fellowship transcends every barrier created by God or set up by man and brings about the highest unity possible among men, the unity in Christ Jesus (Gal. 3:28)."[16] That is to say, unity actually already exists in Christ. The fact that it does not evidence itself among church bodies is a problem, one that those bodies collectively and individually must work to overcome. "Believers exercising their fellowship with God and with one another, and growing strong therein, labor to extend fellowship."[17]

Exactly how much of Part One is directly the result of Franzmann's work and how much of it is the result of the work of the other members of the committee is difficult, if not impossible, to ascertain. The "300 passages" considered by the committee that resulted in the document led to an invigorated interest in extending the bond of fellowship.[18] What is clear is that the document, based on an appraisal of the scriptures and not on an appraisal of the Lutheran Confessions or historical instances, was not well received in the Synodical Conference. For a Synodical Conference that was strained, such a suggestion may have been too much to handle.

---

13. Again, ecumenical should be understood broadly to include dialog between two groups of the same confession. In LCMS and WELS circles inter-Lutheran relations are understood this way. Typically, these inter-Lutheran discussions, as well as discussion between bodies of various confessions, are discussed using terms like "church fellowship" as opposed to the term "ecumenical."

14. "The Theology of Fellowship," 24.

15. "The Theology of Fellowship," 25.

16. "The Theology of Fellowship," 24.

17. "The Theology of Fellowship," 31.

18. "The Theology of Fellowship," 15–16. The historical and confessional appraisal is comprised in Part II of the later version published initially in 1962 and again in 1965.

BAD BOLL

Martin Franzmann's career as an ecumenical figure did not begin with the production of the "Theology of Fellowship." Two years after joining the faculty of Concordia Seminary he was selected to be a commissioner to the 1949 free conferences in Bad Boll, Germany. The conferences had begun a year prior as a means of American Lutherans partnering with German Lutherans to rebuild the physical and spiritual state of the country in the wake of World War II.[19] That first year, 1948, would see important theologians and figures in the life of The Lutheran Church—Missouri Synod interact with equally, if not more, important theologians from the German landscape. Professors from Concordia Seminary in St. Louis, specifically Paul M. Bretscher, Theodore Graebner, and F. E. Mayer were selected as essayists.[20] Karl Arndt was instrumental in securing the location for the conferences.[21] Among other representatives that year were Walter A. Baepler, Alfred O. Fuerbringer, and John Behnken, the president of The Lutheran Church—Missouri Synod.[22] Their German counterparts were well-known theological figures in Germany. Headlining the German contingent of essayists were Werner Elert and Helmut Thielicke, both from Erlangen.[23] The conferences in 1948 met three different times, each for nine days, and were packed with presentations and discussions. Attending these conferences were pastors throughout the war-ravaged country. To say they were successful in bridging the American and German churches' landscapes would be a difficult statement to make. There certainly was impact both ways, but the extent to which they might be considered successful is a matter of debate. One thing was sure, 1948 would not be the only instance of these meetings.

Martin Franzmann would serve as an essayist at Bad Boll in 1949, 1953, and 1956. There was a change between the 1948 and 1949 conferences however. The first conferences essentially "were bilateral between Missouri and the German Free Churches on the one hand and the German 'Landeskirchen' on the other. (The 1949 conferences included the National Lutheran Council Lutherans also, as well as representatives of

---

19. Mayer, *The Story of Bad Boll: Building Theological Bridges*, 7–8.
20. Mayer, *The Story of Bad Boll: Building Theological Bridges*, 9.
21. Mayer, *The Story of Bad Boll: Building Theological Bridges*, 9–10.
22. Mayer, *The Story of Bad Boll: Building Theological Bridges*, 10.
23. Mayer, *The Story of Bad Boll: Building Theological Bridges*, 15–17.

Lutheranism in other European lands.)"[24] Franzmann, in his report on the conference in 1949, remarked that there was a struggle in the years following both World Wars, thanks in part to the impact of the Confessing Church, the renaissance in Luther studies, and the work of Karl Barth. "German Lutheranism, wearied by a long confession struggle under the Nazis and weakened by immediate and desperate physical needs, was in danger of losing what it had newly gained: its Lutheran confessional consciousness, its Lutheran individuality. It faced the threat of Calvinization."[25] In Franzmann's estimation, something was needed to meet the threat. "A decisive testimony for Lutheranism, a strong word of encouragement, was called for."[26] But for Franzmann, such a testimony and word of encouragement were only possible because the theological bridges already existed. "The time is ripe for a renewal of contact: we have the common ground of Scripture as authority and norm and of the Lutheran Confessions as a true exposition of, and witness to, Scripture to meet on."[27] Franzmann's concern was for the needs of the German Lutherans, but he was interested in meeting them only in terms of what the Scriptures and Lutheran Confessions taught. It would do no good to speak solely of what the Confessions had to say to a church experiencing an identity crisis. Those confessions, while useful within Lutheran settings, would not meet the rising challenge of Calvinization without the Scriptures.

The work by the commissioners at Bad Boll was intense. "Glad as we are for the enrichment that the participation has meant for all of us . . . 'such a vacation I wish upon my enemies.' The conferences meant hard work for everybody concerned. We worked with a purpose and with a will."[28] It is important to note this because of the topics under consideration. Franzmann particularly saw that "there was no toying with ecclestical [sic] trivia or academic dealing with peripheral issues. We centered our work on problems and issues that lie at the very heart of our Lutheran existence."[29] He took his work seriously, and in doing so demonstrated again his commitment to teaching people to hear the voice that gives life,

---

24. Franzmann, *Bad Boll*, 2. These were not representatives of the Lutheran World Federation but of distinct Lutheran church bodies across Europe.

25. Franzmann, *Bad Boll*, 4.

26. Franzmann, *Bad Boll*, 5.

27. Franzmann, *Bad Boll*, 4.

28. Franzmann, *Bad Boll*, 5.

29. Franzmann, *Bad Boll*, 5.

the voice that lies at the very heart of the church's existence. His essay in 1949 was later published in the December issue of *Concordia Theological Monthly* entitled, "Augustana II: Of Original Sin." He spent considerable time in the essay dealing with the texts of the Book of Concord, centered but not solely found in the Augsburg Confession, that teach concerning the doctrine of original sin. He did so to indicate the centrality of the doctrine. "The very position of the article on original sin in the Augsburg Confession indicates the importance that the doctrine of original sin had for the consciousness of the Reformation."[30] He explained the significance and depth of the doctrine saying:

> Repeatedly, and blow upon blow, the hammer of the Word of God is made to fall on any self-assertion of man before his God, on every claim to righteousness which man, as man dares make. Nothing is left to the pride and conceit of man. The *whole* man is a sinner, conceived and born in sin, full of concupiscence from his mother's womb; incapable of true fear of God, incapable of trust in God, by nature.[31]

This understanding of original sin, that the human being is wholly a sinner, conceived and born in sin, completely incapable of trust or fear by nature, is nothing revolutionary. He was unpacking what the confessions state.

He was not concerned, however, merely with repeating what the confessions say on the matter. "The Confessions are, and are intended to be, an interpretation of Scripture."[32] This means, for Franzmann, that the Confessions must be put to the test. "Still, as interpretation of Scripture the Confessions demand and require to be continually tested anew on the basis of Scripture. And even a casual testing, if it be a candid one, must concede to the Apology that original sin is in fact a *res manifesta*."[33] It is only because the scriptures teach original sin that the Confessions have validity. "The picture drawn by our Confessions of sin as the total form of man's existence is neither too darkly nor one-sidedly drawn, and one can only marvel at the fact that men could read and proclaim Scripture for

---

30. Franzmann, "Augustana II: Of Original Sin," 882.
31. Franzmann, "Augustana II: Of Original Sin," 883.
32. Franzmann, "Augustana II: Of Original Sin," 890. Emphasis original.
33. Franzmann, "Augustana II: Of Original Sin," 891. *Res manifesta* can be translated as "thing revealed/proved."

centuries without ever taking sin, original sin, really seriously."[34] Franzmann conceded that original sin "is treated in full only by St. Paul, and by him only in Romans 5,"[35] but argued that it is found throughout the New Testament. He cites the genealogy of Luke as an additional example that demonstrates that "the line runs from Adam to all mankind."[36] Regardless of the veracity of his claim, it can be seen that what mattered for Franzmann, especially in confessional discussions, was what the scriptures teach. It is only on the basis of those scriptures that the Augustana has any validity.

Reflecting upon that time in 1949 Martin Franzmann wrote the following: "The Church has but one business on earth: to testify, to upbuild. To do that is the Church's reward, and it seeks no other. But God, the prodigal Giver, gives rewards to them that seek them not, and we can see in this work done at Bad Boll in 1948 and 1949 fruits and rewards for the Missouri Synod."[37] The results of which he was speaking were certainly personal. "All of us who took part in these Free Conferences came away with a renewed sense of our own blessings, a new realization of all that God has given us as a Church . . . a Church with nothing to build it or guarantee it but the Gospel of Jesus Christ."[38] Results also that demonstrated, in no statistically verifiable way, that theology of the Missouri Synod was one that did not stay in the seminary but moved to pulpit and pew.[39] More than these, however, Bad Boll taught Franzmann two important things. First, of the shortcomings of the Missouri Synod:

> Not the least of the fruits of Bad Boll for us was the realization of our shortcomings, the realization, for instance, that we have not worked as we should have with Luther and the Confessions of our Church, that others have outstripped us there as in other fields; that our zeal for the practical has been a one-sided zeal; that here too we must do the one and not neglect the other; that if we are to be a voice in Christendom, we must constantly raise our standards of scholarship, not only for a few experts but for all, clergy, teachers, missionaries, laity—that it must be a real scholarship, no pale and shade-grown intellectualism, but the

---

34. Franzmann, "Augustana II: Of Original Sin," 891.
35. Franzmann, "Augustana II: Of Original Sin," 891.
36. Franzmann, "Augustana II: Of Original Sin," 891.
37. Franzmann, *Bad Boll*, 16.
38. Franzmann, *Bad Boll*, 16.
39. Franzmann, *Bad Boll*, 17.

minds and spirits of men wholly dedicated to searching and seizing God's Word to us and to proclaiming it.[40]

That is to say, Franzmann understood the necessity of education, not for its own sake, but for the sake of "seizing God's Word" and "proclaiming it." Even scholarship is to be sought in service of the Word. Secondly, he learned that gathering around the Word of God could achieve unity.

> Another fruit of great value was the realization that the free conference is *the* means for achieving the Lutheran unity that all desire in a form that all can accept; that this is the one practical way, however long it may take, however "inefficient" it may seem: the free, unhurried, and uninhibited exchange of testimony, the conscience-bound and Word-bound freedom of submitting to God's Word together. It was brought home to us forcibly that testimony, though the testifier may be conscious of his own inadequacy to confess as he ought, is never given in vain; that God's blessing will rest on every honest syllable.[41]

It was clear for Franzmann that gathering around the Word of God, in this kind of unhurried manner, will actually allow people to accomplish unity. Bad Boll, then, was not just an opportunity for Franzmann to flex his academic muscle and explicate a doctrine on the basis of the Confessions and the Scriptures. It was a time that taught him the value of interchurch dialog. Not only would it show the shortcomings that needed to be overcome, it would present viable options for moving forward. All of this is done, however, on the basis of the Scriptures, and in service to their proclamation. Franzmann would serve as commissioner to the free conferences in 1953 and 1956. The locations would change and the topics discussed would vary at these meetings.[42] But it seems that his understanding of the value of these types of interactions, and the basis upon which these interactions would take place, i.e., the Scriptures, would not change much, if at all. Perhaps that is because Franzmann saw that in working with Christians in various lands there came a greater awareness of the work of the church. "The circle of one's intercessions is enlarged by such a mission and such contacts; . . . [I] appeal to all the church to remember in prayer our brethren in England, Germany, and France, men

---

40. Franzmann, *Bad Boll*, 18.

41. Franzmann, *Bad Boll*, 18–19. Emphasis original.

42. See also Koenig, "Free Conferences in Europe"; Franzmann, "Theological Conferences in Europe Summer 1956," 370–71.

striving in weakness like ours to serve the Lord, who is our Lord, struggling with difficulties greater than ours, with means less than ours."[43]

DOCTRINAL UNITY

As a member of the Committee on Doctrinal Unity, Martin Franzmann was intimately involved in the attempts of The Lutheran Church—Missouri Synod to build and maintain relationships with differing church bodies. In 1960, when the Committee on Doctrinal Unity celebrated its twenty-fifth anniversary, Martin Franzmann and Alfred O. Fuerbringer, president of Concordia Seminary in St. Louis, wrote a piece recounting the efforts of the committee. As a concluding sentiment they noted that "these years have not produced striking 'results.' But one can make a number of observations on persistent trends and constant characteristics of the committee's activities during this quarter century."[44] As one might expect from The Lutheran Church—Missouri Synod these characteristic trends involved a stringent adherence to the Scriptures and Lutheran Confessions as the basis for unity. They also noted, however, that "where it could co-operate in externals without violation of its principles, [the committee] has done so."[45] By this they were referring to the possibility of engaging in activities that could not be construed to suggest that disparate groups attained full agreement in all matters of doctrine and practice. Gathering food for distribution would not be as suggestive of unity as a joint worship service and thus could be an external that warranted cooperation.

The existence of this committee within The Lutheran Church—Missouri Synod was indicative of the time in the life of the church worldwide. The ecumenical movement begun in the early part of the twentieth century was in full force after the world wars subsided. It was a time of unprecedented efforts to achieve a wider unity among all church bodies, not just protestant ones. The establishment of the World Council of Churches and Lutheran World Federation after World War II signaled that the efforts would not simply be ongoing, but would be directed at

---

43. Franzmann, "Theological Conferences in Europe Summer 1956," 371.

44. Franzmann and Fuerbringer, "A Quarter-Century of Interchurch Relations: 1935–1960," 13.

45. Franzmann and Fuerbringer, "A Quarter-Century of Interchurch Relations: 1935–1960," 14.

repairing the physical and spiritual cleavage between disparate church bodies across the globe. For a church body like the LCMS, this would not be an easy thing in which to participate. Unity could only come on the basis of full agreement in the Scriptures and Lutheran Confessions. Such a position clearly frustrated efforts to find unity among non-Lutheran groups, but did not completely inhibit it.[46] This commitment would also, however, frustrate efforts among Lutheran groups.

In 1952, the Lutheran World Federation held its second assembly meeting in Hanover, Germany. Martin Franzmann was one of the official observers from The Lutheran Church—Missouri Synod. Others included John Behnken, at the time president of the Missouri Synod, as well as Louis J. Sieck, at the time president of Concordia Seminary. Upon returning from Hanover, Martin wrote a piece reflecting on the delegation's observations, which was published in the *Lutheran Witness*, the synod's periodical. His assessment was less than enthusiastic. He wrote, "the plain and tragic fact that the churches which all subscribe formally to the Lutheran Confessions are in deep disagreement over many issues, issues, moreover, which lie at the very heart of the Reformation's theology—that fact became more evident as the meetings wore on."[47] He claimed that such an assessment was not subjective, "if one wished to be subjective, one could write a much bleaker and more dispiriting report than this."[48] He claimed that his assessment was not shared merely by the Missouri delegation, but also by the Roman Catholic delegation and "the Assembly itself."[49]

This did not mean, however, that Martin took the question of fellowship with the Lutheran World Federation lightly. On the contrary, he took it extraordinarily seriously.

> What shall our relationship to the Lutheran World Federation be? We dare not treat this question as if it were no question; we dare not answer it negatively, against membership, on merely prudential or "practical" grounds (e.g., the necessity of a common front). The Lutheran Church is a confessional Church, bound together in all its diversity of languages, nationalities,

---

46. The Committee on Doctrinal Unity made some effort to dialog with the National Association of Evangelicals. Cf. Franzmann and Fuerbringer, "A Quarter-Century of Interchurch Relations: 1935–1960," 14.

47. Franzmann, "Missouri and the Lutheran World Federation," 124.

48. Franzmann, "Missouri and the Lutheran World Federation," 125.

49. Franzmann, "Missouri and the Lutheran World Federation," 125.

> usages, liturgies, and polities only by its Confessions, that is, by the Word of God therein presented and confessed. The question of membership in a *Lutheran* federation must therefore be considered in its confessional significance.[50]

Here it is plain that Franzmann saw the basis of unity connected to the presentation and confession of the Word of God. It has already been shown that Franzmann adhered to the Confessions because they were a confession of Scripture.[51] His assessment of the Lutheran World Federation, and the seriousness with which he made the assessment, was also on the same basis. "There was no discernable agreement on even such basic things as the formal principle of the Lutheran Reformation, the Scriptures."[52] By formal principle, he meant the thing by which doctrine is to be judged. This lack of discernable agreement, coupled with various levels of confessional adherence by members of the Lutheran World Federation made any suggestion of joining the LWF impossible.

To be sure, this assessment reflects The Lutheran Church—Missouri Synod as much as it does Martin Franzmann. But despite the lack of agreement, Franzmann demonstrated a commitment to working, in whatever way might be possible, with the Lutheran World Federation.

> The particular form in which we work is not so very important; what is important is that the work which needs to be done for Lutheran unity be done. Important also, vastly important, is the spirit in which we define our relationship toward other Lutherans. We dare not give this answer and go this way (which is a somewhat lonely and a difficult way) in pride or self-satisfaction. We must go this way humbly and in grateful recognition of all that God has given us in trust. We are making ourselves a marked Church by this course, and it behooves us to use well the talent which God has given us, to His glory and to the furtherance of His Church. That means daily repentance, for—woe to us if we use this way to further the prestige of Missouri.[53]

Franzmann was keen on denying that kind of pride which may have resulted from denying unity with the Lutheran World Federation. His personal character and continued work toward Lutheran unity suggests these words were not offered in lip service. Over and over again in his

50. Franzmann, "Missouri and the Lutheran World Federation," 148.
51. See section on Bad Boll above.
52. Franzmann, "Missouri and the Lutheran World Federation," 148.
53. Franzmann, "Missouri and the Lutheran World Federation," 149.

writing on ecumenical endeavors his fidelity to the Scriptures evidences itself in this kind of commitment toward Lutheran unity. What he saw as a gift from God was the adherence to the Word of God, so professed, confessed, and contained in the Scriptures. That gift should not be misused for prideful arrogance, but in service to the God of the church, used to make that unity a visible reality.

WHAT KIND OF COOPERATION IS POSSIBLE?

Relationships among international Lutheran bodies were not the only concern of Martin Franzmann in terms of Lutheran unity. The Committee on Doctrinal Unity was also committed to fostering those relationships at home. As mergers between American Lutheran church bodies were happening, a greater push began for the establishment of a single Lutheran church in the United States. The National Lutheran Council, comprised of representatives outside The Lutheran Church—Missouri Synod and the Synodical Conference, sought to create a pan-Lutheran agency that would become known as the Lutheran Council in the United States of America.[54] This agency would foster greater cooperation between Lutheran bodies, not merely in terms of established congregations, but also in terms of pooling resources that could be directed toward efforts of human care. Ultimately a merger among the constituents of LCUSA was a goal. That goal would have to be downplayed in discussions with more conservative elements of The Lutheran Church—Missouri Synod if the National Lutheran Council had any hope of Missouri joining LCUSA.

In April of 1964, in preparation for the 1965 Missouri Synod convention, Martin Franzmann and Alfred Fuerbringer again penned an article recounting the efforts of the National Lutheran Council and the Committee on Doctrinal Unity in establishing LCUSA.[55] Ultimately, they recommended that the synod, in convention, vote to join LCUSA. That did not mean, however, that they saw that work toward Lutheran unity was in anyway finished. "One thing is very clear: theology, the study and discussion of the Gospel in all its fullness and all its meaning for the

---

54. Hereafter LCUSA.

55. Franzmann and Fuerbringer, "The Lutheran Council in the United States of America: A Preliminary Report on the Proposed New Inter-Lutheran Association," 219–227.

life of the church, will be in the center of things."[56] It is this understanding of the Gospel, that is, the depth of what the term "Gospel" means, that was integral to the Missouri discussions with the National Lutheran Council.

Over the course of three meetings in 1960 and 1961, two documents were produced for consumption in the National Lutheran Council and The Lutheran Church—Missouri Synod.[57] The first of the two documents that was published in May of 1961 was a compendium of four papers presented at two meetings in July and November of 1960. The two authors who represented the National Lutheran Council were Conrad Bergendoff, president of Augustan College in Rock Island, Illinois, a member of the then Augustana Synod, and Theodore Tappert, professor at the Lutheran Theological Seminary in Philadelphia, a member of the then United Lutheran Church in America. Missouri's papers were presented by two professors at Concordia Seminary in St. Louis, Martin Franzmann and Herbert J. A. Bouman. The papers presented by Tappert and Bouman focused on the nature and function of subscription to the Lutheran Confessions. They need not be considered at this time. Suffice it to say both authors reflect their constituency. Bergendoff and Franzmann wrote concerning the nature of the gospel according to the scriptures. Martin Franzmann characterizes the difference between the two presentations thusly:

> The NLC presentation tends to view the "doctrine of the Gospel" in antithesis to "whole theological systems" and to emphasize its basic simplicity. The Missouri presentation views the doctrine of the Gospel in its organic connection with the whole divine revelation and therefore tends to stress the innate comprehensiveness and complexity of the doctrine of the gospel.[58]

---

56. Franzmann and Fuerbringer, "The Lutheran Council in the United States of America: A Preliminary Report on the Proposed New Inter-Lutheran Association," 221.

57. These meetings between members of the Committee on Doctrinal Unity and the executive committee of the National Lutheran Council took place July 7-9, 1960 in Chicago, November 18-19, 1960 in St. Louis, and October 30-November 1, 1961 in Chicago. Cf. Franzmann and Fuerbringer, "The Lutheran Council in the United States of America," 220.

58. *Essays on the Lutheran Confessions Basic to Lutheran Cooperation*, 5.

More simply, the two views differ in that one sees the gospel as if it were a finite piece of a jigsaw puzzle and the other sees the gospel as the entire assembled puzzle.

A cursory reading of both essays reveals that Franzmann's assessment is correct. Bergendoff states, "Concerning the 'doctrine of the Gospel,' then we may conclude that there is a message or gospel which is immutable, fixed, certain, which describes what God has done and continues to do for man through Jesus Christ."[59] He goes on to argue that agreement in the proclamation of that Gospel is the basis for unity, and it cannot be more or less.[60] Bergendoff was thereby articulating an understanding of what Article VII of the Augsburg Confession means when it says, "And it is enough for the true unity of the church to agree concerning the teaching of the gospel and the administration of the sacraments."[61] Franzmann would not disagree that agreement concerning the gospel was not more or less than the basis for unity. The disagreement was over how the gospel should actually be defined. He rooted his definition in the closing chapter of Matthew where Jesus commissioned the disciples to make disciples of all nations through baptism and teaching.

> For the Apostles are bidden to teach men "to observe all that I have commanded you," all the riches of the divine self-disclosure which makes the Gospel according to Matthew the most powerful book ever written. And indeed there is in this passage, for all its basic simplicity, a large comprehensiveness: One who has *all* authority in heaven and on earth bids his apostles to make disciples of *all* nations by baptizing them into the fullness of the Trinitarian name and by teaching them to observe *all* that he has commanded them. And he promises to be with them *all* the days until the close of the age.[62]

While clearly Franzmann was privileging his scholarly work in Matthew, he nevertheless argued for an understanding of the gospel that is all

---

59. Bergendoff, "A Lutheran Study of Church Unity," in *Essays on the Lutheran Confessions Basic to Lutheran Cooperation*, 10.

60. Bergendoff, "A Lutheran Study of Church Unity," 13.

61. "Augsburg Confession" in *The Book of Concord*, edited by Robert Kolb and Timothy Wengert, 43. Translation from the German varies slightly but not significantly. "For this is enough for the true unity of the church that there the gospel is preached harmoniously according to a pure understanding and the sacraments are administered in conformity with the divine Word." (Kolb and Wengert, *The Book of Concord*, 42.)

62. Franzmann, "A Lutheran Study of Church Unity," in *Essays on the Lutheran Confessions Basic to Lutheran Cooperation*, 15. Emphasis original.

encompassing of Christian doctrine. He thereby affirms a well-known Missouri Synod position that the gospel is more than just the preaching of the forgiveness of sins. It is that, but it also includes all articles of faith that radiate around the preaching of forgiveness. This includes all that the scriptures claim God has done from the creation of the world to the life, death, and resurrection of Jesus Christ.

Franzmann went on to demonstrate why he believed such a wider definition of the gospel is necessary.

> Jesus will, through the word and sacrament, create the little ones that believe in him. Thus their faith in him is built upon and is sustained by the knowledge that he is such and such, that he has acted thus and thus for us men and for our salvation and will at the close of the age act once more and decisively for all men for ever. They can believe *in* him, be consigned, committed, and obediently devoted to him, only because they believe *that* he is the Christ, the Son of the living God, with all that that believe implies. Faith, being both a "believing *in*" and a "believing *that*," is at the same time completely simple and inexhaustibly complex. And the teaching of the Gospel which creates and sustains faith has both these qualities.[63]

Understanding that faith is both belief in something, i.e., trust, and belief that something, i.e., knowledge, necessitates the broader definition of the gospel. This relates not just to his above description of the Gospel on the basis of Matthew's gospel, but also in terms of his own broader understanding of the scriptures, i.e., their nature and function. They are the voice of God that create trust but also communicate what God has done in history.

Franzmann realized, however, that unity in the church is both an actual reality and one that is worked toward. "The unity of the church both is and becomes. It is both, a divinely given reality and an empirical reality in process of being attained or actualized."[64] That is partly why he also authored the paper in the second published document by the National Lutheran Council and The Lutheran Church—Missouri Synod in November 1961. That document addressed the question: "What Kind of Cooperation Is Possible In View of Discussions to Date?"[65] Again one

---

63. Franzmann, "A Lutheran Study of Church Unity," 15–16.
64. Franzmann, "A Lutheran Study of Church Unity," 21.
65. Franzmann, "What Kind of Cooperation Is Possible in View of Discussions to Date?" in *Toward Cooperation among American Lutherans*, 18.

is not surprised by what Franzmann or his National Lutheran Council counterpart, Alvin Rogness, president of Lutheran Theological Seminary in St. Paul, Minnesota, wrote. Ultimately the National Lutheran Council and the LCMS would align in LCUSA with efforts aimed at common theological study, Christian service to the neighbor, and exploration of further fellowship opportunities.[66] Franzmann spoke of that kind of cooperation as necessary and looked forward to the possibility of more free conferences to achieving the sought after end.[67] He also spoke of it with hope. "Perhaps [God] is leading us in these last days to greater things than we have dared to dream of, to a day when our confessional solidarity will give us an apostolic boldness of witness to which the world and the church will give ear. Perhaps He is preparing us for a missionary march that will make all of our previous little successes seem like stumblings in the dark."[68]

THE NATURE OF THE UNITY WE SEEK

Martin Franzmann's place in the wider American ecumenical realm is cemented in 1957 when he was asked to participate in a symposium, the papers of which were published in the spring issue that year of *Religion in Life*. Other participants included Lesslie Newbigin, then bishop in the Church of South India, Edward John Carnell, then president of Fuller Theological Seminary, Theron D. Price, church history professor at Southern Baptist Seminary, and John Howard Yoder, at the time director of relief activities of the Mennonite Central Committee in France.[69] Each participant wrote on the subject "The Nature of the Unity We Seek."[70] The content of Martin's contribution is a helpful summation of his understanding of the basis and means of achieving unity. It is also, of course, purported to express the Missouri Synod understanding as indicated by

---

66. *Toward Cooperation among American Lutherans*, 4.

67. Franzmann, "What Kind of Cooperation Is Possible in View of Discussions to Date?" 18.

68. Franzmann, "What Kind of Cooperation Is Possible in View of Discussions to Date?" 18.

69. Editorial Note appended to the beginning of Franzmann, "The Nature of the Unity We Seek: A Missouri Synod Lutheran View," 801.

70. Franzmann, "The Nature of the Unity We Seek: A Missouri Synod Lutheran View," 801.

the subtitle, "A Missouri Synod Lutheran View."[71] He defined the unity being sought saying, "we seek unity in the common, free subjection of man to God as the God who has in measureless condescension drawn near to man."[72] Explaining further the meaning of that claim he explicated a typical Missouri understanding of "submission of faith to God" as God has been revealed in the life, death, and resurrection of Jesus Christ.[73]

The paper proceeds from that standpoint, addressing humanity as bound in sin, stuck in the condemnation pronounced by the Law, until the Gospel breathes life. Franzmann connected this unity of faith that results from the work of God to the scriptures in an inextricable way. "Faith holds to the promise, the word of God, against reason, against experience, against feeling. This is what makes the question of the inspiration and the authority of Scripture so important and so crucial in the question of church unity; for 'Scripture' and 'Word of God' belong together, and it is our conviction that they cannot be too tightly bracketed."[74] He allowed for no cleavage between the two.

> The question, "To what extent and in what sense is the Bible God's Word?" is not answered by disquisition and definition; it can be answered only in the act of submission. Only in submitting to the verdict of the law and in accepting the promise of the gospel in the concrete fullness with which Scripture conveys both, do we know the Bible as the word of God, as God's word *to us*, but also as God's word quite independently of our response to it nevertheless.[75]

Unsurprisingly, Franzmann delineated submission to Scripture as God's Word as the basis for unity. This is not a matter of debate for Franzmann, or, for that matter, the Missouri Synod which he represented. "It is this glad and full assent to Scripture as the Word of God that we 'Missourians' painfully miss in large areas of Christendom, including Lutheranism,

---

71. Franzmann, "The Nature of the Unity We Seek: A Missouri Synod Lutheran View," 801.

72. Franzmann, "The Nature of the Unity We Seek: A Missouri Synod Lutheran View," 801.

73. Franzmann, "The Nature of the Unity We Seek: A Missouri Synod Lutheran View," 801.

74. Franzmann, "The Nature of the Unity We Seek: A Missouri Synod Lutheran View," 803.

75. Franzmann, "The Nature of the Unity We Seek: A Missouri Synod Lutheran View," 804. Emphasis original.

today. It constitutes a block to unity, not merely formally . . . but also substantially."[76]

This intractable position should be understood in part an attack on trends relating to historical-critical methods of scriptural interpretation. Franzmann continued in the paper by recounting the problems he saw in attempting to divide history from the revealed words of Scripture as, "God is a God of history and not of myth."[77] He argued against any understanding that allows "the interpreter [to step] as it were, out of his baptism and scrutiniz[e] the words of God 'objectively,' and pu[t] their validity as Gods revelation under question."[78] He was reacting against a perceived trend in biblical studies that sets the reason of the interpreter in judgment of what is or is not historical, and, what is or is not revelatory of God. In the last analysis, for Franzmann "the alliance between 'historical' and 'critical' is therefore theologically not tolerable."[79]

While he spent time in the article noting again that "we treasure and subscribe to the Lutheran Confessions because they are a classic spelling out of the revelation given in Scripture,"[80] he did not argue for unity on their basis, but on the basis of Scripture. Franzmann's entire perspective on unity was shaped not only by the content of the scriptures, e.g., the Gospel, but by the nature and function of the scriptures themselves. "If we Missourians 'still' speak of the verbal inspiration of Scripture, we are primarily confessing the incredible miracle of a divine word spoken to sinful man and are proclaiming that that word, for all its servant's form, is of an inviolable sanctity; that if it means anything, it means everything."[81]

---

76. Franzmann, "The Nature of the Unity We Seek: A Missouri Synod Lutheran View," 804.

77. Franzmann, "The Nature of the Unity We Seek: A Missouri Synod Lutheran View," 805.

78. Franzmann, "The Nature of the Unity We Seek: A Missouri Synod Lutheran View," 805.

79. Franzmann, "The Nature of the Unity We Seek: A Missouri Synod Lutheran View," 806.

80. Franzmann, "The Nature of the Unity We Seek: A Missouri Synod Lutheran View," 807.

81. Franzmann, "The Nature of the Unity We Seek: A Missouri Synod Lutheran View," 807.

GRACE UNDER PRESSURE

"Ecumenicity," wrote Franzmann, "is basic to Christianity, to the church. The church, if it lives in obedience to its Lord, is not 'also' ecumenical; it is ecumenical by definition since the Lord of the church is ecumenical—Lord of all that call upon His name."[82] In co-writing *Grace Under Pressure* with F. Dean Lueking, a well-known pastor in the Missouri Synod, Martin Franzmann was explicating for the wider church what it meant to be ecumenical, biblically speaking. He was not interested in outlining what ecumenicity looked like from an institutional or congregational standpoint, that was the task of F. Dean Lueking. Rather, Franzmann searched the scriptures for a metaphor that could concretize an ecumenical attitude. He found the metaphor in the person of Christ, specifically in what meekness looks like, obedience, weakness, and certitude.[83] All three work in concert with one another, evidenced in Jesus who rides in to Jerusalem on a donkey.

> The meek King comes to Jerusalem in *obedience*. Ever since the confession at Caesarea Philippi, Jesus has spoken of the "must" of God's will that takes Him to Jerusalem, to rejection and the cross (Matt. 16:21). So perfect is His obedience that this must is at the same time Jesus' own free resolve: "Behold, we are going up to Jerusalem! (20:18; cf. Mark 10:32). The meek King comes in *weakness*, without the power and paraphernalia of royalty, riding on the poor man's beast; and His disciples have two swords—that is their total armament! (Luke 22:38). The Meek comes in *certitude* for all that. He takes the initiative; He arranges the procession that is His messianic manifesto to Jerusalem. He knows that He is going to His death; but He also knows, in His confident dependence on His God, that He is going through the depths to the utmost heights, to His royal palace at the right hand of God.[84]

In sketching this picture, Franzmann was forming the mind of his reader to see a pattern worth emulating. The church must be obedient to the voice of the God, specifically in the scriptures. It must demonstrate that it enters in discussion from a position of weakness and not of power. And it must be certain that God's ultimate work in reconciling the world is both

---

82. Franzmann, "Meekness as the Basic Ecumenical Attitude," in Franzmann and Lueking, *Grace Under Pressure: Meekness in Ecumenical Relations*, 3.

83. Franzmann, "Meekness as the Basic Ecumenical Attitude," 7.

84. Franzmann, "Meekness as the Basic Ecumenical Attitude," 9–10.

an actual reality and one that is worked toward. "Meekness is the mark of the Christ; meekness is the mark of the apostles; meekness is the mark of the apostolic church and so also of the church of the Reformation."[85]

The attitude of meekness aids ecumenical work, but it is not the only aspect of it. His goal in writing was much broader than simply instilling an attitude. Franzmann's ecumenical perspective was wholly conceived on the basis of the Scriptures. "To invite men of all confessions to come together under the Word of the Scriptures—to do it in humility and patience, as the word of James suggests—surely that is the basic ecumenical gesture . . . the Scriptural canon is still the common bond, perhaps, the only remaining bond of all Christendom."[86] Such an invitation was an "ecumenical *confession*," that is, it was an expression of the unity that exists and is yet to be realized. Franzmann's life and work in the ecumenical realm was aimed at such a confession whether that confession took place in Bad Boll, Hanover, Chicago, or St. Louis. In fact, for Franzmann, ecumenicity and the life of the church could be nothing else. Neither could ecumenical endeavors exist in isolation from that which gives life.

> We have come a long way round to the practical implementation of ecumenical meekness. But here too the longest way round is the shortest way home. Indeed it is the only way home. For unless the meek Christ and His meek church have grown great before our eyes, unless we have learned from Him who is meek and lowly in heart, unless His Spirit has given us the courage for obedience and weakness and His own unerring certitude, we shall get nowhere either ecumenically or any other way. But with the meekness of Christ implanted in us we can be strong; we shall have confessional strength without rigidity, and we shall have firmness without contempt or malice. And we can be genuinely winning, gracious without weakening or compromising our confession. Whether we shall be "successful" we can leave to the Lord, who bade us to be witnesses to Him. And so we shall be able at the last to stand "with intrepid heart" before His throne.[87]

---

85. Franzmann, "Meekness as the Basic Ecumenical Attitude," 59.
86. Franzmann, "Meekness as the Basic Ecumenical Attitude," 59–60.
87. Franzmann, "Meekness as the Basic Ecumenical Attitude," 61.

6

Weary of All Trumpeting

LET US JUST LAY THE FOOL THING DOWN AND SEE IF IT FITS

In the collection of Martin Franzmann's papers in the archives of Concordia Historical Institute in St. Louis, there is an unpublished handwritten essay. While the document does not bear his signature, someone else rightly wrote his name on the top sheet, as the penmanship is unmistakably Franzmann's. The only marks to identify the context, other than the content, is the title, "Lutheran Church—Missouri Synod, 125th Anniversary, 1972." While it is not clear where this essay was delivered, it is clear that in the poetic flair and dedication to the scriptural word indicative of his pen, Franzmann was appealing to a church in the throes of struggle to find a way forward.

> The 125th anniversary of the Lutheran Church—Missouri Synod promises to be a sober one. As in previous anniversaries, the atmosphere is scented not only with roses and lavender but with the earthier and more acrid smells given off by the machinery of the church militant in motion. There is nothing too unusual or disturbing about that. The Church has always stood and endured because it is stronger than its strongest human link and is never so weak as its weakest human link. All we have ever had to rejoice in is the enduring and stable mercy of God: we endure

and conquer only because the Son of the Living God has said, "I will build my church."[1]

This insightful commentary on the history and future of the church, and of the church body to which Franzmann belonged for part of his life, speaks into a difficult moment. Within two years the Missouri Synod would experience some of the most painful moments in their history. The synod in convention would vote to remove elements deemed not tolerable in God's church. Two-thirds of the student body along with over forty professors, all except five, would stage a walkout protesting the actions of the Board of Control of Concordia Seminary in St. Louis. Although Martin Franzmann had retired and moved to England before these explosive moments, he would not be immune from them. What was the cause of this struggle? In part, a disagreement over the nature, function, and methods of interpreting the scriptural text. "We have discovered, or are discovering, that what we love most troubles us most . . . we are troubled about the sacred Scriptures, the word of God written."[2]

The goal of this chapter is to investigate Franzmann's role in repairing the breach at Concordia Seminary. His distaste for conflict would not insulate him as he was called out of retirement to present at a theological convocation aimed at bringing the disparate sides together. Ever the servant, Martin obliged. Because of his participation, his poetic devotion to the scriptures would be questioned. Sadly, he would stop writing, become physically ill, and ultimately, he would die trying to bring healing to a broken church body. As the anniversary essay shows, he was concerned with maintaining the integrity of the biblical text against any interpreter and methodology that would stand in human judgment of scripture. That did not mean he spoke an anathema against all hypotheses. "I remember a three-year-old boy's remark after hearing all the arguments as to whether a piece of linoleum would fit into a certain space in the neighbor's kitchen: 'Let's lay the fool thing down and see if it fits.' The hypothesis calls for neither adoration nor anathemas. Let us just lay the fool thing down and see if it fits."[3] To a large extent that last sentence describes his attitude. He was not interested in choosing sides amongst peers, but laying all perspectives down in relation to the biblical text to see which ones actually fit. By not choosing a side, or perhaps better put,

---

1. "Lutheran Church—Missouri Synod, 125th Anniversary, 1972," 1.
2. "Lutheran Church—Missouri Synod, 125th Anniversary, 1972," 1.
3. "Lutheran Church—Missouri Synod, 125th Anniversary, 1972," 12.

by siding as he consistently did with the book that grabbed him and did not let him go, he fell victim to the machinations of the church militant.

EXEGETICAL ASPECTS

As discussed elsewhere, Martin Franzmann's tenure as professor and eventual chair of the exegetical department was not free from conflict. The struggle with inspiration and the challenge the Scharlemann situation presented were not the only instances.[4] One essay circulated during his lifetime and three essays originally delivered only to select audiences, two of which ultimately published posthumously, provide insight into Franzmann's work behind the scenes that addressed the needs of the day. Selections of these will be explored in brief, beginning with "Exegesis on Romans 16:17ff." Eventually published under Franzmann's name in January of 1981, the essay had "circulated anonymously when it appeared in 1950."[5] It is unclear why the essay was first circulated anonymously, though, thanks to an investigation by August Suelflow into the papers of former synod president John Behnken, it is clear that Martin Franzmann wrote it.[6] The exegetical investigation took place in order to speak to "the vigorous debate which has been waged over Romans 16:17ff,"[7] a debate that orbited around a discussion on church fellowship. Specifically, it sought to answer the question, "what manner of men were these division-makers and causers of offense against whom the warning is raised?"[8] Franzmann's investigation would "suggest that the interpretation traditional in our circles is essentially sound."[9] Whether or not one agrees with his assessment is irrelevant. Far more important for the purposes of this chapter is the warning that follows.

> It is not the exegete's business, strictly speaking, to go beyond the interpretation of the text itself to its application; but he may

---

4. See chapter 3.

5. Franzmann, "Exegesis on Romans 16:17ff.," 13. The quote above is from an editorial note near the bottom of the page. This was written during a period of rising tensions between The Lutheran Church—Missouri Synod and the Wisconsin Evangelical Lutheran Synod. As Franzmann had only recently made the switch from Wisconsin to Missouri it was likely a personal concern.

6. Franzmann, "Exegesis on Romans 16:17ff.," 13. Again from an editorial note.

7. Franzmann, "Exegesis on Romans 16:17ff.," 13.

8. Franzmann, "Exegesis on Romans 16:17ff.," 13.

9. Franzmann, "Exegesis on Romans 16:17ff.," 19.

with propriety remind the church: 1) that Romans 16:17ff. is not the whole of New Testament teaching on error and errorists and that the whole of that teaching should be brought to bear on any given situation; 2) that the traditional interpretation, which our study has confirmed, does not, by any means, mean an easy way out for the church: the warning both in its breadth and its severity lays upon the church a solemn obligation which can be met only by long, intensive, and loving theological *work*—the church should not be startled to find that the decision on error is not always easy or the question of fellowship always simple; and 3) that the passage is to be applied to ourselves, too, in constant self-scrutiny and self-judgment—a church that complacently deems itself above the possibility of belly service is already dangerously close to serving its belly.[10]

In this concluding statement, Franzmann leaves no room for a short-circuiting of the process necessary for dealing with a perceived error and the person who expresses the perceived error. This early writing is useful because it sets up a framework that Franzmann would emulate as he dealt with matters of controversy during his tenure on the faculty at Concordia Seminary and in his retirement. He perceived, on the basis of the scriptural word, an obligation to intense and loving work.

The challenge presented by the remarks of Martin Scharlemann over the usefulness of historical-critical methods would show Franzmann's commitment to the aforementioned obligation of intense and loving work. Despite the controversy that surrounded the situation, Martin Franzmann did not speak ill of Martin Scharlemann publicly or privately, that is, he did not make known any displeasure with Martin Scharlemann as a person.[11] Rather, forbearing in love, he took the necessary time to address the problem through a critique that sought to call practitioners of the method to give an account. This meant, in part, preparing remarks for faculty consumption. Speaking of historical-critical methods of interpretation he wrote, "the historical-critical method cannot be considered as merely a theologically neutral tool or technique of interpretation, comparable to textual criticism, grammar, or lexicography. None of the latter pass a value judgment on the historical substance of revelation; the historical critical method does."[12] In making this statement to the

---

10. Franzmann, "Exegesis on Romans 16:17ff.," 19.
11. Peter Franzmann spoke of this during the interview on August 25, 2017.
12. Franzmann, "The Historical-Critical Method," 101.

faculty, he is indicting a colleague. In point of fact, the indictment is far more severe than the quote above.

> Those who advocate and practice this method are required, therefore, to ask themselves whether such a method is compatible with their ordination vows, which bound them to Scripture in absolute faith.... It is not a question of coming into conflict with a peculiarly Missourian tradition or idiosyncrasy. The issue raised by the acceptance of this method involves a conflict with the bases of our Lutheran, Christian existence.[13]

Two insights emerge. First, Martin Franzmann was clearly rejecting any methodology, and subsequently indicting practitioners of that methodology, that allows itself to sit in judgment over the historicity of the events of the text. In other words, his position is clear. Second, his comments, as harsh as they are, sought to address the situation involving his colleague, but that address was first privately done. These words were not published until twenty-two years after they were presented to the faculty and were only published with the consent of his widow.[14] The remarks did find their way out of that faculty meeting, as will be demonstrated later, how that happened remains unclear. While Franzmann did, in other places, reject historical-critical methods, the harshest statement he made concerning practitioners was written during the height of the Scharlemann controversy, but it was not written for the public, even if the public consumed it. This is true also of the second document that was published posthumously concerning "The Quest for the Historical Jesus."[15]

An as yet unpublished document, also in the archives at Concordia Historical Institute, provides more insight into how Martin Franzmann sought to engage controversial topics. It centers around a document produced in 1932 entitled, *A Brief Statement of the Doctrinal Position of the Missouri Synod*.[16] This pamphlet was prepared in anticipation of dialog between The Lutheran Church—Missouri Synod and other church bodies. It was meant to be a means by which to disclose, with clarity, the doctrinal position of the Missouri Synod on various topics. While it certainly did function externally that way, internally it became a benchmark

---

13. Franzmann, "The Historical-Critical Method," 102.

14. Franzmann, "The Historical-Critical Method," 101. This appears in an editorial note at the bottom of the page.

15. Franzmann, "The Quest for the Historical Jesus," 102.

16. Hereafter it will be referred to as *A Brief Statement*.

for determining orthodoxy.[17] This officially reached its zenith in 1959 when the synod, which had already adopted *A Brief Statement* in 1932, sought to make official statements binding on individual members of the synod.[18] The 1962 convention repealed the binding nature of synodical statements, assuring that the only means by which matters of doctrine and practice could be decided were the scriptures and Lutheran Confessions.[19] At the same convention an attempt to elevate *A Brief Statement* to be binding in its own right, not only as an official statement of synod, failed to pass on the grounds that it was unconstitutional.[20] Why all the political maneuvering? Because *A Brief Statement* offers a clearly defined picture of how one is to understand the scriptures. That statement reads in part, "Since the Holy Scriptures are the Word of God, it goes without saying that they contain no errors or contradictions, but that they are in all their parts and words the infallible truth, also in those parts which treat of historical, geographical, and other secular matters."[21] The synod tried to assert a clear standard in the midst of the controversy surrounding Martin Scharlemann, who, it should be remembered, officially apologized at the 1962 convention in Cleveland.

As this was happening, sometime prior to 1962, Martin Franzmann penned the unpublished essay mentioned above. It was likely only meant for limited consumption though that is difficult to prove definitively. The document contains no indicators of an audience. Perhaps this also was meant only for the faculty, regardless, it was not intended to be published and indeed has never been. This document is important because

---

17. In many ways it still is. Recent controversy surrounding the age of the earth and creationism within The Lutheran Church—Missouri Synod saw several appeals to *A Brief Statement*. See concordiatheology.org for more information, specifically, Arand, "Regarding the Editorial Process for the Concordia Journal."

18. Members here does not mean members of congregations. It refers to called workers, ordained or commissioned, that is, pastors, teachers, or other church workers, and the congregations as entities. That is to say, congregations had to hold to the document publicly even if individual parishioners disagreed. Violation of the document publicly by a congregation could result in a removal from synod.

19. See Repp, "The Binding Nature of Synodical Statements," 153–162.

20. Per the Missouri Synod constitution, the only things that must be confessed without reservation are the scriptures and the Lutheran Confessions. Although the convention sought to elevate *A Brief Statement* to that level it was unsuccessful. Despite this *A Brief Statement* remained an official statement of synod. This meant that it still had coercive force, even if that force was not necessarily binding in the same way the scriptures and Lutheran Confessions were.

21. *A Brief Statement*, 1.

it provides insight into Franzmann's perspective on the nature of functional statements. Certain documents within the history of the Missouri Synod, chief among them *A Brief Statement*, serve a regulatory function within the synod. These kinds of statements are useful not only in external discussions, as was the original purpose of *A Brief Statement*, but also internally within the synod itself. They provide a standard against which a person or theological opinion might be measured.[22] Such statements are not, however, binding on conscience, as are the scriptures and Lutheran Confessions. Franzmann made his perspective on these kinds of statements clear.

> Documents such as A Brief Statement are functional; they are intended to perform a service and have validity and worth because, and insofar as, they do perform a service. As Lutherans, who receive and embrace the Holy Scriptures as the pure fountains from which the people of God must drink to live, we live in the conviction that the one functioning power in the life of the Church is the Word of God. The exegetical basis and the exegetical substance of a functional document are therefore of critical import; they must be the objects of perpetual and prayerful scrutiny, continually under review.[23]

For Franzmann, then, functional statements, as helpful as they may be, are always subject to review in light of the scriptures. This review is more than ascertaining whether or not the document, or the exegetical basis of that document, is right or wrong.

> Such a review must, in the nature of things, go beyond the question of the "correctness" or "incorrectness" of the exegesis of cited passages, important and necessary as that question is. Such a review must go on to ask whether the voice of God in the Scriptures has been heard and transmitted adequately, that is, it must ask: Is the exegetical base broad enough and is the witness of Scripture full enough to be really functional, to do the work of God for the people of God in these last days? Such a review must go one step further; it must ask: Is our document letting Scripture speak on its own terms? Is it Scripturally structured

---

22. It is not always, or even only, the synodical officials who use them in this way. Any member of synod can use them in this regulatory way because of the status of these statements as official synod positions.

23. Franzmann, "A Brief Statement: Exegetical Aspects," 1. Emphasis original.

and does it present the functioning truth of Scripture in Scriptural perspective?[24]

That is to say, it is not enough that the exegetical basis upon which *A Brief Statement* is founded be correct. The question is whether or not *A Brief Statement* delivers the message of scripture as scripture itself does. Franzmann ultimately agreed that *A Brief Statement* is correct, but he argued that such an agreement with the document must be qualified. His investigation, which he couched as compelled by "the gratitude of dutiful sons who have learned of their fathers to bow to the authority of the Scriptures," reveals how problematic *A Brief Statement* actually is, exegetically speaking. The correctness of the appraisal is not as useful for the present inquiry into his life as is the reason Franzmann presented for his investigation into the document. In other words, what matters is not what he thought about *A Brief Statement*, but what he thought about how functional statements, and indeed theological systems, should be exegetically validated. They should speak with the fullness of the scriptures in the way the scriptures speak about the issue or issues at hand.

All of what has been discussed concerning Franzmann to this point, i.e., the way he handled conflict and the ways he conceived of theological appraisals, would come to a head in 1963. Norman Habel, another professor at Concordia Seminary, delivered an essay to "a combined conference of the College of Presidents of The Lutheran Church—Missouri Synod and the faculties of Concordia Theological Seminary, Springfield, Illinois., and Concordia Seminary, St. Louis, Missouri."[25] The essay sought to "stimulate discussion and [did] not purport to give a final answer to the interpretation of Genesis Three."[26] In it, Habel emphasized the symbolic and figurative aspects of the third chapter of Genesis, spent time unpacking cultural and linguistic issues of relevance, and ultimately, did not affirm the historical facticity of the events. In other words, Habel did not believe that Adam and Eve were real people who took and ate a piece of fruit thereby causing the fall of humanity into sin, resulting in the introduction of death to humanity. Rather he understood the text to be a symbolically represented, yet nevertheless, true story.

Such an understanding is in opposition to traditional Missouri Synod understandings of the text that define it as historical reality. Habel's

---

24. Franzmann, "A Brief Statement: Exegetical Aspects," 1.
25. Habel, *The Form and Meaning of the Fall Narrative*, preface.
26. Habel, *The Form and Meaning of the Fall Narrative*, preface.

essay, which stood in stark contrast to those traditional understandings and was delivered to an assembly of district and synodical officials, necessitated an official response. The goal of such a rebuttal was to present a counterargument to the one that Habel presented. Martin Franzmann was tasked with delivering that response and did so one year later in 1964. His essay, which need not be looked at in detail, exemplifies the way in which he sought to resolve the conflict. He addressed points of agreement, namely that both he and Habel agree,

> In asserting the inspiration, authority, and infallibility of the Holy Scriptures as the Word of God to us . . . in taking seriously the narrative of the Fall as it stands, in its present canonical form and context in Genesis . . . in taking seriously the narrative of the fall as the account of a one-time and once-for-all historical event that determines all the subsequent history of mankind . . . [and] in maintaining that the darkness of the curse on fallen man is lightened by a ray of hope.[27]

The nature of the points of agreement is not as important as the fact that Franzmann clearly outlines them. In doing so, he is affirming Habel before the same crowd that held Habel suspect on the basis of the essay. The assessment also included points of disagreement. Namely, that Habel,

> Diverges from our traditional position: a. in stressing the fact that the mode of the narrative is culturally relevant to the original Israelite audience and in drawing on the historical milieu of ancient Israel in an attempt to determine that relevance. b. in stressing the presence and significance of symbolic or figurative elements in the historical narrative of the Fall. c. in leaving open, or questioning, the "Protoevangelion" character of Gen. 3:14–15. d. in declining to make a simple, direct identification between the Serpent and Satan. . . . e. in maintaining that man was created mortal.[28]

As one would expect from a seasoned professor and chair of the department, Franzmann took time to examine the essay in depth. But, one should notice that his critique, this time in a more public sphere, was not nearly as harsh as the one uttered to the faculty concerning historical-critical methods in 1958. It should also be noted that Habel spoke

---

27. Franzmann, "Hermeneutical Principles Involved in the Appraisal of the 1963 Essay on Genesis 3," 3–4.

28. Franzmann, "Hermeneutical Principles Involved in the Appraisal of the 1963 Essay on Genesis 3," 8.

of Franzmann's assessment saying "[Franzmann] represented [Habel's] basic position admirably" and that "profitable discussions" followed.[29] Additionally, Franzmann refrained from analyzing publicly the section of Habel's essay dealing with mortality so that Habel be given a chance to clarify at least one point that Franzmann thought to be a contradiction.[30] Habel would actually revise his essay in part before publishing it for consumption, thanks to Franzmann's handling of the situation.[31]

What is more, Franzmann outlined at the beginning of his appraisal what he hoped were shared presuppositions. Why?

> By doing so, we shall establish a platform on which we speak to one another and not past one another; we shall reduce the tensions which tend to become exaggerated in the course of a serious and vital discussion such as ours; we shall, one may hope, temper the clash of conflicting opinions and convictions and make possible a fraternally energetic and fruitful interchange of views.[32]

It is Franzmann's commitment to intense and loving work that forced him to begin this way. While it has been said elsewhere that Franzmann certainly had a distaste for conflict, that does not mean he avoided it at all costs. Far from it, he was intimately involved in moments of controversy from his time at Northwestern College until his death in Cambridge. What one sees, however, in view of the above investigation, is that Franzmann is committed to loving the person. Even when Franzmann issued the harsh rebuke in private to Scharlemann, his hope was that his colleague would reexamine himself, not because he wanted to ostracize him. So too, when scrutiny rained down on Habel, he sought to affirm him, at the same time noting points of divergence, so as to forbear with him. What the quote above clearly outlines is Franzmann's commitment to reducing unnecessary tensions by speaking eloquently and clearly.

---

29. Habel, *Form and Meaning of the Fall Narrative*, preface.

30. Franzmann, "Hermeneutical Principles Involved in the Appraisal of the 1963 Essay on Genesis 3," 37.

31. Habel, *Form and Meaning of the Fall Narrative*, preface.

32. Franzmann, "Hermeneutical Principles Involved in the Appraisal of the 1963 Essay on Genesis 3," 1.

THE ART OF EXEGESIS

Such a public display of fraternal fidelity brought with it charges of a change in Franzmann's perspective on the validity of historical-critical methods. By not being as harsh with Habel as he was privately with Scharlemann, and as he was clearly in opposition to it publicly in other forums throughout his career, the charges may be correct. One person to suggest a noticed change in Martin Franzmann's position was Edgar Krentz, a fellow faculty member and neighbor. Reflecting years later he wrote to a friend,

> The radical in the early sixties was the other Martin, Scharlemann. After the Cleveland convention of 1962 their positions began to change. [Scharlemann] turned right, joined later with [Robert] Preus and [Ralph] Bohlmann and [Richard] Klann. [Scharlemann] now attacked historical criticism, which he had earlier defended (along with Horace Hummel). Franzmann was a conservative, absolutely honest scholar. He moved to the left of [Scharlemann]. I recall sitting on our front steps talking with him on a summer evening. We agreed that we did nothing different in interpreting the New Testament than what we both did—or had done—in interpreting classical texts. Franzmann stood for historically conditioned interpretation.[33]

When Krentz stated that Franzmann moved to the left of Scharlemann it indicates more a change in Scharlemann's position than Franzmann's. The role Scharlemann played in the controversy surrounding Concordia Seminary, namely that he became a significant conservative voice against historical-critical methods, is an about-face from his public portrayal in the late fifties and early sixties. Franzmann, however, did not shift, or do an about-face and suddenly embrace historical-critical methods. The shift in the mind of Krentz was in relation the newly positioned Scharlemann. "Was Franzmann a radical critic[?] No way. He admired Adolf Schlatter. . . . [and] Schlatter stressed that exegesis must be free from dogmatic influences and presuppositions. Franzmann imbibed that. He was one of my teachers, from whom I learned a great deal, including the view that the text is the major determiner in exegesis."[34]

33. Personal correspondence from Edgar Krentz to Matthew Becker. See Becker's comment on January 11, 2012 to the following blog post: Becker, "Further Reflections on 1967 LCMS Resolution 2-02."

34. See Becker's comment on January 11, 2012 to the following blog post: Becker, "Further Reflections on 1967 LCMS Resolution 2-02."

Comments regarding a change in Franzmann are not limited to Krentz. Both Richard Gurgel, in his church history thesis, and Daniel Burfiend, in his Master of Sacred Theology thesis, speak about Franzmann's comments in a series of taped correspondence course lectures called *The Art of Exegesis*. The major content of those lectures represents material he had used throughout his career to teach people how to read and interpret the bible. In those lectures Franzmann stated, "I confess that I do not have much faith, as it grows less as I grow older, in things like form criticism and redaction criticism and other behind the beyond techniques."[35] Gurgel questioned how much faith Franzmann had to begin with and what the level of faith was to which he was now referring.[36] Burfiend's critique is stronger. He notes that the series of lectures include references to different resources than Franzmann's previous work. Whereas the early "Essays in Hermeneutics" refer to Schlatter as a resource, *The Art of Exegesis* lectures required two books, *Interpreting the Bible* by J. C. K. von Hoffmann and a book of the same title by Berkely Mickelson with *From Luther to Kierkegaard* by Jaroslav Pelikan as one of three suggested books. Burfiend believed that the shift in and emphasis of the material demonstrates a change.[37] Franzmann even went so far as to say that von Hoffmann "baptized all that is sound and sensible in the historical-critical method and made it useful for the church."[38] This led Burfiend to conclude that Franzmann had shifted.

> Franzmann's willingness to even suggest that the historical-critical method can be "made useful for the church" is a significant change from even his statements in his 1960 essay, "Revelation-Scripture-Interpretation," where he criticizes even the "conservative practitioners of the method', [sic] noting where they questioned the accuracy of the Word of God and noting that they had no good reason to do so."[39]

---

35. *The Art of Exegesis*, audio recording.

36. Gurgel, "The Life and Legacy of Martin Hans Franzmann: Lutheran Poet, Scholar, and Professor," III-4.

37. Burfiend, "A Third Way? Martin Franzmann's Contributions to Discussions of the Nature and Interpretation of Scripture in The Lutheran Church—Missouri Synod," 90. Particularly revealing of Burfiend is footnote 279 which points to Franzmann's suggestion that both J. C. K. von Hoffmann's and Jaroslav Pelikan's books be read twice, once before the course and once after it.

38. *The Art of Exegesis*, audio recording.

39. Burfiend, "A Third Way?" 91.

Burfiend's critique, however, does not say that Franzmann embraced historical-critical methods. Rather, he argued that over the course of time he believes Franzmann softened his position on such methods, evidenced in part, by the lack of accusatory statements against well-known practitioners in *The Art of Exegesis* lectures.

Is this critique valid? The preponderance of the evidence suggests otherwise. Even if Franzmann admitted a waning interest in types of criticism, he stated flat out he never had much faith in it anyway. The shift in suggested resources for a study of hermeneutics could just as easily reflect what is readily available to the public as much as it does anything else. Franzmann actually said as much in the bibliographic overview.[40] The comment made by Franzmann regarding von Hoffman baptizing what was useful in historical-critical methods is part of a greater explanation that seeks to set von Hoffmann within his context, which was not the twentieth but, rather the nineteenth century. His inclusion of von Hoffmann in the bibliography is to help the hearers of the lectures develop an appreciation for the biblical text in light of historical and linguistic developments from a conservative voice a century earlier, whose work had only been recently translated into English in 1959. All of Franzmann's discussion in those lectures about the bibliography set all of the required and suggested text under, and in service to, the biblical word.

Moreover, an argument based on what Franzmann does not say in reference to modern trends is not nearly as strong as an argument based upon what he actually said. There is no direct statement made by Franzmann concerning a substantial change in his understanding or affinity for historical-critical methods of inquiry. The remainder of this chapter endeavors to demonstrate not only that Franzmann did not make any substantial shift, but that he remained committed to his position. He would address the current needs of the church, but he would not be inventing something new. For example, a cursory reading of one Franzmann's most famous pieces, "Seven Theses on Reformation Hermeneutics," a piece that has since been reprinted two more times since his death, does not see Franzmann adopting new understandings when he made a comment using the language of "radical gospel."[41] In actuality, Franzmann was defining the gospel in much the same way as he did in his

---

40. *The Art of Exegesis*, audio recording.
41. See Appendix: Another Franzmann Bibliography.

1951 essay, "Quick and Powerful."[42] The perceived shift in Franzmann over the waning years of his career was not because he actually shifted. The difference, not unlike the situation with Scharlemann as described by Krentz, is that the landscape surrounding him did. In doing so, thereby being caught in the middle of warring factions, he suffered greatly.

ON CHANGE IN THEOLOGY

The story surrounding the walkout of the student body and faculty of Concordia Seminary in St. Louis is too involved to be told in its entirety here.[43] However, because of the necessity of situating the end of Martin's life within the proper context, a brief history of the events leading up to and including those events is necessary. As a theologically conservative and stridently confessional denomination, The Lutheran Church—Missouri Synod has rarely made attempts to innovate or change theological and biblical perspectives since its founding in 1847. One reason is the fact that the immigrants fled Saxony in order to avoid being forced into a church union. The Lutherans who settled in Missouri and other states were not particularly interested in being American Lutherans, but rather, being German Lutherans who could live in America and benefit from the freedoms therein. This meant they would be able to found schools and congregations, maintain their native German, and keep their Lutheran beliefs without being forced to give them up or compromise confessionally. None of this is particularly unique to The Lutheran Church—Missouri Synod, but it is clear that Missouri was able to maintain this parochial system for a much longer time than other immigrant church bodies. With a fierce loyalty to their synod president, C. F. W. Walther, the synod grew to become a large Lutheran denomination. While it

42. Franzmann, "Quick and Powerful," 161–9.

43. Full accounts from opposite perspectives are available. What follows is not an attempt to tell the entire history of the events, but to give enough context relative to Franzmann. The following list of resources is not exhaustive but provides a helpful introduction into some of the most difficult days in the life of the Missouri Synod. The list represents both conservative and moderate perspectives. Danker, *No Room in the Brotherhood: The Preus-Otten Purge of Missouri*; Burkee, *Power, Politics, and the Missouri Synod: A Conflict That Changed American Christianity*; Tietjen, *Memoirs in Exile: Confessional Hope and Institutional Conflict*; Marquart, *Anatomy of An Explosion*; Zimmerman, *A Seminary in Crisis: The Inside Story of the Preus Fact Finding*; The Board of Control of Concordia Seminary, St. Louis, *Exodus From Concordia: A Report on the 1974 Walkout*.

participated in dialog, some of which was not always kind or fruitful, it was rather reticent to merge with other Lutherans. Missouri was far from being a lone wolf as it was affiliated with some other conservative Lutheran bodies as part of the Evangelical Lutheran Synodical Conference of North America. This relationship, not without its own struggle, lasted for ninety years until two members of the conference noticed a change in the Missouri Synod. What exactly was that change? In part, it was a willingness and openness on the part of the LCMS to seek altar and pulpit fellowship with the American Lutheran Church, another, less conservative Lutheran denomination. But the dissolution of the Synodical Conference over Missouri's relationship with the American Lutheran Church is only part of the story.

Concurrent with the shift in openness to inter-Lutheran relationships was a shift at Concordia Seminary in St. Louis. Beginning with Martin Scharlemann, who later recanted and repented of his actions, historical-critical methods of biblical interpretation gained a foothold in the exegetical department. These methods, which are in one sense difficult to define, are by no means universal. They involve a critical appraisal of the biblical text from a literary, historical, and social perspective. That is, historical-critical methods involve attempts to explain the situation that gave rise to the biblical text. This includes making determinations about what sources were used by authors or editors in compiling biblical books, examining the social situation that would have given rise to the need for the text to be written, and making determinations about what could or could not, should or should not, be understood as factual history and what was symbolically true. Those methods stood in opposition to the long held and utilized historical-grammatical method used for decades prior to the mid 1950s.[44] The historical-grammatical method sought to unpack texts on the basis of the linguistic and historical situation of the text. It did not try to peer beyond the words of the page to make determinations of authenticity and historicity. Perhaps the biggest difference between the historical-critical and historical-grammatical methods is a presupposition. Those who advocated the use of historical-critical methods endeavored to treat the text of the bible as they would any other secular book. The scriptures would receive no special treatment. It would be subject to the same stringent standards as any piece of literature in antiquity. The advocates of the historical-grammatical method, on the other

---

44. See, for example, Graebner, "The Practice of Exegesis," 22–32.

hand, would not allow the standards of secular history and literature be applied to the biblical material, which, although it was another book, was unlike any other book ever written.

The partial shift within the Missouri Synod from a predominantly historical-grammatical methodology to the embracing of historical-critical methods did not happen instantaneously. Other denominations had struggled with a similar shift in the early part of the twentieth century. The methods had been in use since the eighteenth and nineteenth centuries. This happened later, in the life of The Lutheran Church—Missouri Synod, beginning in the 1950s with Martin Scharlemann. Scharlemann, like other eventual practitioners of the method in the LCMS, e.g., Ralph Klein and Edgar Krentz, was introduced to the methods in graduate study, through the pursuit of Doctor of Philosophy degrees in America and Europe. Universities like the University of Chicago, Union Theological Seminary, or the University of Erlangen became training grounds for the best and brightest graduates from Concordia Seminary. After continuing their education, they returned to teach what they had learned.

Over the course of time, conservatives within The Lutheran Church—Missouri Synod became vocally concerned over the moderate shift taking place. The 1962 convention at Cleveland did not silence the critics even if it welcomed Scharlemann back with open arms. Requests to investigate the shift in methods continued for years. This conservative backlash resulted in the surprise election of J.A.O. Preus as president of synod in 1969. Jacob A.O. Preus was raised and educated in the Evangelical Lutheran Synod and had been instrumental in suspending fellowship with The Lutheran Church—Missouri Synod.[45] It was Jacob and his brother Robert who led that charge in the early sixties. Both ended up earning doctorates, but when the Evangelical Lutheran Synod became too small for their academic endeavors, both took up positions at seminaries in the LCMS, Jacob in Springfield and Robert in St. Louis. Jacob would rise to the position of president of the seminary in Springfield before he became the president of the synod and was selected to be the leader of the conservative elements within the LCMS. Not only was he a theologically and politically conservative, he was not afraid to be confrontational when it was needed.

That same year John H. Tietjen was selected to fill the presidency at Concordia Seminary in St. Louis. Tietjen had grown up within the

45. His life is explained in Adams, *Preus of Missouri and the Great Lutheran Civil War*.

educational system of the LCMS. He attended college in Bronxville and was a graduate of Concordia Seminary. Tietjen earned his doctorate at Union Theological Seminary in New York, with his dissertation focusing on ways to Lutheran unity. He was the ideal candidate to lead the seminary that was shifting theologically to reflect a more moderate position. Not only was he educated, he was well known within Lutheran circles because of his role in public relations with The Lutheran Council in the USA.[46] Tietjen would prove just as capable of digging in his heels when he felt it was necessary.

After Preus and Tietjen were elected, investigations began into the position of faculty members.[47] After the investigations concluded, the Board of Control declared each faculty member innocent of teaching any false doctrine. Conservatives, undeterred by such a declaration, refocused their efforts on creating a means by which faculty members could be found guilty. The document that did that is called *A Statement of Scriptural and Confessional Principles*. It outlines traditional understanding of doctrine, argues against historical-critical methods, and left no room for moderate perspectives on inter-Lutheran relationships. This was no accident, as the document was written by one of the five faculty members who stood in opposition to their forty-five colleagues. Ralph Bohlmann, who would become president of both Concordia Seminary and then the LCMS, wrote it. The other two members of the "faithful five," as they were eventually called, worth mention at this point are Robert Preus, brother of Jacob, who would become president of Concordia Theological Seminary in Springfield, and Martin Scharlemann, who would become acting president of Concordia Seminary.

At the synod convention in 1973, Concordia Seminary would be dealt a devastating blow. Not only would *A Statement of Scriptural and Confessional Principles* be accepted as a benchmark for determining orthodoxy, the assembly would narrowly vote to deal with the faculty. In point of fact, the convention, echoing the Formula of Concord, resolved to remove elements and perspectives that "could not be tolerated in the church of God." Over the next few months John Tietjen, who had openly advocated for and protected his faculty, would be suspended. Martin Scharlemann, who led the charge as a conservative against his

---

46. See chapter 5 for a fuller discussion on LCUSA. Tietjen's life is explained in detail in his *Memoirs in Exile: Confessional Hope and Institutional Conflict*.

47. These investigations are detailed in Zimmerman, *A Seminary in Crisis: The Inside Story of the Preus Fact Finding Committee*.

fellow faculty members, was named acting president. The faculty would in turn recognize Tietjen's suspension as their own. The students then declared a moratorium on all classes until the Board of Control identified which faculty members were guilty of teaching false doctrine. All but five faculty honored that moratorium. After nearly a month, the Board of Control issued an ultimatum, if the faculty did not return to class they would be found in violation of their contract and terminated. When the faculty did not heed the ultimatum, they were fired. The next day, on February 19, 1974, over two-thirds of the student body voted to follow their faculty into exile.

Now, the question needs to be asked, what did Martin Franzmann have to do with any of the events from 1969 to 1974? In reality, not much. Franzmann retired in 1969 from Concordia Seminary. He was not among the faculty accused of teaching false doctrine at any point nor did he participate in any of the walkout activities. He did, however, in the mid-sixties, address the perceived change in theological perspective. "Change," he said, "is not only inevitable; it is desirable."[48] Here he is affirming change in terms of "linguistic, cultural, liturgical, architectural, administrative, homiletical, evangelistic, and journalistic"[49] areas. The purpose of the essay is to be honest in saying that a shift was taking place.

> In general it would seem to be true that our theology is today more directly and explicitly "exegetical" than formerly; there is today a larger sense of the historical qualification in both exegesis and dogma; our asseverations are more frequently qualified and our polemics less sweeping than they tended to be in the past; a greater ecumenical openness is so obvious it hardly needs mentioning. Whether this "change" amounts to "change *and decay*," that is the question that needs to be raised and answered.[50]

Admitting a change in perspective did not in and of itself mean passing a value judgment on the change. Following the quote Franzmann attempted to unpack whether or not change meant decay. He concluded with a warning.

> Every change involves risk, man being what he is in this time where the aeons overlap. And there are dangers in this trend. There are those that are endemic in the shaded domains of

---

48. Franzmann, "On Change in Theology," 5.
49. Franzmann, "On Change in Theology," 5.
50. Franzmann, "On Change in Theology," 7.

> exegetical scholarship; the one-sidedness of the specialists, misplaced or perverse ingenuity, parallelomania, pegomania (a mad passion for non-extant sources), behind-the-beyond historical thinking (explaining the obscure by means of the unknown), and so on. These are not to be underrated; but the Bible has a way of arising every so often and shaking them off, as a damp dog shakes off water. The paths of exegetical scholarship are inevitably wet with the drip of discarded hypotheses.[51]

That is to say, Franzmann, while admitting change, was not giving it a free pass. He was suggesting that the exegetical scholarship at the seminary needed to be vigilant in guarding against the danger. He went on to suggest that the entire theological enterprise need to be concerned toward that end.

> There is one major threat, however, insidiously pervasive. That is the secularization of historical thought and historical inquiry. Our God is more than Aristotle's First Cause Uncaused; but if we lose sight of Him amid our carefully collected clutter of subordinate casualties, we shall have regressed to a point somewhere behind Aristotle. To this problem theology must address itself with all the vigor and capable acumen.[52]

Here Franzmann was clear, there is a pervasive threat and it must not be ignored.

What can be deduced from the above article is that Franzmann admitted change was taking place, but also, that such change was not without its perils. In this paper, he attempted to give voice to the helpful changes of which the larger church are beneficiaries while commenting on the fact that the exegetical changes are not to be ignored or downplayed. Two years later Franzmann would retire. Perhaps it is because of the change taking place, combined with his distaste for conflict, that led him to see a confrontation between conservative and moderate elements within the synod as inevitable, and thus, something he could avoid through retirement. At least one person has suggested that he saw the writing on the wall and did not want to be forced to choose between friends and colleagues.[53]

---

51. Franzmann, "On Change in Theology," 8–9.
52. Franzmann, "On Change in Theology," 9.
53. Interview with James W. Voelz, July 25, 2017.

In what was likely the last sermon he preached at Concordia Seminary Martin Franzmann said the following.

> This seminary has gone under the name Concordia for many years; it is a good name and a true one—I have found much love here in the concord of this teaching brotherhood. But one of these days there is bound to be a committee which will propose a renaming of this venerable place; and I should like to get my suggestion in early. Call it *Beth Selichah*, the House of Forgiveness. There let the exegetes spell it out, parse it out, trilingually and eloquently. Let the systematicians pack it up and stack it up in its divinely wondrous symmetry. Let the historians trace the footsteps of the Forgiver through all the intricate ways of man's sad and glorious history. Let the practical men preach it, teach it, visual-aid it, televise it *ad maiorem Dei gloriam*. Let the musicians sing it, flute it, oboe it, kettle drum it, cymbal it, diapason it till the house is filled with smoke and the seraphim marvel at it.[54]

That plea for Concordia to be a house full of forgiveness would go unheeded.

THE HISTORICAL-CRITICAL METHOD

In 1965 Franzmann addressed a group of pastors in Brazil and then subsequently in America on "The Hermeneutical Dilemma: Dualism in the Interpretation of Holy Scripture." The presentation is a masterful outlining of the role of historical study in relation to the scriptures. It recounts much of what Franzmann said elsewhere and exhibits his trademark poetic theologizing. It concludes, however, with a prescient question. "We have not yet, as a church participated in [a] flight from dogma. But perhaps we should ask ourselves: Has the sight of the dissolution of dogma after dogma under the onset of historical-critical exegesis so terrified us that we have not taken a flight *into* dogma?"[55] This perceptive question would demonstrate itself to be a reality when it came to the events that led to the massive walkout at Concordia Seminary. Conservatives had

---

54. Franzmann, unpublished sermon on Micah 7:18–29, quoted in Robin Leaver, *Come to the Feast*, 114–5.

55. Franzmann, "The Hermeneutical Dilemma: Dualism in the Interpretation of Holy Scripture," 531.

indeed resorted to dogma as a means of protecting the synod from what they perceived to be a moderate threat.

Martin Franzmann, however, was not part of those events. He had retired, moved to Cambridge, and had served at Westfield House as tutor until his retirement there in 1972, after which he and Alice moved to Wells. He spent two quarters in 1973 at Concordia Theological Seminary in Springfield teaching courses, including one entitled "The Art of Exegesis." It was not until 1975 that Martin Franzmann was asked to give his voice to the struggles taking place in the life of The Lutheran Church—Missouri Synod. This would happen at a theological convocation on "The Nature and Function of Holy Scripture" in April of 1975 on the campus of Concordia Seminary in St. Louis. The purpose of the convocation was to try to find consensus between the moderate and conservative factions within the synod. Each of the presenters would have two responders, one representing each side. All materials were prepared in advance of the convocation so as to give time for all participants to reflect upon the material. Almost 300 delegates from various districts within the LCMS attended the event.[56] Several media outlets including the *Lutheran Witness*,[57] *Missouri in Perspective*,[58] *Christian News*,[59] and the *St. Louis Globe-Democrat*[60] covered the event.

Martin was asked to deliver a paper, one he titled "Historical-Critical Method." In that paper Martin sought to redefine the terms *historical* and *critical*. In many ways, the goal was a recapitulation of his work in 1964 aimed at teachers of the bible.[61] He was attempting to set limits to the terms that were broad enough yet faithful enough to the scriptures. Much of the paper unpacks his understanding of *historical* and *critical* in relation to the biblical text. "Historical," he wrote, "means simply that we are content to walk where our God walks and reveals Himself for our salvation on earth, amid persons and events. It does not mean that we

---

56. "Five Presenters Air Views on Scripture," 1.

57. See the following issue which contains numerous articles concerning the event: *Lutheran Witness* 94 (April 27, 1975).

58. The periodical of the moderate wing. "Five Presenters Air Views on Scripture," 1.

59. The periodical of the conservative wing. "Hundred's Attend Concordia Lecture," 1.

60. A local paper. Teuscher, "Lutherans Again Debate Interpretation of Bible."

61. "Problems and Principles of Interpretation," see chapter 4 of this work for a fuller exploration.

delude ourselves into believing that their hypotheses are of equal weight with one observable documentable fact, however useful and helpful a careful hypothesis may be, within its limitation."[62] Being historical in an approach to scripture means taking seriously the means by which God entered into history. It means to walk where God has walked. This is hardly a surprising definition. It matches exactly with his perspective as he has espoused it throughout the years. The same can be said of his definition of the term *critical*, which "means simply involving the use of the faculty of discriminating (χρίνω!) appreciation, that we discriminate between the inspired words of Paul, 'Drink a little wine for thy stomach's sake' (1 Tim. 5:23) and the inspired words of Paul when he writes, "Christ died for our sins, according the Scriptures" (1 Cor. 15:3)."[63] The discrimination made by the interpreter is not a decision over which words are inspired, but the value of the inspired words for the faith and life of the hearer. He concluded his introduction with a clear articulation of his goal. "We *can* decide to avoid the terms 'historical' and 'critical' when they have become ambiguous or misleading. We *cannot* decide to be unhistorical and uncritical. For if we do, the living word of God will rise up and make damned fools of us all."[64]

Responding to the paper from the moderate side was Ralph Klein, a member of the faculty who had walked out in 1974. He began by attempting to use Franzmann's definition of critical as a starting point to defend his own understanding of what it means to approach the scriptures critically. In actuality, he used Franzmann's definition as a means of demonstrating that words can have different definitions, and in doing so, Klein filled the word *critical* with his own definition. "Martin Franzmann has shown us that there are varieties of ways in which the Historical-Critical Method can be defined . . . we can speak most meaningfully if we define historical criticism as it has been used among us."[65] He went on to define it using words provided by G. E. Ladd, someone Klein notes is a conservative practitioner.[66] The remainder of his time was spent speak-

---

62. Franzmann, "Historical-Critical Method," in *The Nature and Function of Holy Scripture*, 16.

63. Franzmann, "Historical-Critical Method," 16.

64. Franzmann, "Historical-Critical Method," 16. Emphasis original.

65. *The Nature and Function of the Holy Scripture: Theological Convocation, St. Louis, Mo., April 14–18, 1975*, audio recording.

66. *The Nature and Function of the Holy Scripture: Theological Convocation, St. Louis, Mo., April 14–18, 1975*, audio recording.

ing about what he found valuable in historical-critical methodological approaches while also making noticeably transparent critiques of the synod and the historical-grammatical method.[67] What is clear from the audio recording of that convocation is that Klein was more concerned with advocating for his position than interacting with what Franzmann actually had to say.[68]

The response from the conservative side is even worse. Harold Buls, professor at Concordia Theological Seminary in Springfield, Illinois, presented that response. He thanked Martin for the call to repentance in his essay but says, "we have to say more than that we are in trouble."[69] A printed version of the response essay is even more emphatic. "With all due respect to Dr. Franzmann's personal stand in the matter, it must be said very frankly that his essay for this convocation, though very devotional, does not really come to grips with the issues . . . When I first read Dr. Franzmann's essay I thought it my duty to inform this convention what the Historical-Critical Method is all about and then to treat it point by point."[70] The audio reveals an impassioned Buls doing just that, a point by point treatment not just of historical-critical methods but of how Martin Franzmann failed to address it. Buls goes so far as to say that historical-critical methods will disrupt the central teaching of the church, "justification by faith," because ultimately those methods are a "clear enemy of the Word of God."[71] In his response, Buls used Franzmann's supposed failure to address issues as a pretext for Buls's own misgivings on the matter.

It is also important to take a moment to review the question and answer session following Franzmann's presentation and the presentation of the responses. The questions of two people during that time are important. The first person clearly and directly asked Franzmann if his essay was an about face or change from his previous works or perspective. In asking the question, the unnamed questioner quoted from Franzmann's

---

67. *The Nature and Function of the Holy Scripture: Theological Convocation, St. Louis, Mo., April 14–18, 1975*, audio recording.

68. Klein's response was also published. Klein, "The Historical-Critical Method: A Response," 12.

69. *The Nature and Function of the Holy Scripture: Theological Convocation, St. Louis, Mo., April 14–18, 1975*, audio recording.

70. Buls, "The Historical-Critical Method: A Reaction," 13.

71. *The Nature and Function of the Holy Scripture: Theological Convocation, St. Louis, Mo., April 14–18, 1975*, audio recording.

own appraisal of the historical-critical methods during the height of the Scharlemann controversy intended for faculty consumption.[72] The person asking the question said he had been a student for eight years at the seminary and studied under Martin Franzmann. After the man finished quoting at length Franzmann's document on historical-critical methods Martin replied.

> I do not consider my essay today as an about face from anything I said about the method previously. I was speaking then of the historical-critical method as it appears in the majority of cases, as it appears in modern theology. I was trying to portray it today as a new possibility, as an application of valid and undeniable truths concerning scripture to our approach to scripture. Perhaps I wasn't successful. But if I was guilty of a contradiction of what I said before of those words said before in a polemical context, I am heartily sorry for them. I don't believe I was. I was speaking there of the historical-critical method as it was predominantly practiced in the nineteenth and twentieth century, from a purely secular point of view. I was trying to re-baptize the term to make a good Lutheran of it, to make a good Missourian of it, by putting it into the neutral framework, what do the words historical and critical mean? Are they permitted, are we even commanded, by scripture, to be historical and to be critical? And it is my conviction, a conviction of faith, that we are. I realize that this probably has issued in statements that are a seeming contradiction. But I hope you will believe me that, from my mind and heart, they are simply a seeming contradiction. That basically what the words themselves mean, quite apart what men have done with them, what the words themselves intend, quite apart from what rationalism may have done with it, the words themselves are good, neutral, positive and useful words and it's our privilege and our duty, as Christian men who read the word of God to make use of them.[73]

Anyone who would suggest that Martin Franzmann shifted his position or perspective on historical-critical methods has to reckon with these words. He saw how a person could conceive of a contradiction because he affirmed that people must be historical and critical. But he asked to be understood in context and flat out states he did not believe he is caught in a contradiction. Perhaps he was trying to save face, or, perhaps he

---

72. Franzmann, "The Historical-Critical Method," *Concordia Journal*, 101–2.
73. *The Nature and Function of the Holy Scriptures*, audio recording.

was trying to bring two disparate sides together around a redefinition of terms. The question and answer session suggests the latter. It does so not only because of the above quote, but also because Franzmann, when asked about why he sought to re-baptize the terms, said the following:

> I'm not the proud godfather to the term, and I don't hold any particular brief for it. If someone can find a similar and adequate term I'd be very happy. And it's not my position here to fight for the term one way or the other. For me, to me, it seems a completely neutral term *per se* and can be used *per se*. You gentlemen who are working actively in the church probably see the thing from a somewhat clearer and better point of view than my own. And I would urge you to find a clearer and better term that you may use. It's not a point that I wish to get very controversial about.[74]

The terms in use where not of his choosing. He was doing what he could to repair the breach. He was not doing an about face, rather, he was trying to serve a church in crisis.

Franzmann left the convocation a broken man.[75] He stopped writing, his health deteriorated quickly, and just less than a year after speaking these words he would be dead. This was due to the fact that his attempts failed. He could not bring the sides back together. This servant of the church was attacked by conservatives for not going far enough. He was used by moderates to advance a cause he had no interest in advancing. What is even more intriguing, when Franzmann died, no major encomiums or tributes poured out from conservatives or moderates within the LCMS.[76] The *Lutheran Witness*, a publication to which Franzmann contributed multiple times, barely published a death notice and obituary.[77] Even if Franzmann's death came at a time when the Missouri Synod was still embroiled in a major conflict, as his death coincided with the pending and ultimate removal of district presidents within the LCMS, the lack of recognition for the passing of this poetic and faithful servant of the church, combined with the way he was treated by both sides in the last year of his life, was more than negligence, it was a failure at every

---

74. *The Nature and Function of the Holy Scripture: Theological Convocation, St. Louis, Mo., April 14–18, 1975*, audio recording.

75. Many sources suggest this, among them his son Peter Franzmann.

76. A brief death notice does appear in *Missouri in Perspective*, "Cambridge, England," 6.

77. "Scholar Dies," 185; "Obituary: Martin Hans Franzmann," 220.

level. Franzmann passed away somewhat forlorn, thinking he had failed the synod. In reality, however, he was a victim of a church so divided it would not see his attempt as a plea for genuine reconciliation.

WEARY OF ALL TRUMPETING

One of the last hymns Franzmann wrote, "Weary of All Trumpeting," was commissioned by composer Jan Bender, who wanted to redeem a tune of Hugo Distler. Distler composed a melody "under duress" in 1934 for the Third Reich which, "was in a jubilant mood after its annexation of Austria and wished to celebrate this enforced union."[78] The first verse of that hymn is as follows:

> Weary of all trumpeting,
> Weary of all killing,
> Weary of all songs that sing
> Promise, nonfulfilling.
> We would raise, O Christ, one song:
> We would join in singing
> That great music pure and strong,
> Wherewith Heav'n is ringing.[79]

Richard Brinkley, among others, has suggested that Franzmann's lyrical contribution to the Distler tune reflects more than just the tune's tragic origins.[80] Could it reflect Franzmann's own perspective of the events taking place in 1972, events that led to a cleavage yet to be repaired? Given what is known about Franzmann's final year, this is more than plausible.

The autobiographical possibility is further enhanced when one considers Alice Fletcher's comments about how her parents raised her. "I do remember my parents saying 'those who have a lot, must give a lot,' and they practiced this in monetary and personal ways. We were brought up to understand that there really was no boundary between the sacred and the secular, but life was to be lived as a godly whole."[81] The hymn's second verse echoes this self-giving that reflects what Christ had done.

---

78. Leaver, *Come to the Feast*, 112. Distler ended up taking his own life in regret for his forced role in the Third Reich.

79. Franzmann, "Weary of All Trumpeting," in Leaver, *Come to the Feast*, 81.

80. Brinkley, "The Hymns of Martin Franzmann: A Perspective," 155–63.

81. Personal correspondence, Alice Franzmann Fletcher, February 2018.

> Captain Christ, O lowly Lord,
> Servant King, Your dying
> Bade us sheathe the foolish sword,
> Bade us cease denying.
> Trumpet with Your Spirit's breath
> Through each height and hollow:
> Into Your self-giving death,
> Call us all to follow.[82]

Whatever may be true about this hypothesis, the hymn demonstrates again Franzmann's poetic flair. "Poetry," Franzmann said in his *Art of Exegesis* lectures, "is the language of religion."[83] He named those lectures the way he did because he believed that the word *art* painted a better picture than the word *methodology*.[84] And the goal of exegesis was to paint a picture. "Real exegesis leads to proclamation . . . [which is] all uttering of the hope that is in us."[85] The hymn's final verse speaks to that hope.

> To the triumph of Your cross
> Summon all men living;
> Summon us to live by loss,
> Gaining all by giving.
> Suffering all, that men may see
> Triumph in surrender;
> Leaving all, that we may be
> Partners in Your splendor.[86]

Franzmann's consistent and unwavering dedication to the text that grabbed him and would not let him go was, in actuality, a dedication to the cross of Christ. As his life and work demonstrate, he never failed to teach men and women to listen to the Christ enthroned on the cross. He never failed to approach the text as he would suggest anyone should, as a beggar at the foot of cross. His words concerning the cross need no explanation:

---

82. Franzmann, "Weary of All Trumpeting," in Leaver, *Come to the Feast*, 81.
83. Franzmann, *The Art of Exegesis*, audio recording.
84. Franzmann, *The Art of Exegesis*, audio recording.
85. Franzmann, *The Art of Exegesis*, audio recording.
86. Franzmann, "Weary of All Trumpeting," in Leaver, *Come to the Feast*, 81.

The cross marks the spot where the disciples failed, and it marks the spot where we all, we theologians, too, must fail. The cross marks the spot where the exegete ceases to be proud of his exegetical niceties, is shaken out of his scholarly serenity and cries out for his life in terms of the first Beatitude. The cross marks the spot where the systematician sees his system as the instrument which focuses his failure; where the practical theologian realizes that there is only one practical thing to do, and that is to repent and abhor himself in dust and ashes; where the historian leaves his long and sanely balanced view of things and goes desperately mad. The cross marks the spot where we all become beggars—and God becomes king. Amen.[87]

---

87. Franzmann, *Ha! Ha! Among the Trumpets*, 45.

Appendix
Another Franzmann Bibliography

OVERVIEW

TWO MAJOR BIBLIOGRAPHIES OF Martin Hans Franzmann's work have been published. The first was published in 1971 in *Concordia Theological Monthly*. It was composed by Victor Bartling, a colleague of Franzmann at Concordia Seminary in St. Louis. The second was appended to *Preaching Notes According to St. Luke* which was published posthumously. Two substantial unpublished bibliographies also exist. One was compiled by Richard Gurgel as part of his Church History Thesis and the other by Shawn Barnett which is in the possession of Concordia Historical Institute. Gurgel and Barnett's bibliographies, which clearly build upon the published two, include references to the earliest work of Franzmann published in *The Black and Red*. The present annotated bibliography builds upon the four by making minor corrections to the content where necessary and by including a listing of Franzmann's work published in *The British Lutheran*. The bibliography is arranged by type of material with the individual citations organized alphabetically. Annotations are meant to inform the researcher of the content and are not intended to provide an evaluation of it. No doubt this bibliography will need to be updated over the course of time as the output of Martin Hans Franzmann was vast. One of the goals of my analysis of the life and work of Franzmann is to ignite in others a desire to read more of his work. This appendix is meant to help facilitate that engagement.

BOOKS

Alive with the Spirit. St. Louis: Concordia Publishing House, 1973.

A series of devotions rooted in various passages of the New Testament. The devotions unpack what the life of the Holy Spirit means for the church as individuals and as a collective.

Bad Boll. St. Louis: The Lutheran Church—Missouri Synod, 1950.

A recounting of events that took place in 1949 at one of the free conferences held at Bad Boll. Franzmann recounts the events of each day, presentations, and the reception of those presentations. He also suggests the benefits and points of learning derived from the conferences.

Follow Me: Discipleship According to St. Matthew. St. Louis: Concordia Publishing House, 1961.

This commentary on Matthew discusses the content of the gospel in relation to discipleship. A major theme is the kingdom of God. Though not a traditional commentary, which unpacks verse by verse, it addresses the content of Matthew sequentially by section.

Ha! Ha! Among the Trumpets. St. Louis: Concordia Publishing House, 1966.

A collection of Franzmann's sermons organized according to liturgical dates and events. It was republished, with a different preface, in 1994.

New Courage for Daily Living: Devotions for Adults. The Family Worship Series. St. Louis: Concordia Publishing House, 1963.

A composition of devotions rooted in Colossians. The devotions work through the text one pericope at a time.

Pray for Joy. St. Louis: Concordia Publishing House, 1970.

A collection of prayers addressing various situations. Those situations include a prayer for before meals, over a glass of wine, and even a prayer for the right use of language. They are structured as poetry.

Preaching Notes on the Gospel According to Luke. St. Louis: Concordia Publishing House, 1976.

Published posthumously, this book unpacks the isagogic material relevant to Luke as well as offers commentary on major elements of the usage of Luke in year C of the three-year lectionary used in The Lutheran Church—Missouri Synod.

Romans. Concordia Commentary. St. Louis: Concordia Publishing House, 1968.

A commentary on the book of Romans that is part of the *Concordia Commentary* series. Franzmann's exegesis moves through Romans one pericope at a time. It reflects conservative scholarship.

The Revelation to John. St. Louis: Concordia Publishing House, 1976.

A commentary on Revelation, not part of the *Concordia Commentary* series, but published by Concordia Publishing House nevertheless. The exegesis moves through Revelation one pericope at a time.

Scripture and Interpretation. Springfield: Concordia Seminary Print Shop, 1961.

A book intended to serve as a substantive statement on hermeneutics. It is a compilation of Franzmann's 1948 "Essays in Hermeneutics" and his 1960 essays "Revelation—Scripture—Interpretation" and "The Posture of the Interpreter." It was used as an introductory textbook at Concordia Theological Seminary in Springfield, Illinois.

The Way of the Servant: Devotions for Lententide. St. Louis: Lutheran Laymen's League, 1967.

A Lenten devotional focusing on Christ as servant. The devotional is framed by the "Servant Songs" in Isaiah with individual devotions focusing on various verses in Luke's gospel.

The Word of the Lord Grows: A First Historical Introduction to the New Testament. St. Louis: Concordia Publishing House, 1961.

Isagogic material relative to the entire New Testament. Franzmann offers a discussion on canon, composition, dates, authorship, and major themes relative to each book. The book is thematically tied together by an exploration of the character of the New Testament, as the title, which utilizes a phrase from Acts, suggests.

Franzmann, Martin and F. Dean Lueking. *Grace Under Pressure: Meekness in Ecumenical Relations*. The Witnessing Church Series. St. Louis: Concordia Publishing House, 1966.

Franzmann's portion of the book unpacks ecumenicity relative to the traits of Jesus, namely obedience, weakness, and certitude. He then discusses how those traits showed themselves in the apostles and the church.

Franzmann, Martin and Walter Roehrs. *Concordia Self-Study Commentary: An Authoritative In-Home Resource for Students of the Bible*. St. Louis: Concordia Publishing House, 1979.

This text offers isagogic material relative to each book in the bible as well as exegetical insight into specific passages. Franzmann's portion covers the entire New Testament as well as the minor prophets. Much of the content regarding the New Testament mirrors *The Word of the Lord Grows*.

RESEARCH ESSAYS

"The Apocalypse." In *Interpreting and Teaching the Bible: A Resource for Teachers of the Bible, Pastors, Directors of Education, Bible Class Leaders*, edited by Oscar E. Feucht. St. Louis: The Lutheran Church—Missouri Synod, 1964. 103–15.

Part of a series of lectures on the biblical text. Franzmann, who also presented on the "Problems and Principles of Interpretation" walks through elements of the book of Revelation. This is not a point by point exegetical analysis, but an overview of the book.

"The Apostolate: Its Enduring Significance in the Apostolic Word." *Concordia Theological Monthly* 28, no. 3 (March 1957) 174–97.

An exegetical exploration of the theological and historical significance of the apostolate. It investigates both the apostle and the apostle's word with regard to their enduring significance for the life of the church.

"Augustana II: Of Original Sin." *Concordia Theological Monthly* 20, no. 12 (December 1949) 881–93.

This essay was first delivered at the Bad Boll Free Conferences in 1949. It explores the doctrine of original sin in the Lutheran Confessions and evaluates the doctrine exegetically.

"Beggars Before God: The First Beatitude." *Concordia Theological Monthly* 18, no. 12 (December 1947) 889–98.

An exploration of the place of first beatitude in the life of a Christian interpreter.

"A Brief Statement: Exegetical Aspects." Unpublished manuscript at Concordia Historical Institute, 1962.

This unpublished manuscript investigates the exegetical basis for elements of *A Brief Statement of the Doctrinal Position of the Missouri Synod* published in 1932. It comments on the nature and function of the document within the synod and whether or not such a statement is one to which a person could assent.

"Christ, the Hope of Glory." *Concordia Theological Monthly* 24, no. 12 (December 1953) 881–900.

This essay was first presented at the Bad Boll Free Conferences in 1953. It focuses on the hope for the church that is in Christ. It is eschatologically oriented and speaks of the resurrection and consummation of all things.

"The Christian Hope and Our Fellow Man." *Concordia Theological Monthly* 26, no. 10 (October 1955) 764–71.

———. *Concordia Theological Monthly* 26, no. 11 (November 1955) 831–41.

Both articles above were part of a presentation delivered at the 1954 Institute of the Lutheran Association for Human Relations at Valparaiso University. The articles include an appraisal of the relationship between Christians and other human beings, in terms of detachment and involvement, on the basis the New Testament in general, and James specifically.

"Critique of the Revised Standard Version of the Epistle of James." *Concordia Theological Monthly* 26, no. 1 (January 1955) 48–52.

A critique of the translation of James from the Revised Standard Version. It focuses on general benefits, explores the deficiencies of specific stylistic choices, and comments on matters of interpretation.

"Essays in Hermeneutics." *Concordia Theological Monthly* 19, no. 8 (August 1948) 595–605.

The first in a series of essays meant to serve as an introduction to hermeneutics. This essay explores hermeneutics generally as well as establishes and explains the "circle of language." The "circle of language" is Franzmann's designation for the role of linguistic study in the exegetical task.

"———." *Concordia Theological Monthly* 19, no. 9 (September 1948) 641–52.

A continuation of the hermeneutics essays focusing on the "circle of history." The "circle of history" is Franzmann's designation for the role of historical investigation in the exegetical task.

"———." *Concordia Theological Monthly* 19, no. 10 (October 1948) 738–46.

A continuation of the hermeneutics essays focusing on the "circle of scripture." The "circle of scripture" is Franzmann's designation to denote that the biblical text is the voice of God which calls to the hearer.

"Exegesis on Romans 16:17ff." *Concordia Journal* 7, no. 1 (January 1981) 13–20.

Initially circulated anonymously in 1950, the article explores what is meant in this section of Romans regarding fellowship with erring or heretical Christians. John Behnken's personal papers make clear that Franzmann wrote it.

"The Hermeneutical Dilemma: Dualism in the Interpretation of Holy Scripture." *Concordia Theological Monthly* 36, no. 8 (September 1965) 502–33.

An essay, first presented in Brazil and later at a conference of pastors in Missouri, that explores trends in exegetical study and approaches to historical investigation of the scriptures.

"Hermeneutical Principles Involved in the Appraisal of the 1963 Essay on Genesis 3." In *Essays Delivered at the Meeting of College Presidents and Seminary Faculties, November 30–December 2, 1964*. St. Louis, 1964. 1–39.

A response and rebuttal of Norman Habel's *The Form and Meaning of the Fall Narrative* presented one year earlier to district and synodical representatives. Franzmann notes points of agreement and divergence with Habel regarding the interpretation of Genesis 3. As a result of this paper Habel partially revised and published his essay in 1965.

"The Hermeneutics of Fulfillment: Is. 7:14 and Matt. 1:23." In *A Project in Biblical Hermeneutics*, edited by Richard Jungkuntz. St. Louis: The Commission on Theology and Church Relations of The Lutheran Church—Missouri Synod, 1969. 19–38.

This essay, which is part of a work by the Commission on Theology and Church Relations of The Lutheran Church—Missouri Synod, unpacks the relationship between the Old and New testaments. The discussion centers around the virgin birth narrative in Matthew and its supposed counterpart in Isaiah. A particular focus is also the meaning of the term "fulfillment" as it relates to the exegetical task.

"The Historical-Critical Method." *Concordia Journal* 6, no. 3 (May 1980) 101–02.

An exploration and evaluation of historical-critical methodology first written in 1958 for faculty consumption. Franzmann deems certain presuppositions of those methods unfit for Missouri Synod exegetes. It was later published with the consent of Alice Franzmann.

"The Inclusiveness and the Exclusiveness of the Gospel, as Seen in the Apostolate of Paul." *Concordia Theological Monthly* 27, no. 5 (May 1956) 337–51.

An exegetical exploration of the gospel in terms of Paul's life and work. It pays close attention to Galatians as it investigates how the gospel is inclusive and exclusive, i.e., its unifying and polemic qualities. Moreover, it speaks about how the anathema must accompany inclusion for fraternity to be genuine.

"A Lutheran Study of Church Unity." In *Essays on the Lutheran Confessions Basic to Lutheran Cooperation*. St. Louis: The Lutheran Church—

Missouri Synod and New York: The National Lutheran Council, 1961. 15–23.

Franzmann served as one of the essayists at this gathering of representatives from The Lutheran Church—Missouri Synod and the National Lutheran Council. Franzmann's essay explored the nature and depth of the gospel relative to inter-church relationships.

"The Marks of the Theologian." *Concordia Theological Monthly* 24, no. 2 (February 1953) 81–93.

An exegetically rich essay describing theologians as fools, children, and slaves.

"The Nature of the Unity We Seek: A Missouri Synod Lutheran View." *Concordia Theological Monthly* 28, no. 11 (November 1957) 801–09.

An investigation of the Missouri Synod's insistence on agreement concerning doctrine and practice as the basis for fellowship. It involves a lengthy exploration of why the Missouri Synod insists on the agreement concerning the nature and function of the biblical text.

"A New Lexicon." *Concordia Theological Monthly* 28, no. 9 (September 1957) 654–59.

An evaluation of the English translation of the Bauer-Danker-Arndt-Gingrich lexicon.

"The New Testament View of Inspiration." *Concordia Theological Monthly* 25, no. 10 (October 1954) 743–48.

An exegetical appraisal of verbal inspiration. It was written to address an issue on the campus of Concordia Seminary in St. Louis.

"Our Fellowship Under Scripture." Essay in *Conference of Theologians*. Oakland, CA, 1959.

This essay was delivered at an international conference of Lutheran theologians in June of 1959. It explores the relationship of the interpreter to the biblical text. Using the example of the apostles as exemplary, the characterization of that relationship is summed up in the word "*mimesis*." The content was later published in 1960 under the title, "The Posture of the Interpreter."

"Problems and Principles of Interpretation." In *Interpreting and Teaching the Bible: A Resource for Teachers of the Bible, Pastors, Directors of Education, Bible Class Leaders*, edited by Oscar E. Feucht. St. Louis: The Lutheran Church—Missouri Synod, 1964. 31–60.

This series of lectures unpacks much of Franzmann's perspective on hermeneutics. They focus on how meaning is derived through language, history, and revelation. It also offers a discussion on the appropriate ways to be historical and critical of the biblical text.

"The Quest for the Historical Jesus." *Concordia Journal* 6, no. 3 (May 1980) 102–6.

An exploration and evaluation of the so-called "Quest for the Historical Jesus." Franzmann expresses a disdain for the quest's understanding and use of historical inquiry. Initially meant for faculty consumption, it was later published with the consent of Alice Franzmann.

"Quick and Powerful." *Concordia Theological Monthly* 22, no. 3 (March 1951) 161–69.

An evaluation of the word of God and its place in the preaching and teaching of the church.

"The Posture of the Interpreter." *Concordia Theological Monthly* 31, no. 3 (March 1960) 149–64.

This essay was delivered at an international conference of Lutheran theologians in June of 1959. It explores the relationship of the interpreter to the biblical text. Using the example of the apostles as exemplary, the characterization of that relationship is summed up in the word "*mimesis*." The content was first part of the compilation, *Conference of Theologians*.

"A Ransom for Many: *Satisfactio Vicaria*." *Concordia Theological Monthly* 25, no. 7 (July 1954) 497–515.

An exegetical appraisal and evaluation of the "ransom saying," i.e., that Jesus comes to give his life as a ransom for many. It not only an appraisal from a New Testament perspective but includes an investigation of how that saying fits with the Old Testament.

"Reconciliation and Justification." *Concordia Theological Monthly* 21, no. 2 (February 1950) 81–93.

An analysis of the confessional and exegetical basis of the doctrine of justification by grace through faith. It was reprinted by Concordia Theological Seminary in Springfield, Illinois as part of a collection compiled by Robert Preus focusing on the subject of objective justification. See Robert Preus ed., *Selected Articles on Objective Justification* (Fort Wayne, IN: Concordia Theological Seminary Press.)

"Return to the Primacy of Exegesis." *Concordia Theological Monthly* 18, no. 6 (June 1947) 449–50.

An evaluation of a new periodical which explores relevant trends in exegetical study.

"Revelation—Scripture—Interpretation." In *A Symposium of Essays and Addresses given at the Counselors Conference: Valparaiso, Indiana September 7–14, 1960.* St. Louis: The Lutheran Church—Missouri Synod, 1960. 44–68.

This presentation explores revelation, scripture, and interpretation in light of current controversy. In sum, revelation is God's constant action in Christ; scripture is a recital of God's action in history; interpretation is an attempt at understanding that recital. This presentation was later combined with Franzmann's "Essays in Hermeneutics" and "The Posture of the Interpreter" under the title *Scripture and Interpretation*, which was used as a textbook for hermeneutics at Concordia Theological Seminary in Springfield, Illinois.

"Seven Theses on Reformation Hermeneutics." *Concordia Theological Monthly* 40, no. 4 (April 1969) 235–46.

A paper adopted by the Commission on Theology and Church Relations of The Lutheran Church—Missouri Synod. It explores the central features of reformation hermeneutics, with specific regard to justification by faith and the "radical gospel," and discusses the importance of that perspective in the life of the church. It has been reprinted twice; *Concordia Journal* 15, no. 3 (July 1989) 337–50; *Concordia Journal* 36, no. 2 (Spring 2010) 120–32.

"Studies in Discipleship." *Concordia Theological Monthly* 31, no. 10 (October 1960) 607–25.

———. *Concordia Theological Monthly* 31, no. 11 (November 1960) 670–89.

Both articles above are a preview of, respectively, chapters one and two of *Follow Me: Discipleship According to Saint Matthew* which would be published in 1961.

"Three Aspects of the Way of Christ and the Church: An approach to the Fellowship Problem." *Concordia Theological Monthly* 23, no. 10 (October 1952) 705–20.

An exegetically grounded exploration of differing perspectives on church fellowship. It investigates doxological, antagonistic, and soteriological approaches to the problem.

"Truth in the New Testament." In *Essays Delivered at the Meeting of College Presidents and Seminary Faculties, November 26-28, 1962 at Concordia Seminary, St. Louis, MO*. St. Louis, 1962. 1–13.

An exploration of the the word "truth" primarily on the basis of its usage in Romans and John. It also explores the relationship between truth and inerrancy.

"What Kind of Cooperation Is Possible in View of the Discussions to Date?" In *Toward Cooperation Among American Lutherans*. St. Louis: The Lutheran Church—Missouri Synod and New York: The National Lutheran Council, 1961. 18–22.

This essay was presented at a follow-up meeting between The Lutheran Church—Missouri Synod and the National Lutheran Council. It explored what kinds of relationships might be possible moving forward in light of expressed differences. There is special attention paid to pulpit and altar fellowship as well as human care effort.

"What is Truth." *What Has God Done Lately? Christian Perspectives for the Church School Teacher*. Edited by Dale E. Griffin. St. Louis: Concordia Publishing House, 1971. 44–50.

An edited version of the 1962 essay "Truth in the New Testament." It explores the the word "truth" primarily on the basis of its usage in Romans and John. It also discusses the relationship between truth and inerrancy.

"The Word of the Lord Grew: The Historical Character of the New Testament Word." *Concordia Theological Monthly* 30, no. 8 (August 1959) 563–81.

A preview of the first chapter of *The Word of the Lord Grows* which would be published in 1961.

Franzmann, Martin H. and Alfred O. Fuerbringer. "A Quarter-Century of Interchurch Relations: 1935–1960." *Concordia Theological Monthly* 32, no. 1 (January 1961) 5–14.

A reflection on the work of the Committee on Doctrinal Unity of The Lutheran Church—Missouri Synod. It includes an appraisal of events as well as a look toward the future work of that committee.

Franzmann, Martin H. and Alfred O. Fuerbringer. "The Lutheran Council in the United States of America: A Preliminary Report on the Proposed New Inter-Lutheran Association." *Concordia Theological Monthly* 35, no. 4 (April 1964) 219–27.

An appraisal of the discussions between the Committee on Doctrinal Unity of The Lutheran Church—Missouri Synod and the National Lutheran Council. It includes an evaluation of the proposed Lutheran Council in the United States of America and suggests the relationship the Missouri Synod should have with that group.

BOOK REVIEWS

Review of *Einleitung in Das Neue Testament*, by Alfred Wikenhauser. *Concordia Theological Monthly* 31, no. 4 (April 1960) 259.

Franzmann's review of this work is balanced and favorable.

Review of *The Epistle of James*, by C. Leslie Mitton. *Concordia Theological Monthly* 38, no. 11 (December 1967) 740–41.

Franzmann's review is brief and favorable.

Review of *The Epistle of Paul to the Galatians*, by Joh. Ph. Koehler, translated from the German by E. E. Sauer. *Concordia Theological Monthly* 30, no. 11 (November 1959) 862.

Franzmann's review of this translation expresses a fondness for the work and author.

Review of *The Epistles of St. John*, by Brooke Foss Westcott. *Concordia Theological Monthly* 38, no. 11 (December 1967) 741.

Franzmann's review is brief and favorable.

Review of *Interpreting the New Testament, 1900–1950*, by Archibald M. Hunter. *Concordia Theological Monthly* 25, no. 5 (May 1954) 399–400.

Franzmann's review of the book is well balanced.

Review of *Lange's Commentary on the Holy Scriptures*, translated from the German and edited by Philip Schaff. *Concordia Theological Monthly* 23, no. 12 (December 1952) 940.

Franzmann's review of the work is favorable although he admits he does not use it personally.

Review of *Lutherischer Rundblick: Informationsblatt Für Luterische Kirche und Theologie*, edited by W. M. Oesch and Hans Kirsten. *Concordia Theological Monthly* 27, no. 1 (January 1956) 70.

Franzmann's review of this periodical is favorable.

Review of *Ministers of Christ: A Commentary on the Second Epistle of Paul to the Corinthians*, by John P. Meyer. *Concordia Theological Monthly* 36, no. 5 (May 1965) 341.

Franzmann's review of the work is more a review of the author and the impact the author had on Franzmann's own theological development. As such the review of the work is favorable.

Review of *The New Testament, Its Making and Meaning*, by Albert E. Barnett. *Concordia Theological* Monthly 18, no. 3 (March 1947) 234–35.

Franzmann's review suggests that the book is of a "Liberal critical opinion" and that it would not prove valuable beyond an example of that opinion.

Review of *A Pattern For Life, An Exposition of the Sermon on the Mount*, by Archibald M. Hunter. *Concordia Theological Monthly* 25, no. 5 (May 1954) 400–1.

Franzmann's review of the book is rather critical but still positive.

Review of *Practical Exposition of James*, by J. Nieboer. *Concordia Theological Monthly* 21, no. 12 (December 1950) 951–52.

Franzmann's critique of this book is harsh, stating that it is "prolix" and "dogmatic."

Review of *Principles of Biblical Interpretation*, by L. Berkhoff. *Concordia Theological Monthly* 22, no. 1 (January 1951) 67–68.

Franzmann's critique is certainly critical. It is, however, also generous as he finds good in the book overall.

Review of *Problems of New Testament Translation*, by Edgar J. Goodspeed. *Concordia Theological Monthly* 18, no. 8 (August 1947) 640.

Franzmann's brief review of this book is generally favorable.

Review of *Sola Fide: Eine Exegetische Studie Ueber Jakobus 2 Zur Reformatorischen Rechtertigungslehere*, by Max Lackmann. *Concordia Theological Monthly* 21, no. 12 (December 1950) 950–51.

Franzmann's critique of this book is rather balanced but not overly supportive.

Review of *St. Paul the Traveler and the Roman Citizen*, by W. M. Ramsay. *Concordia Theological Monthly* 22, no. 1 (January 1951) 71.

Franzmann's brief review is supportive.

Review of *Voraussetzungen Der Neutestamentlichen Exegese*, by Ernst Lerle. *Concordia Theological Monthly* 23, no. 12 (December 1952) 939–40.

Franzmann's review of the work is favorable.

EDITORIALS

"Apollo in Spectacles." *The Black and Red* 30, no. 5 (October 1926) 164.

A commentary on the misreading of morals into poetry.

"The Apostolic Psha!" *Concordia Theological Monthly* 22, no. 12 (December 1951) 908–11.

Written as part of a *festschrift*, this article explores the attitudes and perspectives of which a theologian should rightly be dismissive.

"Be Thyself." *The Black and Red* 29, no. 6 (November 1925) 193–94.

An exhortation to writers to demonstrate humor and character in their compositions.

"Campus and Classroom." Column in *The Black and Red* 29, no. 1–10 (April 1925–March 1926) 26–29, 67–69, 116–19, 143–45, 177–80, 209–12, 244–47, 279–83, 317–21, 365–69.

A lighthearted and comedic column edited by Franzmann.

"Christian Poetry." *Northwestern Lutheran* 33 (1946) 134, 154, 172, 185.

A four-part essay on the merits of poetry in general and Christian poetry specifically. Franzmann speaks generally as well as specifically with regard to specific examples of poetry.

"Classics in the Senior College." *Concordia Theological Monthly* 21, no. 7 (July 1950) 522–26.

An evaluation of classics as a discipline and its value in the preparation of pastors. It is also an exhortation to include classics in the development of a new curriculum at a college in the Missouri Synod system.

"Cockcrow Manor." *British Lutheran* 14, no. 10 (December 1969) 2–3.

An exploration of worship in light of the Christmas season. Part of the recurring column, "Westfield's Window."

"Concerning Class Numbers." *The Black and Red* 31, no. 6 (November 1927) 181.

An editorial note on what constitutes worthy submissions for an upcoming issue.

"Confession." *The Black and Red* 31, no. 10 (March 1928) 313.

An appraisal of his travails as editor of the periodical.

"The Convention Proceedings." *Northwestern Lutheran* 30 (September 1943) 279–85.

An overview of the events that took place during the twenty-seventh convention of the Wisconsin Synod. Highlights include appraisal of doctrinal essays, worship services, mission work, and financial developments.

"Cynicism." *The Black and Red* 31, no. 4 (September 1927) 121.

A commentary defining the usefulness of cynicism.

"Diapason of Joy." *Lutheran Witness* 72 (January 6, 1953) 3, 13.

A meditation on the nature of joy in light of the Epiphany season.

"Der Baum Ist Nicht Dick Sondern Gruen." *Concordia Theological Monthly* 23, no. 12 (December 1952) 922–24.

An exploration of false antitheses and their place within the church.

"Dr. John Henry Ott." *Northwestern Lutheran* 32 (December 1945) 292–93.

An obituary demonstrating a fondness for John Henry Ott.

"Editorial." *Concordia Theological Monthly* 31, no. 1 (January 1960) 1.

A brief commentary on expectations of the new year for the theological journal which is said only to be good insofar as it is a churchly journal.

"An Educational Ideal." *Lutheran School Bulletin* 11 (February 1941) 1–3.

An article that seeks to establish an educational ideal, which is a wholly formed Christian life of worship. It discusses the realization of that ideal, which is understood to be a long process. Finally, it explores the ideal's relevance for the future, which he believes necessitates, in part, investing in teachers.

"Familiar and Fresh." *British Lutheran* 15, no. 9 (December 1970) 2.

A brief meditation on the merits of recovery from illness. Part of the recurring column, "Westfield's Window."

"Final Concert and Graduation at Northwestern." *Northwestern Lutheran* 30 (June 1943) 198.

An informative and endearing appraisal of two events that mark the close of the year at Northwestern college, the final concert and graduation.

"The Genius of Shakespeare." *The Black and Red* 32, no. 3 (June 1928) 60–63.

A senior English oration where Franzmann explores and describes the works, skills, and talent of William Shakespeare.

"In Praise of Cramming." *The Black and Red* 31, no. 8 (January 1928) 248–49.

A commentary conveying the merits of cramming before exams.

"Keep Off the Grass." *The Black and Red* 30, no. 4 (September 1926) 128–30.

An exploration of contentment and restraint.

"The Last Look." *British Lutheran* 16, no. 6 (November/December 1971) 2.

A reflection on Franzmann's last days as tutor at Westfield House and a look ahead to his retirement. Part of the recurring column, "Westfield's Window."

"A Little Candle." *British Lutheran* 16, no. 5 (August/October 1971) 8–9.

A commentary on Franzmann's impressions of the life of a synod within the Evangelical Lutheran Church of England.

"Locals." Column in *The Black and Red* 30, no. 1–10 (April 1926–March 1927) 23–24, 68–70, 114–15, 144–46, 177–80, 209–12, 244–47, 279–83, 317–21, 365–69.

A running commentary on current events relative to the campus and students edited by Franzmann.

"Missouri and the Lutheran World Federation." *Lutheran Witness* 72 (April 14, 1953) 124, 133–134.

"———." *Lutheran Witness* 72 (April 28, 1953) 148–49.

Both of the above articles recount Franzmann's impressions of time spent at the Hanover meeting of the Lutheran World Federation. He explores the benefits and weakness of his time and expresses a clear perspective on whether or not, and on what grounds, the Missouri Synod should join the federation.

"The New Year and All Things." *Concordia Theological Monthly* 34, no. 1 (January 1962) 5–7.

A meditation on the new year, based on Colossians 1:17, especially as it relates to the life of the church.

"Of a Man and Four Rivers." *British Lutheran* 14, no. 8 (October 1969) 6–7.

An article intended to introduce the Evangelical Lutheran Church of England to Martin Franzmann. He uses four rivers as a scheme for unpacking his biographical information.

"The Old Fire and The New." *Lutheran Witness* 74 (June 7, 1955) 207.

A meditation on taming the flames of sinful behavior in light of Pentecost.

"On Change in Theology." *Concordia Theological Monthly* 38, no. 1 (January 1967) 5–9.

An evaluation of the curriculum changes taking place at Concordia Seminary. It includes an appraisal of the merits and dangers of those changes as well as other trends in exegetical study.

"On Filling Your Head." *The Black and Red* 30, no. 9 (February 1927) 330–31.

A commentary on the merits of education and the proper attitude to have toward the educational process.

"On Smiles." *The Black and Red* 30, no. 1 (April 1926) 4–6.

A commentary on the types and values of smiles.

"¿Pastor Versus Proffesor?" *Revista Theológica* 12, no. 48 (Cuarto Trimestra, 1965) 30–32.

This article explores tension between pastors and professors. Franzmann speaks about what temptations exist for both individuals and contains a plea for the tensions to cease. No published translations of this article appear to exist. A translation was made available to this author by Rev. James Sharp.

"Proem." *The Black and Red* 31, no. 1 (April 1927) 14–15.

A commentary on the intentions of the editorial staff for the upcoming volume.

Reply to editorial. *Lutheran Outlook* (December 1952).

Franzmann responds to an editorial that explores a church fellowship dilemma in the Missouri Synod. Franzmann critiques the editorial and suggest the dilemma is in actuality a trilemma due to Missouri's relationship with the Synodical Conference.

"Seven Ways to Use a Sundial." *The Black and Red* 31, no. 4 (September 1927) 113–14.

A commentary on the installation of a new sun dial on campus.

"So We Preach." *Lutheran Witness* 66 (April 22, 1947) 132.

An essay celebrating the one hundredth anniversary of The Lutheran Church—Missouri Synod. It focuses on the nature and function of the gospel.

"Sure—But Not Complacent." *Lutheran Witness* 80 (November 28, 1961) 572–73.

An advent meditation on the difference between confidence and complacency concerning the grace of God.

"Theologians in Lent." *British Lutheran* 15, no. 2 (February 1970) 2–3.

An exhortation to theologians not to succumb to the temptation of pride and a plea for the right use of theology. Part of the recurring column, "Westfield's Window."

"Theological Conferences in Europe: Summer 1956." *Lutheran Witness* 75 (September 25, 1956) 370–71.

A recounting of his time spent at conferences throughout Europe. He explores the benefits and concerns brought about by those free conferences which began at Bad Boll in 1948.

"Thou Art Mad." *Concordia Theological Monthly* 21, no. 3 (March 1950) 215–17.

An exploration on the merits of practical theology and the practically minded theologian.

"Toward the Mark." *Lutheran Witness* 73 (January 5, 1954) 5.

A meditation comparing the Christian's life to the life of an athlete.

"Vita Monastica." *The Black and Red* 29, no, 8 (January 1926) 259–60.

An exploration of the merits and pitfalls of a life lived in seclusion.

"We Look Before and After." *Northwestern Lutheran* 31 (August 1944) 172.

An exploration of the benefits the church has by being able to look back to the garden of Eden and forward to the age to come. This is put in comparison to the vision the world possesses. Franzmann also expresses a desire for people to understand teaching not as a job but as life.

"Westfield's Window." *British Lutheran* 14, no. 9 (November 1969) 2–3.

An article, which is part of a recurring column titled "Westfield's Window," that explores theological education taking place at Westfield House in Cambridge, England. Specifically, it addresses a weekly textual study.

"Westfield's Window. *British Lutheran* 15, no. 4 (April 1970) 2–3.

An exploration of what the benefits of being taught the "radical Gospel" by God are for the Evangelical Lutheran Church of England, a specific unnamed student, and all people.

"Westfield's Window." *British Lutheran* 16, no. 2 (February/March 1971) 2.

A commentary on the communal nature of the church in light of a postal strike.

"Westfield's Window." *British Lutheran* 16, no. 5 (August/October 1971) 2.

An exploration of the present and future from the perspective of a theology teacher in light of eschatological realities.

"What a Dumb Lot We Are." *The Black and Red* 31, no. 2 (May 1927) 50.

A commentary on the value of humility for a student.

"Why So Many Bibles?" *Lutheran Witness* 81 (March 20, 1962) 134–35.

An exploration of the situation which gave rise to different English translations and an evaluation of some specific translations. Franzmann notes his personal preference for the Revised Standard Version.

"Words of Life." Column in *Lutheran Witness* 75 (January 3, 1956– December 18, 1956) 7, 23, 47, 63, 79, 95, 119, 135, 151, 175, 199, 215, 253, 275, 311, 327, 343, 367, 383, 399, 423, 437, 459, 483.

An ongoing column focusing on themes such as the Kingdom of God and discipleship. The majority of meditations stem from the gospel of Matthew.

"Ye Who Are About to Learn." *The Black and Red* 29, no. 1 (April 1925) 5–7.

A commentary about learning how to swim.

SPEECHES AND SERMONS

"Approved Workman: In Memoriam John Theodore Mueller." *Concordia Theological Monthly* 38, no. 8 (September 1967) 499–500.

A sermon preached at the funeral of John Theodore Mueller.

"Chapel Address." *Concordia Theological Monthly* 40, no. 8 (September 1969) 578–79.

Sermon on Isaiah 57:15. The sermon features an exploration of what happens when theologians act like "slobs" and "kooks."

"Commencement Address." *Lutheran School Bulletin* 13 (September 1942) 2–4.

A meditation on Psalm 116: 12–13. It emphasizes the work of God who created, redeemed, and sustained believers. Additionally, it focuses on the benefits of time spent reading the scriptures.

"The Forgiveness of Sin and the Unity of the Spirit." *Proceedings of the Forty-Second Convention of the Evangelical Lutheran Synodical Conference of North America*. 1952. 12–57.

This convention essay begins by exploring the forgiveness of sins relative to grace alone, faith alone, and word alone. It continues with a discussion of the self-denying love of Jesus Christ. And finally iterates how it may be possible to preserve unity.

"I Believe in One God: Trinity Sunday/Romans 10:10A." In *The Concordia Pulpit for 1970*. St. Louis: Concordia Publishing House, 1969. 136–40.

The first in a series of sermons aimed at unpacking the content of the Nicene Creed. This initial sermon explores the phrase, "I believe in one God." This exploration revolves around belief in the heart and the sermon structure reflects that.

"If We Walk in the Light." *Lutheran Witness* 72 (January 20, 1953) 3.

An Epiphany meditation on walking between light and darkness. Republished in *Ha! Ha! Among the Trumpets*.

"Installation of a Theological Professor." In *The Concordia Pulpit for 1950*. Vol. XXI. St. Louis: Concordia Publishing House, 1949. 368–74.

A copy of the sermon preached at the installation of Dr. Alfred von Rohr Saur, professor of Old Testament at Concordia Seminary in St. Louis. It focuses on the beatitude, "blessed are the poor in spirit." The sermon was reprinted in *Ha! Ha! Among the Trumpets* in 1966.

"James II—The Working Faith." *Proceedings of the Thirtieth Convention of the Northern Illinois District of The Lutheran Church—Missouri Synod*. 1952. 5–25.

This convention essay unpacks the context and content of the epistle of James, with special reference to chapter two, and sets it within the context of the New Testament. It explores how James presents understandings of God, Jesus Christ, humanity, soteriology, and faith. Furthermore, it investigates the relationship between faith, favoritism, and verbal profession.

"Lutheran Church—Missouri Synod, 125th Anniversary, 1972." Unpublished manuscript at Concordia Historical Institute, 1972.

This unpublished work celebrates the anniversary of the synod realistically, noting the current struggles. It is divided into sections focusing on the radical gospel and the place of hypothesis in the interpretive process.

"Milwaukee Convention Essay." Unpublished manuscript at Concordia Historical Institute, 1950.

Delivered in installments at The Lutheran Church—Missouri Synod's 1950 convention in Milwaukee, this essay unpacks the relevance of the seven letters written to church in Revelation. Co-essayist at the convention was Dr. Martin Walker. Franzmann's portion covers Revelation 2:1–29. Although the convention proceedings indicate that this manuscript should have been published, no record of its publication has been found. The proceedings also indicate that it should be potentially titled "The Living Church." The manuscript itself has another potential title at the top, "The Seven Letters or Call to Complete Surrender to Christ." The essay is cited as it is due to a lack of clarity on the actual title.

"Quick to Hear, James 1:19–21." *Lutheran Witness* 67 (June 15, 1948) 191–92.

A sermon on hearing God's voice in the biblical text. It was preached at a chapel service at Concordia Seminary in St. Louis around the time of Pentecost.

"The Resurrection of the Dead: The Beating Heart of All Our Hope." *Lutheran Witness* 78 (March 24, 1959) 128–29.

An Easter meditation on the entire chapter of 1 Corinthians 15. It focuses on the nature and hope of the resurrection. Republished in *Ha! Ha! Among the Trumpets*.

"The Royal Banners Forward Go." *Concordia Theological Monthly* 32, no. 3 (March 1961) 157–61.

Three Lenten meditations, based on Matthew 21:28–32, 21:33–43, and 22:1–14, which are focused on the the nature of God and God's children as expressed in the parables. They were reprinted in *Ha! Ha! Among the Trumpets*.

"Theology Must Sing." *Parish Leadership* 2 (Summer 1994) 14–15.

A reprinting of a Reformation sermon on hymnody bearing the same title originally published in *Ha! Ha! Among the Trumpets*.

"Who Cares?" *Lutheran Witness* 76 (December 3, 1957) 584–85.

An Advent meditation on John the Baptist. Republished in *Ha! Ha! Among the Trumpets*.

"Who Is a God Like Thee?" *The Springfielder* 37, no. 2 (September 1973) 81–83.

Sermon delivered at Concordia Theological Seminary in Springfield, Illinois on May 22, 1973. It focuses on the nature and result of forgiveness.

"The Young Man Who Fled." *Lutheran Witness* 71 (February 19, 1952) 3, 7.

A meditation, based on Mark 14:51–52, that explores the nature of discipleship. Republished in *Ha! Ha! Among the Trumpets*.

AUDIO RECORDINGS

All in Each Place: Church Fellowship at the Local Level. St. Louis: Concordia Seminary Media Services, July 20–24, 1964.

Franzmann begins by noting his lack of experience in parish ministry but nevertheless endeavors to unpack what local church fellowship looks like. He speaks about ecumenicity as being integral to the church. Much of the content is reminiscent of the book he coauthored with F. Dean Leuking, *Grace Under Pressure*. The Concordia Seminary library record indicates that this lecture was delivered at the 8th annual Institute on Parish Administration held on the campus of Concordia Seminary July 20–24, 1964.

The Art of Exegesis. St. Louis: Concordia Publishing House, 1972.

A series of lectures unpacking the methodology behind scriptural interpretation. Much of the content is reminiscent of his "Problems and Principles of Interpretation" published in 1964.

Memorial Service for Professor J. T. Mueller. St. Louis: Concordia Seminary Media Services, 1967.

Franzmann serves as preacher at this memorial service for former faculty member J.T. Mueller. The sermon was published in 1967 under the title "Approved Workman: In Memoriam John Theodore Mueller."

The Nature and Function of Holy Scripture: Theological Convocation, St. Louis, Mo., April 14–18, 1975. St. Louis: Concordia Publishing House, 1975.

Franzmann delivers an essay entitled "The Historical-Critical Method" in which he affirms what it means to approach the text historically and critically. The audio also contains an abbreviated question and answer session.

Theological Study Today: Have We Changed? St. Louis: Concordia Seminary Media Services, June 6–10, 1966.

This address, as noted in the Concordia Seminary library record, is delivered to a vicarage supervisors conference. It seeks to unpack the curriculum changes taking place at Concordia Seminary and offers comments on their validity and potential dangers. The content mirrors the essay published in January 1967, "On Change in Theology."

Truth According to the New Testament. Phonotape [Cl-2l] recorded at the Audio-Visual Center of Concordia Seminary, St. Louis, Mo., November 13, 1961.

A discussion on the nature of revelation and truth and their usage in the New Testament. The content of this audio mirrors his essay "Truth in the New Testament," which was published in 1962.

HYMNS

Due to the exceptional work of Richard Brinkley, *Thy Strong Word: The Enduring Legacy of Martin Franzmann,* and Robin Leaver, *Come to the Feast: The Original and Translated Hymns of Martin H. Franzmann,* the hymns below appear without annotation. The hymns reflect Robin Leaver's assessment of Franzmann's hymnody.

Original

"In Adam We Have All Been One."
"Lord, We Will Remember Thee."

"Lord Jesus Christ, In Hidden Ways."
"O Fearful Place, Where He Who Knows Our Heart."
"O First and Greatest of All Servants."
"O God, O Lord of Heaven and Earth."
"O Kingly Love, That Faithfully."
"O Thou Who Hast of Thy Pure Grace."
"O Thou Who On Th'Accursed Ground."
"O Thou Whose Fiery Blessing."
"Our Lord Has Laid His Benison."
"Our Paschal Lamb, That Sets Us Free."
"Preach You the Word."
"Thee, Lord, Would I Serve."
"Thou Whose Glory None Can See."
"Though Wisdom All Her Skills Combine."
"Thy Strong Word Did Cleave the Darkness."
"Thy Word Has Been Our Daily Bread."
"Weary of All Trumpeting."
"You Spoke Your Word of Truth."

Translations

"Christ, Our Lord, Arose."
"Isaiah in a Vision Did of Old."
"Jesus Only, Naught But Jesus."
"O Lord, We Praise Thee."
"Praise Thou the Lord, My Soul."
"Rise Again, Ye Lion-Hearted."
"The Dawn Has Driven Dark Night Away."
"To Songs of Joy Awake Thee."
"With High Delight Let Us Unite."

POETRY & PROSE

These titles appear without annotation as they are divided into categories indicating their type of literature.

English Poetry

"Apology for Greek Syntax." *The Black and Red* 31, no. 6 (November 1927) 169.

"Autumn." *The Black and Red* 26, no. 6 (November 1922) 154.

"Beginning and End." *The Black and Red* 27, no. 1 (April 1923) 1.

"Belshazzar." *The Black and Red* 27, no. 10 (March 1924) 310–11.

"Christmas." *The Black and Red* 28, no. 7 (December 1924) 187–88.

"Day-Dreams." *The Black and Red* 27, no. 6 (November 1923) 166.

"Drunken Sailor." *The Black and Red* 31, no. 8 (January 1928) 248.

"Hellas." *The Black and Red* 31, no. 2 (May 1927) 37.

"Mark Antony to a Dull Mistress." *The Black and Red* 30, no. 3 (June 1926) 93.

"The Morn." *The Black and Red* 27, no. 3 (June 1923) 66–67.

"Northwestern Credo." *The Black and Red* 31, no. 3 (June 1927) 86–87.

"October." *The Black and Red* 28, no. 5 (October 1924) 127.

"The Old and the New." *The Black and Red* 26, no. 8 (January 1923) 213.

"A Railroad Carol." *The Black and Red* 27, no. 7 (December 1923) 198.

"Return." *The Black and Red* 30, no. 9 (February 1927) 316.

"River Dam, Mississippi." *The Black and Red* 29, no. 9 (February 1926) 284.

"Senior." *The Black and Red* 31, no. 10 (March 1928) 315.

"Song for the Weary," *The Black and Red* 28, no. 1 (April 1924) 1.

"A Sonnet" *The Black and Red* 29, no. 6 (November 1925) 181.

"The Sprinter (In February)." *The Black and Red* 31, no. 9 (February 1928) 300–1.

"Three Green Candles." *The Black and Red* 30, no. 5 (October 1926) 150.

"To Any Genius." *The Black and Red* 31, no. 10 (March 1928) 303.

"To the Mississippi." *The Black and Red* 26, no. 9 (February 1923) 243.

"Vale Pick and Shovel." *The Black and Red* 30, no. 4 (September 1926) 119.

"When We Go Forth." *The Black and Red* 28, no. 3 (June 1924) 61.

"Who Weds a Goddess." *The Black and Red* 30, no. 7 (December 1926) 218.

Fables

"For the Sake of a Plot." *The Black and Red* 29, no. 4 (September 1925) 120–23.

"For Small Children." *The Black and Red* 31, no. 8 (January 1928) 247–48.

German Poetry

"Fruehlingstraum." *The Black and Red* 26, no. 10 (March 1923) 271.

"Heil'ge Nacht." *The Black and Red* 26, no. 7 (December 1922) 181.

MISCELLANEOUS CONTRIBUTIONS

"Cantate: The Fourth Sunday After Easter." *Concordia Theological Monthly* 35, no. 4 (April 1964) 234–36.

Sermonic study of James 1:16–21. Franzmann speaks about what God's promise is and what it means to desire that promise. It concludes with a paragraph on application.

EN-101c Introduction to the New Testament. Concordia Seminary Correspondence Course, 1965.

A correspondence course workbook mirroring his other New Testament isagogic material.

EN-561c Sermon on the Mount. Concordia Seminary Correspondence Course, 1966.

A correspondence course workbook focusing on the sermon on the mount in Matthew. Some of the material is reflective of Franzmann's work in that gospel.

"The Fourth Sunday after Easter: James 1:16–21." In *Sermonic Studies: The Standard Epistles*. Vol. 1. St. Louis: Concordia Publishing House, 1957. 328–36.

This sermon study explores the context of the epistle as well as its content. Within that exploration are suggestions related to other readings assigned for the day. Finally, it offers a possible outline for a sermon.

"Hear Ye Him: Training the Pastor in the Holy Scriptures." In *Toward a More Excellent Ministry*, edited by Richard R. Caemmerer and Alfred O. Fuerbringer. St. Louis: Concordia Publishing House, 1964. 81–90.

An essay reflecting Franzmann's perspective on training future pastors written to celebrate the one hundred twenty-fifth anniversary of Concordia Seminary. Franzmann notes that his aim in training pastors is to teach people to listen to the voice of God in the scriptures.

"Historical Meditations on Saint John." In *The Devotional Bible*. St. Louis: Concordia, 1948. 319–23.

There are two brief meditations. One focuses on what is known about the author of John. The other focuses on the content of the gospel. Both meditations conclude with prayer.

Introducing the New Testament. St. Louis: Concordia Seminary Print Shop.

A course workbook Franzmann prepared for a course he taught on New Testament isagogics. This material reflects much of what would be published in the 1961 book *The Word of the Lord Grows*.

"Jesus Wills Unity." Unpublished manuscript at Concordia Historical Institute, September 1968.

This manuscript works through sections focusing on the titles, call, words, and death and resurrection of Jesus and how those things relate to church unity. The context of the manuscript is not clear. Handwritten and typed versions exist in the archives.

"Rogate: The Fifth Sunday After Easter." *Concordia Theological Monthly* 35, no. 4 (April 1964) 236–37.

Sermonic study of James 1:22–27. Franzmann suggests the theme of the text has to do with loving, facing, staying with, and doing what God commands. It concludes with a paragraph on application.

A Workbook in the New Testament Theology: Basileia Tou Theou. Revised Edition, 1956.

A course workbook Franzmann created for a course on "the kingdom of God" as expressed throughout the scriptures, not solely in the New Testament.

Voigt, Gottfried. "The Speaking Christ in His Royal Office." Translated by Martin H. Franzmann. *Concordia Theological Monthly* 23, no. 3 (March 1952) 161–75.

Franzmann translated this article which was delivered by Voigt at a theological conference. The topic of the article is an exploration of Christ's relationship with the church.

Bibliography

PRIMARY SOURCES

Franzmann, Martin H. *Alive With The Spirit*. St. Louis: Concordia Publishing House, 1973.

———. *All in Each Place: Church Fellowship at the Local Level*. St. Louis: Concordia Seminary Media Services, July 20–24, 1964.

———. *The Art of Exegesis*. St. Louis: Concordia Publishing House, 1972.

———. "The Apocalypse." In *Interpreting and Teaching the Bible: A Resource for Teachers of the Bible, Pastors, Directors of Education, Bible Class Leaders*, edited by Oscar E. Feucht. St. Louis: The Lutheran Church—Missouri Synod, 1964. 103–15.

———. "Apollo in Spectacles." *The Black and Red* 30, no. 5 (October 1926) 164.

———. "Apology for Greek Syntax." *The Black and Red* 31, no. 6 (November 1927) 169.

———. "The Apostolate: Its Enduring Significance in the Apostolic Word." *Concordia Theological Monthly* 28, no. 3 (March 1957) 174–97.

———. "The Apostolic Psha!" *Concordia Theological Monthly* 22, no. 12 (December 1951) 908–11.

———. "Approved Workman: In Memoriam John Theodore Mueller." *Concordia Theological Monthly* 38, no. 8 (September 1967) 499–500.

———. "Augustana II: Of Original Sin." *Concordia Theological Monthly* 20, no. 12 (December 1949) 881–893.

———. "Autumn." *The Black and Red* 26, no. 6 (November 1922) 154.

———. *Bad Boll*. St. Louis: The Lutheran Church—Missouri Synod, 1950.

———. "Belshazzar." *The Black and Red* 27, no. 10 (March 1924) 310–11.

———. "Be Thyself." *The Black and Red* 29, no. 6 (November 1925) 193–94.

———. "Beggars Before God: The First Beatitude." *Concordia Theological Monthly* 18, no. 12 (December 1947) 889–98.

———. "Beginning and End." *The Black and Red* 27, no. 1 (April 1923) 1.

———. "A Brief Statement: Exegetical Aspects." Unpublished manuscript at Concordia Historical Institute, 1962.

———. "Campus and Classroom." Column in *The Black and Red* 29, no. 1–10 (April 1925–March 1926) 26–29, 67–69, 116–19, 143–45, 177–80, 209–12, 244–47, 279–83, 317–21, 365–69.

———. "Cantate: The Fourth Sunday After Easter." *Concordia Theological Monthly* 35, no. 4 (April 1964) 234–36.

———. "Chapel Address." *Concordia Theological Monthly* 40, no. 8 (September 1969) 578–79.

———. "Christ, the Hope of Glory." *Concordia Theological Monthly* 24, no. 12 (December 1953) 881–900.

———. "The Christian Hope and Our Fellow Man." *Concordia Theological Monthly* 26, no. 10 (October 1955) 764–71.

———. "The Christian Hope and Our Fellow Man." *Concordia Theological Monthly* 26, no. 11 (November 1955) 831–41.

———. "Christian Poetry." *Northwestern Lutheran* 33 (1946) 134, 154, 172, 185.

———. "The Convention Proceedings." *Northwestern Lutheran* 30 (September 1943) 279–85.

———. "Christmas." *The Black and Red* 28, no. 7 (December 1924) 187–88.

———. "Classics in the Senior College." *Concordia Theological Monthly* 21, no. 7 (July 1950) 522–26.

———. "Cockcrow Manor." *British Lutheran* 14, no. 10 (December 1969) 2–3.

———. "Commencement Address." *Lutheran School Bulletin* 13 (September 1942) 2–4.

———. "Concerning Class Numbers." *The Black and Red* 31, no. 6 (November 1927) 181.

———. "Confession." *The Black and Red* 31, no. 10 (March 1928) 313.

———. "Critique of the Revised Standard Version of the Epistle of James." *Concordia Theological Monthly* 26, no. 1 (January 1955) 48–52.

———. "Cynicism." *The Black and Red* 31, no. 4 (September 1927) 121.

———. "Day-Dreams." *The Black and Red* 27, no. 6 (November 1923) 166.

———. "Der Baum Ist Nicht Dick Sondern Gruen." *Concordia Theological Monthly* 23, no. 12 (December 1952) 922–24.

———. "Diapason of Joy." *Lutheran Witness* 72 (January 6, 1953) 3, 13.

———. "Dr. John Henry Ott." *Northwestern Lutheran* 32 (December 1945) 292–93.

———. "Drunken Sailor." *The Black and Red* 31, no. 8 (January 1928) 248.

———. "Editorial." *Concordia Theological Monthly* 31, no. 1 (January 1960) 1.

———. "An Educational Ideal." *Lutheran School Bulletin* 11 (February 1941) 1–3.

———. *EN-101 Introduction to the New Testament*. Concordia Seminary Correspondence Course. 1965.

———. *EN-561c Sermon on the Mount*. Concordia Seminary Correspondence Course, 1966.

———. "Essays in Hermeneutics." *Concordia Theological Monthly* 19, no. 8 (August 1948) 595–605.

———. "Essays in Hermeneutics." *Concordia Theological Monthly* 19, no. 9 (September 1948) 641–52.

———. "Essays in Hermeneutics." *Concordia Theological Monthly* 19, no. 10 (October 1948) 738–46.

———. "Exegesis on Romans 16:17ff." *Concordia Journal* 7, no. 1 (January 1981) 13–20.

———. "Familiar and Fresh." *British Lutheran* 15, no. 9 (December 1970) 2.

———. "Final Concert and Graduation at Northwestern." *Northwestern Lutheran* 30 (June 1943) 198.

———. *Follow Me: Discipleship According to St. Matthew*. St. Louis: Concordia Publishing House, 1961.

———. "For Small Children." *The Black and Red* 31, no. 8 (January 1928) 247–48.
———. "For the Sake of a Plot." *The Black and Red* 29, no. 4 (September 1925) 120–23.
———. "The Forgiveness of Sin and the Unity of the Spirit." *Proceedings of the Forty-Second Convention of the Evangelical Lutheran Synodical Conference of North America*. 1952. 12–57.
———. "The Fourth Sunday after Easter: James 1:16–21." In *Sermonic Studies: The Standard Epistles*. Vol. 1. St. Louis: Concordia Publishing House, 1957. 328–36.
———. "Fruehlingstraum." *The Black and Red* 26, no. 10 (March 1923) 271.
———. "The Genius of Shakespeare." *The Black and Red* 32, no. 3 (June 1928) 60–3.
———. *Ha! Ha! Among the Trumpets*. St. Louis: Concordia Publishing House, 1966.
———. "Hear Ye Him: Training the Pastor in the Holy Scriptures." In *Toward a More Excellent Ministry*, edited by Richard R. Caemmerer and Alfred O. Fuerbringer. St. Louis: Concordia Publishing House, 1964. 81–90.
———. "Heil'ge Nacht." *The Black and Red* 26, no. 7 (December 1922) 181.
———. "Hellas." *The Black and Red* 31, no. 2 (May 1927) 37.
———. "The Hermeneutical Dilemma: Dualism in the Interpretation of Holy Scripture." *Concordia Theological Monthly* 36, no. 8 (September 1965) 502–33.
———. "Hermeneutical Principles Involved in the Appraisal of the 1963 Essay on Genesis 3." In *Essays Delivered at the Meeting of College Presidents and Seminary Faculties, November 30–December 2, 1964*. St. Louis, 1964. 1–39.
———. "The Hermeneutics of Fulfillment: Is. 7:14 and Matt. 1:23." In *A Project in Biblical Hermeneutics*, edited by Richard Jungkuntz. St. Louis: The Commission on Theology and Church Relations of The Lutheran Church—Missouri Synod, 1969. 19–38.
———. "The Historical-Critical Method." *Concordia Journal* 6, no. 3 (May 1980) 101–02.
———. "The Historical-Critical Method." In *The Nature and Function of the Holy Scripture: Theological Convocation, St. Louis, Mo., April 14–18, 1975*. St. Louis: Concordia Publishing House, 1975.
———. "Historical Meditations on Saint John." In *The Devotional Bible*. St. Louis: Concordia, 1948. 319–23.
———. "I Believe in One God: Trinity Sunday/Romans 10:10A." In *The Concordia Pulpit for 1970*. St. Louis: Concordia Publishing House, 1969. 136–40.
———. "If We Walk in the Light." *Lutheran Witness* 72 (January 20, 1953) 3.
———. "In Praise of Cramming." *The Black and Red* 31, no. 8 (January 1928) 248–49.
———. "The Inclusiveness and the Exclusiveness of the Gospel, as Seen in the Apostolate of Paul." *Concordia Theological Monthly* 27, no. 5 (May 1956) 337–51.
———. *Introducing the New Testament*. St. Louis, MO: Concordia Seminary Print Shop.
———. "James II—The Working Faith." *Proceedings of the Thirtieth Convention of the Northern Illinois District of The Lutheran Church—Missouri Synod*. 1952. 5–25.
———. "Jesus Wills Unity." Unpublished manuscript at Concordia Historical Institute.
———. "Keep Off the Grass." *The Black and Red* 30, no. 4 (September 1926) 128–30.
———. "The Last Look." *British Lutheran* 16, no. 6 (November/December 1971) 2.
———. "A Little Candle." *British Lutheran* 16, no. 5 (August/October 1971) 8–9.
———. "Locals." Column in *The Black and Red* 30, no. 1–10 (April 1926–March 1927) 23–24, 68–70, 114–15, 144–46, 177–80, 209–12, 244–47, 279–83, 317–21, 365–69.

———. "Lutheran Church—Missouri Synod, 125th Anniversary, 1972." Unpublished manuscript at Concordia Historical Institute, 1972.

———. "A Lutheran Study of Church Unity." In *Essays on the Lutheran Confessions Basic to Lutheran Cooperation*. St. Louis: The Lutheran Church—Missouri Synod and New York: The National Lutheran Council, 1961. 15–23.

———. "Mark Antony to a Dull Mistress." *The Black and Red* 30, no. 3 (June 1926) 93.

———. "The Marks of the Theologian." *Concordia Theological Monthly* 24, no. 2 (February 1953) 81–93.

———. *Memorial Service for Professor J. T. Mueller*. St. Louis: Concordia Seminary Media Services, 1967.

———. "Milwaukee Convention Essay." Unpublished manuscript at Concordia Historical Institute, 1950.

———. "Missouri and the Lutheran World Federation." *Lutheran Witness* 72 (April 14, 1953) 124, 133–34.

———. "Missouri and the Lutheran World Federation." *Lutheran Witness* 72 (April 28, 1953) 148–49.

———. "The Morn." *The Black and Red* 27, no. 3 (June 1923) 66–67.

———. *The Nature and Function of the Holy Scripture: Theological Convocation, St. Louis, Mo., April 14–18, 1975*. St. Louis: Concordia Publishing House, 1975.

———. "The Nature of the Unity We Seek: A Missouri Synod Lutheran View." *Concordia Theological Monthly* 28, no. 11 (November 1957) 801–09.

———. *New Courage for Daily Living: Devotions for Adults*. The Family Worship Series. St. Louis: Concordia Publishing House, 1963.

———. "A New Lexicon." *Concordia Theological Monthly* 28, no. 9 (September 1957) 654–59.

———. "The New Testament View of Inspiration." *Concordia Theological Monthly* 25, no. 10 (October 1954) 743–48.

———. "The New Year and All Things." *Concordia Theological Monthly* 34, no. 1 (January 1962) 5–7.

———. "Northwestern Credo." *The Black and Red* 31, no. 3 (June 1927) 86–87.

———. "October." *The Black and Red* 28, no. 5 (October 1924) 127.

———. "Of a Man and Four Rivers." *British Lutheran* 14, no. 8 (October 1969) 6–7.

———. "On Change in Theology." *Concordia Theological Monthly* 38, no. 1 (January 1967) 5–9.

———. "On Filling Your Head." *The Black and Red* 30, no. 10 (March 1927) 330–31.

———. "On Smiles." *The Black and Red* 30, no. 1 (April 1926) 4–6.

———. "The Old and the New." *The Black and Red* 26, no. 8 (January 1923) 213.

———. "The Old Fire and The New." *Lutheran Witness* 74 (June 7, 1955) 207.

———. "Our Fellowship Under Scripture." Essay in *Conference of Theologians*. Oakland, CA, 1959.

———. "¿Pastor Versus Proffesor?" *Revista Theológica* 12, no. 48 (Cuarto Trimestra, 1965) 30–32.

———. *Pray for Joy*. St. Louis: Concordia Publishing House, 1970.

———. *Preaching Notes on the Gospel According to Luke*. St. Louis: Concordia Publishing House, 1976.

———. "Problems and Principles of Interpretation." In *Interpreting and Teaching the Bible: A Resource for Teachers of the Bible, Pastors, Directors of Education, Bible*

Class Leaders, edited by Oscar E. Feucht. St. Louis: The Lutheran Church—Missouri Synod, 1964. 31–60.

———. "The Posture of the Interpreter." *Concordia Theological Monthly* 31, no. 3 (March 1960) 149–64.

———. "Proem." *The Black and Red* 31, no. 1 (April 1927) 14–15.

———. "The Quest for the Historical Jesus." *Concordia Journal* 6, no. 3 (May 1980) 102–6.

———. "Quick and Powerful." *Concordia Theological Monthly* 22, no. 3 (March 1951) 161–69.

———. "Quick to Hear, James 1:19–21." *Lutheran Witness* 67 (June 15, 1948) 191–92.

———. "A Railroad Carol." *The Black and Red* 27, no. 7 (December 1923) 198.

———. "A Ransom for Many: *Satisfactio Vicaria*." *Concordia Theological Monthly* 25, no. 7 (July 1954) 497–515.

———. "Reconciliation and Justification." *Concordia Theological Monthly* 21, no. 2 (February 1950) 81–93.

———. Reply to editorial. *Lutheran Outlook* (December 1952).

———. "The Resurrection of the Dead: The Beating Heart of All Our Hope." *Lutheran Witness* 78 (March 24, 1959) 128–29.

———. "Return." *The Black and Red* 30, no. 9 (February 1927) 316.

———. "Return to the Primacy of Exegesis." *Concordia Theological Monthly* 18, no. 6 (June 1947) 449–50.

———. "Revelation—Scripture—Interpretation." In *A Symposium of Essays and Addresses given at the Counselors Conference: Valparaiso, Indiana September 7–14, 1960*. St. Louis: The Lutheran Church—Missouri Synod, 1960. 44–68.

———. *The Revelation to John*. St. Louis: Concordia Publishing House, 1976.

———. Review of *A Pattern For Life, An Exposition of the Sermon on the Mount*, by Archibald M. Hunter. *Concordia Theological Monthly* 25, no. 5 (May 1954) 400–01.

———. Review of *Einleitung in Das Neue Testament*, by Alfred Wikenhauser. *Concordia Theological Monthly* 31, no. 4 (April 1960) 259.

———. Review of *Interpreting the New Testament, 1900–1950*, by Archibald M. Hunter. *Concordia Theological Monthly* 25, no. 5 (May 1954) 399–400.

———. Review of *Lange's Commentary on the Holy Scriptures*, translated from the German and edited by Philip Schaff. *Concordia Theological Monthly* 23, no. 12 (December 1952) 940.

———. Review of *Lutherischer Rundblick: Informationsblatt Für Luterische Kirche und Theologie*, edited by W. M. Oesch and Hans Kirsten. *Concordia Theological Monthly* 27, no. 1 (January 1956) 70.

———. Review of *Ministers of Christ: A Commentary on the Second Epistle of Paul to the Corinthians*, by John P. Meyer. *Concordia Theological Monthly* 36, no. 5 (May 1965) 341.

———. Review of *Practical Exposition of James*, by J. Nieboer. *Concordia Theological Monthly* 21, no. 12 (December 1950) 951–52.

———. Review of *Principles of Biblical Interpretation*, by L. Berkhoff. *Concordia Theological Monthly* 22, no. 1 (January 1951) 67–68.

———. Review of *Problems of New Testament Translation*, by Edgar J. Goodspeed. *Concordia Theological Monthly* 18, no. 8 (August 1947) 640.

———. Review of *Sola Fide: Eine Exegetische Studie Ueber Jakobus 2 Zur Reformatorischen Rechtertigungslehere*, by Max Lackmann. *Concordia Theological Monthly* 21, no. 12 (December 1950) 950–51.

———. Review of *St. Paul the Traveler and the Roman Citizen*, by W. M. Ramsay. *Concordia Theological Monthly* 22, no. 1 (January 1951) 71.

———. Review of *The New Testament, Its Making and Meaning*, by Albert E. Barnett. *Concordia Theological Monthly* 18, no. 3 (March 1947) 234–35.

———. Review of *The Epistle of James*, by C. Leslie Mitton. *Concordia Theological Monthly* 38, no. 11 (December 1967) 740–41.

———. Review of *The Epistle of Paul to the Galatians*, by Joh. Ph. Koehler, translated from the German by E. E. Sauer. *Concordia Theological Monthly* 30, no. 11 (November 1959) 862.

———. Review of *The Epistles of St. John*, by Brooke Foss Westcott. *Concordia Theological Monthly* 38, no. 11 (December 1967) 741.

———. Review of *Voraussetzungen Der Neutestamentlichen Exegese*, by Ernst Lerle. *Concordia Theological Monthly* 23, no. 12 (December 1952) 939–40.

———. "River Dam, Mississippi." *The Black and Red* 29, no. 9 (February 1926) 284.

———. "Rogate: The Fifth Sunday After Easter." *Concordia Theological Monthly* 35, no. 4 (April 1964) 236–37.

———. *Romans*. Concordia Commentary. St. Louis: Concordia Publishing House, 1968.

———. "The Royal Banners Forward Go." *Concordia Theological Monthly* 32, no. 3 (March 1961) 157–61.

———. *Scripture and Interpretation*. Springfield: Concordia Seminary Print Shop, 1961.

———. "Senior." *The Black and Red* 31, no. 10 (March 1928) 315.

———. "Seven Theses on Reformation Hermeneutics." *Concordia Theological Monthly* 40, no. 4 (April 1969) 235–46.

———. "Seven Theses on Reformation Hermeneutics." *Concordia Journal* 15, no. 3 (July 1989) 337–50.

———. "Seven Theses on Reformation Hermeneutics." *Concordia Journal* 36, no. 2 (Spring 2010) 120–32.

———. "Seven Ways to Use a Sundial." *The Black and Red* 31, no. 4 (September 1927) 113–14.

———. "So We Preach." *Lutheran Witness* 66 (April 22, 1947) 132.

———. "Song for the Weary," *The Black and Red* 28, no. 1 (April 1924) 1.

———. "A Sonnet" *The Black and Red* 29, no. 6 (November 1925) 181.

———. "The Sprinter (In February)." *The Black and Red* 31, no. 9 (February 1928) 300–1.

———. "Studies in Discipleship." *Concordia Theological Monthly* 31, no. 10 (October 1960) 607–25.

———. "Studies in Discipleship." *Concordia Theological Monthly* 31, no. 11 (November 1960) 670–89.

———. "Sure—But Not Complacent." *Lutheran Witness* 80 (November 28, 1961) 572–73.

———. "Theologians in Lent." *British Lutheran* 15, no. 2 (February 1970) 2–3.

———. "Theological Conferences in Europe: Summer 1956." *Lutheran Witness* 75 (September 25, 1956) 370–71.

———. *Theological Study Today: Have We Changed?* St. Louis: Concordia Seminary Media
Services, June 6-10, 1966.

———. "Theology Must Sing." *Parish Leadership* 2 (Summer 1994) 14-15.

———. "Three Aspects of the Way of Christ and the Church: An Approach to the Fellowship Problem." *Concordia Theological Monthly* 23, no. 10 (October 1952) 705-20.

———. "Three Green Candles." *The Black and Red* 30, no. 5 (October 1926) 150.

———. "Thou Art Mad." *Concordia Theological Monthly* 21, no. 3 (March 1950) 215-17.

———. "To Any Genius." *The Black and Red* 31, no. 10 (March 1928) 303.

———. "To the Mississippi." *The Black and Red* 26, no. 9 (February 1923) 243.

———. "Toward the Mark." *Lutheran Witness* 73 (January 5, 1954) 5.

———. *Truth According to the New Testament.* Phonotape [Cl-2l] recorded at the Audio-Visual Center of Concordia Seminary, St. Louis, Mo., November 13, 1961.

———. "Truth in the New Testament." In *Essays Delivered at the Meeting of College Presidents and Seminary Faculties, November 26-28, 1962 at Concordia Seminary, St. Louis, MO.* St. Louis, 1962. 1-13

———. "Vale Pick and Shovel." *The Black and Red* 30, no. 4 (September 1926) 119.

———. "Vita Monastica." *The Black and Red* 28, no, 8 (January 1925) 259-60.

———. *The Way of the Servant: Devotions for Lententide.* St. Louis: Lutheran Laymen's League, 1967.

———. "We Look Before and After." *Northwestern Lutheran* 31 (August 1944) 172.

———. "Westfield's Window." *British Lutheran* 14, no. 9 (November 1969) 2-3.

———. "Westfield's Window." *British Lutheran* 15, no. 4 (April 1970) 2-3.

———. "Westfield's Window." *British Lutheran* 16, no. 2 (February/March 1971) 2.

———. "Westfield's Window." *British Lutheran* 16, no. 5 (August/October 1971) 2.

———. "What a Dumb Lot We Are." *The Black and Red* 31, no. 2 (May 1927) 50.

———. "What Kind of Cooperation is Possible in View of the Discussions to Date?" In *Toward Cooperation Among American Lutherans.* St. Louis: The Lutheran Church—Missouri Synod and New York: The National Lutheran Council, 1961. 18-22.

———. "What is Truth." *What Has God Done Lately? Christian Perspectives for the Church School Teacher.* Edited by Dale E. Griffin. St. Louis: Concordia Publishing House, 1971. 44-50.

———. "When We Go Forth." *The Black and Red* 28, no. 3 (June 1924) 61.

———. "Who Cares?" *Lutheran Witness* 76 (December 3, 1957) 584-85.

———. "Who Is a God Like Thee?" *The Springfielder* 37, no. 2 (September 1973) 81-83.

———. "Who Weds a Goddess." *The Black and Red* 30, no. 7 (December 1926) 218.

———. "Why So Many Bibles?" *Lutheran Witness* 81 (March 20, 1962) 134-35.

———. "The Word of the Lord Grew: The Historical Character of the New Testament Word." *Concordia Theological Monthly* 30, no. 8 (August 1959) 563-81.

———. *The Word of the Lord Grows: A First Historical Introduction to the New Testament.* St. Louis: Concordia Publishing House, 1961.

———. "Words of Life." Column in *Lutheran Witness* 75 (January 3, 1956–December 18, 1956) 7, 23, 47, 63, 79, 95, 119, 135, 151, 175, 199, 215, 253, 275, 311, 327, 343, 367, 383, 399, 423, 437, 459, 483.

---. *A Workbook in the New Testament Theology: Basileia Tou Theou.* Revised Edition, 1956.

---. "Ye Who Are About to Learn." *The Black and Red* 29, no. 1 (April 1925) 5–7.

---. "The Young Man Who Fled." *Lutheran Witness* 71 (February 19, 1952) 3, 7.

Franzmann, Martin H. and Alfred O. Fuerbringer. "A Quarter-Century of Interchurch Relations: 1935–1960." *Concordia Theological Monthly* 32, no. 1 (January 1961) 5–14.

---. "The Lutheran Council in the United States of America: A Preliminary Report on the Proposed New Inter-Lutheran Association." *Concordia Theological Monthly* 35, no. 4 (April 1964) 219–27.

Franzmann, Martin H. and F. Dean Leuking. *Grace Under Pressure: Meekness in Ecumenical Relations.* The Witnessing Church Series. St. Louis: Concordia Publishing House, 1966.

Franzmann, Martin H. and Walter Roehrs. *Concordia Self-Study Commentary: An Authoritative In-Home Resource For Students of the Bible.* St. Louis: Concordia Publishing House, 1979.

Voigt, Gottfried. "The Speaking Christ in His Royal Office." Translated by Martin H. Franzmann. *Concordia Theological Monthly* 23, no. 3 (March 1952) 161–75.

SECONDARY SOURCES

Adams, James Edward. *Preus of Missouri and the Great Lutheran Civil War.* New York: Harper & Row, 1977.

Albrecht, Michael. "John Philipp Koehler (1859–1951) and the Wauwatosa Theology." *Lutheran Quarterly* 24, no. 4 (2010) 424–46.

"Ancient Stone Used in Lutheran Ceremony." *British Lutheran* 14, no. 9 (November 1969) 11.

Backer, Bruce. *Lutheran Worship: A Course Guide.* 4th ed. New Ulm: Luther College, 1988.

Barnbrock, Christoph, Thomas Egger, Alfonso Espinosa, Jeffrey Holtan, and Charles Schaum. *C. F. W. Walther: Churchman and Theologian.* St. Louis: Concordia Publishing House, 2001.

Bartling, Victor. "A Martin Franzmann Bibliography." *Concordia Theological Monthly* 42, no. 8 (September 1971) 485–87.

---. Review of *Follow Me: Discipleship According to Saint Matthew,* by Martin H. Franzmann. *Concordia Theological Monthly* 33, no. 1 (January 1962) 45–46.

Bauer, W., F. W. Danker, W. F. Arndt, F. W. Gingrich. *A Greek-English Lexicon of the New Testament and Other Early Christian Literature.* 3rd ed. Chicago: University of Chicago Press, 2000.

Beard, Mary and John Henderson. *Classics: A Very Short Introduction.* Oxford: Oxford University Press, 1995.

Becker, Matthew. "Further Reflections on 1967 LCMS Resolution 2–02." *Transverse Markings: One Theologian's Notes* (blog). January 10, 2012. http://matthewlbecker. blogspot.com/20 12/01/further-reflections-on-1967-lcms.html.

Braun, Mark. "The Protes'tant Controversy and Its Impact on the Wisconsin Synod." *Lutheran Historical Conference* 20 (2002) 76–98.

A Brief Statement of the Doctrinal Position of the Missouri Synod. St. Louis: The Lutheran Church—Missouri Synod, 1932.

Brinkley, Richard N. "Of Four Rivers: A Biographical Sketch of Martin Franzmann." *Journal of the Good Shepherd Institute* 8 (2007) 123–37.

———. "The Hymns of Martin Franzmann: A Perspective." *Journal of the Good Shepherd Institute* 8 (2007) 155–63.

———. Personal correspondence. July, August, and October 2017.

———. *Thy Strong Word: The Enduring Legacy of Martin Franzmann*. St. Louis: Concordia Publishing House, 1993.

The Board of Control of Concordia Seminary, St. Louis, Missouri. *Exodus from Concordia: A Report on the 1974 Walkout*. St. Louis: Concordia College, 1977.

Bretscher, Paul. M. "William Frederick Arndt: 1880–1957." *Concordia Theological Monthly* 28, No. 6 (June 1957) 401–8.

Buls, Harold. "The Historical-Critical Method: A Reaction." *Christian News* 8, no. 16 (April 25, 1975) 13–14.

Burfiend, Daniel. "A Third Way? Martin Franzmann's Contributions to Discussions on the Nature and Interpretation of Scripture in The Lutheran Church—Missouri Synod." Master of Sacred Theology Thesis, Concordia Theological Seminary, 2016.

Burkee, James C. *Power, Politics, and the Missouri Synod: A Conflict That Changed American Christianity*. Minneapolis: Fortress, 2011.

Caemmerer, Richard R. "Essays on the Interpretation of Scripture." *Concordia Theological Monthly* 25, no. 10 (October 1954) 738.

———. "Preaching in Lent." *Concordia Theological Monthly* 31, no. 1 (January 1960) 38–44.

"Cambridge, England." *Missouri in Perspective* 3, no. 12 (April 12, 1976) 6.

The Commission on Theology and Church Relations. *Theology and Practice of the Divine Call*. St. Louis: The Lutheran Church—Missouri Synod, 2003.

Danker, Frederick W. *No Room in the Brotherhood: The Preus-Otten Purge of Missouri*. Clayton: Clayton Publishing House, Inc., 1977.

Essays on the Lutheran Confessions Basic to Lutheran Cooperation. St. Louis: The Lutheran Church—Missouri Synod and New York: The National Lutheran Council, 1961.

"A Festival of Hymns of Martin Franzmann." St. Louis: Concordia Seminary, 1996. Audio recording.

Feuerhahn, Carol. Interview by author. St. Louis, Missouri. September 26, 2017.

———. Personal correspondence. September 2017 and February 2018.

Feurhahan, Ronald. "Preface." In *Ha! Ha! Among the Trumpets: Sermons by Martin H. Franzmann*. St. Louis: Concordia Publishing House, 1994.

"Five Presenters Air Views on Scripture" *Missouri In Perspective* 2, no. 11 (April 14, 1975) 1.

Fletcher, Alice. Personal correspondence. February 2018.

Four Statements on Fellowship. St. Louis: Concordia Publishing House, 1960.

Franzmann, Peter. Telephone interview by author. August 30, 2017.

Friedrich, E. J. "They Studied Christian Doctrine." *Lutheran Witness* 79 (October 18, 1960) 538–39, 551, 556.

Gingrich, Felix Wilbur. "The Classics and the New Testament." *Anglican Theological Review* 15, no. 4 (October 1933) 300–4.

Graebner, A. L. "The Practice of Exegesis." *Theological Quarterly* 2, no. 1 (January 1898) 22–32.
Granquist, Mark. *Lutherans in America: A New History*. Minneapolis: Fortress, 2015.
Gurgel, Richard. "The Life and Legacy of Martin Hans Franzmann: Lutheran Poet, Scholar, and Professor." Church History Thesis, Wisconsin Lutheran Seminary, 1986.
Habel, Norman C. *The Form and Meaning of the Fall Narrative*. St. Louis: Concordia Seminary Print Shop, 1965.
Hoenecke, Gerald. "Dr. Martin H. Franzmann." *Wisconsin Lutheran Quarterly* 73, no. 3 (July 1976) 226.
"Hundreds Attend Concordia Lecture." *Christian News* 8, no. 16 (April 21, 1975) 1.
Jungkuntz, Richard. "Editorial." *Concordia Theological Monthly* 43, no. 6 (June 1972).
———. Review of *The Word of the Lord Grows*, by Martin H. Franzmann. *The Springfielder* 25, no. 3 (1961) 37–38.
Just Jr., Arthur A. "'Glorious Now, We Press Toward Glory:' The Primary Theology of Paul Gerhardt and Martin Franzmann." *Journal of the Good Shepherd Institute* 8 (2007) 99–121.
Katt, Arthur F. *Critical Comments on the Proposed New Hymnal*. Shaker Heights, OH. Compiled July 15–September 15, 1939.
Klatt, Dennis. "The Brothers Franzmann: A Strengthening Influence on the Bible-Based Theology of the Wisconsin Synod." Church History Thesis, Wisconsin Lutheran Seminary, 1988.
Koch, John B. *When the Murray Meets the Mississippi: A Survey of Australian and American Lutheran Contacts 1838–1974*. North Adelaide: Lutheran Publishing House of South Australia, 1975.
Koehler, John Philipp. "Analogy of Faith" *Faith-Life* 24–25 (October, 1951 to May, 1952).
———. "Legalism and the Evangelical Church." *Concordia Theological Monthly* 60, no. 3 (March 1969) 131–48.
———. *The History of the Wisconsin Synod*. Edited by Leigh Jordahl. St. Cloud: Faith-Life, The Protes'tant Conference, 1970.
Koenig, Paul. "Free Conferences in Europe." *Lutheran Witness* 72 (September 15, 1953) 319–20.
Kolb, Robert and Timothy Wengert, eds. *The Book of Concord*. Minneapolis: Fortress, 2001.
Korby, Kenneth F. "Notes from the Editor's Notebook." *The Cresset* 40, no. 1 & 2 (November/December 1976) 4–5.
Krentz, Edgar. *The Historical-Critical Method*. Eugene: Wipf and Stock Publishers, 2002. First published 1975 by Augsburg Fortress (Minneapolis).
Kretzmann, Karl. "News from Concordia Seminary." *Lutheran Witness* 65, no. 25 (December 3, 1946) 410.
Leaver, Robin A. *Come to the Feast: The Original and Translated Hymns of Martin H. Franzmann*. St. Louis: MorningStar Music Publishers, 1994.
"Light from Above." *Lutheran Witness* 73 (October 26, 1954) 362.
Lutheran Service Book. St. Louis: Concordia Publishing House, 2006.
Lutheran Witness 94 (April 27, 1975).
Marquart, Kurt. *Anatomy of an Explosion: Missouri in Lutheran Perspective*. Fort Wayne, IN: Concordia Theological Seminary Press, 1977.

Mayer, F. E. *The Story of Bad Boll: Building Theological Bridges*. St. Louis: The Lutheran Church—Missouri Synod, 1949.

Mayer, Herbert T. Review of *The Word of the Lord Grows*, by Martin H. Franzmann. *Concordia Theological Monthly* 33, no. 1 (January 1962) 49–50.

Memorial Service for Dr. Martin H. Franzmann. April 2, 1976. Audio Recording.

Moeller, Elmer J. Review of *Follow Me: Discipleship According to Saint Matthew*, by Martin H. Franzmann. *The Springfielder* 26, no. 1 (1962) 63–64.

Mordhorst, Robert. Telephone interview by the author. August 25, 2017.

The Nature and Function of the Holy Scripture: Theological Convocation, St. Louis, Mo., April 14–18, 1975. St. Louis: Concordia Publishing House, 1975.

Nelson, E. Clifford. *The Lutherans in North America*. Minneapolis: Fortress, 1980.

"News From Our Churches." *British Lutheran* 14, no. 8 (October 1969) 8.

Nordquist, N. Leroy. Review of *The Word of the Lord Grows*, by Martin H. Franzmann. *Lutheran Quarterly* 13, no. 4 (November 1961) 374.

"Obituary: Martin Hans Franzmann." *Lutheran Witness* 95 (May 16, 1976) 220.

Pearce, E. George. "The Stones of All Hallows—Speak." *British Lutheran* 14, no. 9 (November 1969) 6–9.

Pelikan, Jaroslav. "John Philipp Koehler (1859–1951)." *Concordia Theological Monthly* 23, no. 1 (January 1952) 50–51.

Pless, Joel. "Wauwatosa Titan: The Life, Contributions and Lasting Legacy of John Philipp Koehler." *Lutheran Historical Conference* 19 (2000) 111–28.

Polack, W. G. *The Handbook to the Lutheran Hymnal*. 3rd ed. St. Louis: Concordia Publishing House, 1958.

Prange, Peter. "Pastor E. Arnold Sitz and the Protes'tants: Witnessing to the Wauwatosa Gospel." Church History Thesis, Wisconsin Lutheran Seminary 1998, Revised 2004.

———. "The Wauwatosa Gospel and The Synodical Conference: A Generation of Pelting Rain." *Logia* 12, no. 2 (2003) 31–45.

Price, Jay M. *Temples for A Modern God: Religious Architecture in Postwar America*. Oxford: Oxford University Press, 2013.

Report of the Commission on Theology and Church Relations: Theology of Fellowship. St. Louis: The Lutheran Church—Missouri Synod, 1965.

Repp, Arthur C. "The Binding Nature of Synodical Statements." *Concordia Theological Monthly* 42, no. 3 (March 1971) 153–62.

Rutz, Karl. "Ha! Ha! Among the Trumpets." *Response* 17, no. 1 (1977).

Seddon, Constance Buszin. "Memories of the Franzmann Family and the Origins of the Franzmann Hymn 'Thy Strong Word.'" *Journal of the Good Shepherd Institute* 8 (2007) 139–53.

"Service Bulletin: Martin Hans Franzmann." St. Louis: Concordia Historical Institute, rev. 2012.

Scharlemann, Martin H. Review of *Romans*, by Martin H. Franzmann. *Concordia Theological Monthly* 41, no. 3 (March 1970) 184–85.

Scheibert, Harold W. "The Hymn and the Liturgy." *Concordia Theological Monthly* 29, no. 5 (May 1958) 321–43.

"Scholar Dies." *Lutheran Witness* 95 (April 25, 1976) 185.

Shorey, Paul. "A Symposium on the Value of Humanistic, Particularly Classical Studies: The Classics and the New Education. III: The Case For Classics." *The School Review* 18, no. 9 (November 1910) 585–17.

Storaasli, Olaf K. Review of *Follow Me: Discipleship According to Saint Matthew*, by Martin H. Franzmann. *Lutheran Quarterly* 14, no. 2 (May 1962) 181–82.

Stuempfle, Herman. "Hymn Interpretation." *The Hymn* 52, no. 1 (January 2001) 46–47.

Tanner, Eugene S. Review of *Follow Me: Discipleship According to Saint Matthew*, by Martin H. Franzmann. *Journal of Biblical Literature* 80, no. 4 (December 1961) 398.

Tappert, Theodore, ed. *Luther's Works*. Vol. 54. Philadelphia: Fortress, 1967.

Teuscher, Robert. "Lutherans Again Debate Interpretation of Bible." *St. Louis Globe-Democrat* (April 16, 1975).

"Theses on Church Fellowship." Wisconsin Evangelical Lutheran Synod. Accessed April 5, 2018. https://wels.net/about-wels/what-we-believe/doctrinal-statements/church-fellowship/.

Tietjen, John H. *Memoirs in Exile: Confessional Hope and Institutional Conflict*. Minneapolis: Fortress, 1990.

Todd, Mary. *Authority Vested: A Story of Identity and Change in the Lutheran Church—Missouri Synod*. Grand Rapids: Eerdmans, 2000.

Toward A More Excellent Ministry. St. Louis: Concordia Publishing House, 1964.

Toward Cooperation Among American Lutherans. St. Louis: The Lutheran Church—Missouri Synod and New York: The National Lutheran Council, 1961.

Vieker, Jon D. "Hymn Festival Commentary." *Journal of the Good Shepherd Institute* 8 (2007) 165–70.

Voelz, James W. Telephone interview by the author. July 25, 2017.

Webber, F. R. "The Fine Arts in the Service of the Church." *American Lutheran* 20, no. 6 (June 1937) 9–10.

Werth, Charles E. "The Wauwatosa Theology: John Philipp Koehler and His Exegetical Methodology." *Church History* 55, no. 2 (June 1986) 206–17.

Zimmerman, Paul. *A Seminary in Crisis: The Inside Story of the Preus Fact Finding Committee*. St. Louis: Concordia Publishing House, 2007.

www.ingramcontent.com/pod-product-compliance
Lightning Source LLC
Chambersburg PA
CBHW070321230426
43663CB00011B/2189